The present situation and trends of research
in the field of special education

The present situation
and trends of research
in the field of special education

Four studies: Sweden and other Scandinavian countries

Union of Soviet Socialist Republics

United States of America

Uruguay

Unesco Paris 1973

36734

Published by the United Nations
Educational, Scientific
and Cultural Organization
7 Place de Fontenoy, 75700 Paris
Printed by Arts graphiques Coop Suisse, Basle

ISBN 92-3-101106-5
French edition: 92-3-201106-9

Preface

The present publication is a study initiated under Unesco's programme of studies on special education for handicapped children and young people. Special education is not one field but many in as far as it involves handling children and young people with learning difficulties caused by visual, hearing, motor or mental handicaps. Any improvement in methods for helping the handicapped to develop into productive and well-adjusted members of the community does not merely benefit the handicapped themselves, but may also lead to improvements in ordinary education. It is worth noting that the basic philosophy underlying special education—to adapt the school to the child and not the child to the school—is now widely accepted.

Four specialists were asked to describe the present situation of special education research and the trends of future development within their own geographical areas—Latin America and, in particular, Uruguay; Sweden and the other Scandinavian countries; the Union of Soviet Socialist Republics; and the United States of America.

The author of the Latin American chapter is Mrs Eloisa Garcia Etchegoyhen de Lorenzo, Head of the Mental Retardation Section, Inter-American Children's Institute, Uruguay. Dr Karl-Gustaf Stukát, Professor at the Pedagogical Institution of the Gothenburg School of Education, Sweden, is responsible for the study concerning the Scandinavian countries, and Dr William P. Hurder, former Director of the Institute for Research on Exceptional Children at the University of Illinois, for the study on special education research in the United States. The joint authors of the Soviet study are Professors V. I. Lubovsky and T. A. Vlasova, of the Institute of Defectology, Academy of Pedagogical Sciences, U.S.S.R.

An introductory chapter and a conclusion have been provided by Professor John McKenna, Director of Psychology, Child Guidance Clinic, Dublin, Republic of Ireland.

It is hoped that this publication will be of interest not only to teaching staff dealing with handicapped children of different ages and levels, but also to others in contact with such children and young people, e. g. psychologists, psychiatrists, social workers and nurses. Since, however, the essential aim is to ensure that the handicapped are integrated in the community, administrators and teachers in the field of ordinary education should likewise find it of value.

The opinions expressed are those of the authors and do not necessarily reflect the views of Unesco.

Contents

John McKenna

Introduction

In 1968 a meeting of consultants was convened to consider and discuss with the Secretariat the long-term development of Unesco's programme for special education.

After intensive discussion the group recorded in a brief report (ED/SPECED/2) its opinions on important considerations and principles relevant to the provision of special education. There was general agreement that Unesco should continuously attempt to define the field of special education and to present facts to governments in a way that would promote development in thought and in action for the handicapped. The group tentatively defined special education as 'an enriched form of general education aimed at enhancing the quality of the lives of those who labour under a variety of handicapping conditions; enriched in so far as it makes use of specially trained educational personnel who are aware of the application of methodological advances in education and of technological equipment to offset certain types of handicap. In the absence of such intervention, many handicapped are likely to suffer a degree of social incompetence and inadequacy and to live well below the level of their potential'.

Many solutions to the problem of affording special services to the handicapped were put forward and discussed and, while it was agreed that varied approaches have proved to be partially effective, there was no tendency to suggest that perfect solutions had been, or indeed will ever be, achieved. Our growing knowledge of developmental changes in children, of differential growth rates in intelligence, of the effects and of the unintentional side effects of various forms of intervention, and of education as a social process, underline the necessity for constant re-evaluation of our concepts and for a dynamic approach which can both identify needs and innovate effective practices.

It was generally agreed that national policies with regard to special education should be directed to providing equal access for all to education and integrating all citizens into the economic and social life of the community. The aims of special education for those who suffer from mental, sensorial, physical or emotional handicaps are similar to those of education in general, that is, offering the child the maximum opportunity to develop cognitive, scholastic and social skills to the highest possible level. It was felt that, ideally, educational planning is necessary for each child from an early age, with a corresponding flexibility in the organization of programmes.

Programmes have been evolved in some countries which aim at ensuring integration of the handicapped in the ordinary educational provisions for children; in other countries it is hoped to achieve the goal of preparing the handicapped for independent participative roles in society by a process of differentiation within the system of education, creating diversified educational establishments for every type of handicap and for different combinations of multiple handicaps. Again there was general agreement that while institutions for both short- and long-term care will for many reasons remain necessary, steps should be taken to offset the negative effects of institutionalization, by well-considered programme planning in the light of contemporary research on social, emotional and cognitive development. In the past decade, exciting developments in the field of medical, biological and psychological research have raised the hopeful possibility that a marked reduction can be made in the deleterious consequences of initial handicapping factors which afflict a large part of the human race. The key to advance lies mainly in early identi- fication and treatment of problems and in provision for an adequate integra- tion of services. When the individual's handicaps have been diagnosed and, equally, their assets determined, progress has been made towards a clearer definition of the kind of programme and treatment appropriate in each case. This led the group to conclude that preventive and remedial measures in education must be based on a thorough study of the learners themselves, taking into account their emotional, social and psychological growth.

Some guiding principles for Unesco's programme were tentatively put forward at this meeting and included the following important sugges- tions:

1. In planning activities, priority should be accorded to handicaps in relation to their frequency and to the social and personal disruption they occasion in the absence of treatment.

2. The development of special education may be facilitated by including it within the general educational system where advantage can be taken of the existing educational infrastructure and services.

3. Surveys, studies and research are important so that action is based on a thorough knowledge of the situation in each country.

4. Unesco should seek co-operation with local and national associations set up by the parents and families of handicapped children and should under- take to play a part in informing the public of the problems and needs of the handicapped.

5. Existing training and research centres should be used on a multinational basis until all countries have adequate services.

6. There should be greater collaboration with the United Nations, the Specialized Agencies and competent non-governmental organizations, greater use being made of their documentation and statistical and other information regarding requirements for the various categories of the handi- capped and the services available in different countries.

Patterns of care

There are wide divergencies in the patterns and in the quality of the educational experiences and expectations to which the handicapped are exposed in many countries. Contemporary research and practice have revealed immense possibilities for modification and amelioration of the lot of the handicapped and the pessimistic overtones which in many places circumscribed the work of those dealing with the handicapped are being replaced by programmes of optimistic action. A clearer conception of the plasticity of human beings, of the potential of many once held to be irremediable, and of the modifiability of their behaviour has led to the hope that the removal of barriers to personal and social development and the provision of support to offset or prevent the blighting effects of many types of handicapping conditions will contribute in no small way to the welfare of mankind. The modifiability of humans is paralleled by a similar capacity for change in the cultural groups of which they are members and in the social institutions within which their growth and development takes place.

It is widely hoped that the spread of knowledge about patterns of care, and the methods, interests and theoretical models in a variety of countries will contribute to a better understanding of these problems and will effect changes in the social processes favourable to the acceptance of worth-while ideas and their application in practice.

Progress in the scientific advance of special education cannot be expected by focusing on individuals without some attempt to generalize or to seek for what may be universally valid in our approach. There are differences in the patterns of care for the handicapped from country to country and even from region to region within the same country. We may ask what are the roots of these differences and whether they are necessary. If they are not, are they worth preserving? There must have been preceding differences in the structure of society and in the social institutions underlying these differences. Each country has its own specific problems and develops its own methods of dealing with them. Many of the problems which are the object of our interest may have international relevance, and attempts to find solutions may have universal validity. In the past decade important international conferences on various aspects of handicap have voiced more clearly the demand for research information, for collaborative projects and for international exchange. However, exchange of information and of knowledge, no matter how useful, does not of itself ensure that the communicated ideas will be translated into action programmes, especially when cultural boundaries have to be crossed. In such circumstances, international organizations with members having different sets of values and an appreciation of cultural differences may act as effective mediators.

Against such a background, Unesco initiated projects in four Member States—Sweden, Uruguay, the Union of Soviet Socialist Republics and the United States of America. These studies were intended to cover the following points, emphasizing the substance rather than the organization and administrative aspects of research:

1. The main fields of research in special education during the past ten years, the most important achievements, including work of an experimental nature, their scientific and pedagogical results and ways of applying these results in educational practice.
2. The main lines and orientation of research for the next five or six years.
3. Liaison of research with the training of teachers for handicapped children.
4. Organization of research: bodies and institutions (public and private) involved.
5. Co-ordination of research work at a national level and dissemination of results.
6. Exchange of information at international level concerning on-going research and results of work carried out.

Sources of the reports

Sweden

The Education Act of 1962 reformed the Swedish educational system and Sections 2a, 6, and 24 of that Act provided for special education for certain categories of handicapped children. Similar provisions were made in the General School Statute of 1962 and further developed in the Special School Statute No. 478 of 1965.

The application of these legislative provisions is effected through regulations issued by the National Board of Education.

Legislation is passed at the national level and is enforced, according to subject-matter, either by the State (special schools for handicapped in sight or hearing) or by county councils (schools for the mentally retarded and boarding schools for the motor-handicapped) or again by municipalities (special teaching within regular schools).

The Ministry of Education, through the National Board of Education, is responsible for all special education within the general education system and for schools operating under the Special School Statute (paragraph 8). It is jointly responsible with the Ministry of Social Welfare and Health for special schools for the mentally retarded and for boarding schools for the motor-handicapped.

In the course of an enquiry into the problem of handicapped children the government arrived at the following definition: 'A handicapped person is one who, for physical or psychological reasons, encounters major difficulties in daily existence.' The Education Act of 1962 contains a first catalogue of various deficiencies and the General School Statute of the same year, dealing with attendance at special classes attached to comprehensive schools, provides the following enumeration: slow learners, hearing impaired, partially sighted, motor-handicapped, reading and writing disorders, retarded maturity, those whose health demands open air.

In addition, special regulations issued by the National Board of Education in 1966 and 1968 mention schools for the visually handicapped, the hearing-impaired, the speech-handicapped and the mentally retarded.

The education of the handicapped young is based on the principle of the pupil's participation in the collective life of the school and of his retention among ordinary children. To this end, a system of special courses and classes corresponding to the deficiencies listed above has been created within regular municipal schools side by side with ordinary classes.

For the more seriously affected children (hearing, sight or speech deficiencies, children with multiple handicaps, motor-handicapped and mentally retarded cases) there are special schools of the boarding type, also providing medical care. In boarding schools for the motor-handicapped, teaching is provided at the nearest regular school.

Vocational training is included in the study programmes of special schools, while professional re-education falls under the responsibility of the National Council for the Labour Market, acting in conjunction with the National Board of Education.

Although this report draws heavily on Swedish sources to exemplify the situation and trends of research in special education, several insights are offered concerning the situation in other Scandinavian countries and methods of co-ordination and dissemination of research information at national and international level. This concern for the effective spread of knowledge is a feature of the report. Projects are directed towards practical problems and their findings are useful only to the extent that they reach relevant social targets. In the past the application of research findings in special education has been limited by the small-scale nature of many studies and by the fact that the majority of these studies were concerned with the learner rather than the instructional process. The emergence of an interest in the educational process is now clear with the recent growth of large-scale projects which are expected to have radical implications for special education. Central to the current debate and typical of the lively discussion which inspires research in

Sweden is the 'differentiation-integration' problem. Arguments for the integration of children of average and of superior ability have long since been
advanced on the grounds of social equality but handicapped pupils had not
been considered prior to this. It was well into the sixties before traditional
organizational models for the education of the handicapped were challenged
by 'integrationists' not on the grounds of social equality, but of efficacy, and
questions were raised as to whether special classes or special schools really
supplied the kinds of environment which could best achieve the basic aims
of special education.

While practical experiments with alternative models are being carried on,
current development of special instruction reflects the impact of such research,
with a reduction in the number of special classes, an increase in the number
of pupils taking special lessons from special teachers in ordinary classes, and
a tendency to replace special schools by special classes.

Despite the fact that interest is being focused on the learning process
rather than on the learner, the goal of educators is ideally that of individually
adapted instruction and an attempt on the part of the school to satisfy the
needs of each pupil rather than obliging the pupil to satisfy the demands of
the school. Acknowledgement is made of the fact that true individualization
is seldom found but the masterly analysis of the criteria of individualization
by Stukát and Engström has important implications for the realization of
this goal and for special education in general.

Concentration of recent research on what the handicapped can do rather
than what they cannot do has led to new insights and to a greater exercise
of ingenuity on the part of teachers. There is a heightened awareness of the
fact that it is not so much that many handicapped children have failed to
learn as that many schools have failed to teach.

Union of Soviet Socialist Republics

The preparation and adoption of legislative or regulatory measures concerning special education may take place at the Soviet Union level or at the
level of the republics. Specific questions of a concrete character are settled at the
regional or local level, in particular by executive committees in the territories
and districts.

Three ministries are concerned with special education: Public Instruction,
Public Health and Social Security.

The Ministry of Public Instruction has competence over pre-school
establishments for physically handicapped children and over schools for all
categories of physically or mentally handicapped subjects. It provides general
and vocational training for all pupils and is also in charge of the training of
teaching staff for every type of special establishment. It has a Section of
Special Education.

The Ministry of Public Health has general charge of handicapped children up to the age of 3, of kindergartens for the mentally backward, and of sanatoria for various categories of deficients. It provides medical care in every type of school and deals with the vocational training and employment of mentally handicapped youth in special workshops.

The Ministry of Social Security is concerned with the vocational training and placement of the deaf and the blind in special school workshops. It also sees to the payment of pensions to every category of handicapped young— physically or mentally affected.

An Institute of Research on Deficiencies (or 'Defectology') attached to the Soviet Academy of Pedagogical Sciences was created by decrees of the Council of Peoples' Commissars of the U.S.S.R. of 6 October 1943 and of the Council of Peoples' Commissars of the R.S.F.S.R. of 14 February 1944. Its task is to study physical and mental deficiencies and to plan appropriate systems of education as well as the structure of special schools.

The earliest definitions of categories of handicapped children appear in the decree of 1919. They distinguish: nervous children or children suffering from psychic disturbance; backward children; and the physically handicapped (with three subdivisions for the deaf-mute, the blind and the crippled). Other legislative texts mention children handicapped in sight, hearing or speech and the mentally deficient.

The report from the U.S.S.R. is a systematic presentation of all that happens in special education throughout their country. The system of State supervision facilitates the introduction of a uniform structure and organization of special schools with similar curricula and programmes for each type of handicap. It ensures that textbooks, visual aids and manuals for teachers are available for every school and that for each type of handicap research is co-ordinated and implemented without delay. The rapid application of scientific knowledge is further enhanced by the Scientific Research Institute of Defectology at the U.S.S.R. Academy of Pedagogical Sciences where continuous work is carried out on the education and vocational training of the blind, the deaf, the mentally retarded, the educationally disadvantaged and the speech-impaired. According to the report, action is being taken on a wide front to ensure that every disadvantaged child, whatever his disability may be, and wherever he may be located, has access to the kind of educational environment which will best appreciate the nature of his disability and take steps where possible to remedy or to offset the systemic effects of the initial handicapping factor. This is made possible by trained teachers who are aware of the psychoeducational abilities and disabilities of their charges and who have a critical understanding of the educational demands of specific learning tasks in relation to specific kinds of disability.

The following are the most characteristic trends in the development of special education in the U.S.S.R.:

1. The ever-increasing process of differentiation within the system of education for handicapped children accomplished by: (a) special schools for children with partial defects (e. g. schools for partially sighted pupils are

separable from schools for blind pupils); (b) special sections within special schools determined by specific features of the pupils' handicap (e.g. in schools for the hearing-impaired, sections determined by the onset of defects or in schools for the speech-impaired, special sections for stammerers); (c) individualization of the learning process within each class depending on the level of mental development of each pupil and on the degree of their special defects; (d) the setting up of schools for multiple handicapped pupils.

2. Research into early development and the establishment of pre-school facilities for children with defects of hearing, vision or speech, and for mentally retarded children.

3. The raising of the level of general education in all special schools.

4. The perfection of vocational education programmes making possible an increasing range of vocational outlets for handicapped persons.

5. The use of activity and work programmes to develop cognitive activities.

6. The development of evaluation techniques for the selection of pupils for various schools.

7. Improved teaching methods based on: (a) research in cognitive activity; (b) more refined technical equipment; and (c) programmed instruction.

The report contains chapters on research in education of the mentally retarded, the deaf, the blind and the speech-impaired, and on the vocational training and special psychological studies appertaining to each type of handicapping condition. It deals with the substance of research in each of these categories and the principal trends, and then demonstrates how this knowledge is disseminated at national and international levels.

United States of America

Education is decentralized and legislative provisions relating to special education are found at two levels, that of individual states and that of the federal government. Each of the fifty states has its own laws governing its educational structure, and these laws show great variety.

Further legislation is of a State character and is individual to each of the separate states. Enforcement is the responsibility of the local authorities within each community, but schools are administered by boards of education. Federal legislation mainly takes the form of budgetary grants and of agreements with various public or private entities concerned with special education.

The U.S. Office of Education (USOE), which has authority over most matters connected with education, is a unit of the Federal Department of Health, Education and Welfare. Special education of the handicapped is in the hands of a distinct branch within that office, namely the Bureau for the Education and Training of the Handicapped, created by a law of 1966 (P-L. 89-750) to promote and administer all activity in this field. Within the separate states it is generally the state educational authority which has charge of special education, although a few medical establishments are under the control of the state health and welfare authorities.

An official classification of handicapped children is found in the Act of 1963 (P-L. 88-164, Section 301) concerning the training of professional personnel, which enumerates: 'mentally retarded, hard of hearing, deaf, speech impaired, visually handicapped, seriously emotionally disturbed, crippled or otherwise health-impaired children who, by reason thereof, require special education.' This enumeration was subsequently taken up in a variety of legislative texts issued by federal authorities. Nevertheless each state adopts its own terminology in this field, thus leading to a great diversity in state classifications—sometimes more restrictive than the federal enumeration, but sometimes adding further categories of children entitled to special education. Thus Illinois speaks among others of multiple handicapped children, while Oklahoma mentions children with special health problems.

Because of the volume of potentially significant research in the United States, the following criteria helped to determine for inclusion in the report research which would give a sense of the direction and substance of current work in the field of special education:

1. Research of immediate relevance conducted by individuals or bodies whose primary concern is special education, e.g.: (a) academic departments of special education; (b) doctoral dissertations in special education; (c) research sponsored or conducted by state and local departments of education.

2. Research of intermediate relevance which aims to improve the conditions underlying educability.

3. Research, with a more remote degree of relevance, which though not necessarily service-oriented or of immediate utility to the education of the handicapped is based on theoretical concern with such conditions of cognition as cerebral function, perception, learning, memory, motivation and socialization.

The report is based therefore on a selection of the research, demonstration and development efforts funded by the Bureau of Education for the Handicapped of USOE, on reviews and research sponsored by the National Education Association (NEA) and the Council Exceptional Children on (CEC), on original research publications and on data from specialized clearing houses.

The organization of the report is based on the classification of handicaps used by USOE which comprises the following seven categories: crippled or otherwise health-impaired; emotionally disturbed; hearing-impaired; mentally retarded; speech-impaired; visually impaired; multiple cross disability.

Systematic consideration is given to each of the above handicaps, emphasizing the aims and approach of research as it has developed through each year of the past decade and indicating where possible the findings and conclusions of research projects and programmes.

It is clear that the field of special education in the United States is in a state of flux: not only because of the recent dramatic growth of interest and of available funds for development, but also because of shifts in the patterning of its own subject-matter and responsibilities. One does not get the impression so much of a steady advance on a broad front as of intensive bursts of energy and enterprise depending on individuals and on groups of individuals with a common purpose. Backed by the findings of contemporary research, individuals and groups often open up new perspectives and influence the decisions of policy makers about the funding of programmes and the deployment of resources which affect the emphasis and directions of work in the field.

In the recent history of special education in the United States many groups figure prominently—the Joint Commission on Mental Illness and Health, the President's Panel on Mental Retardation, the National Institute of Child Health and Human Development (NICHHD), the Joint Commission on Mental Health for Children, the Council on Exceptional Children (CEC) of the National Education Association (NEA), the Bureau for Education for the Handicapped of USOE, the National Association for Retarded Children, the American Association for Mental Deficiency. So much activity has been generated by these groups and the dramatic increase in the handicapped, as evidenced by the quantity and quality of reported research, is such that one could almost hope for an advance of 'breakthrough' proportions in the near future.

The report is permeated with concern to ensure that access to special educational opportunities is freely available to all children. How this is done throughout the United States is not made fully explicit. Possibly this is a direct consequence of the protean nature of the administration of school systems and the high degree of decentralization which allows for a wide variation of services from community to community. Under these conditions it is essential that community leaders and administrators have a clear understanding and acceptance of new findings and a willingness to make their applications effective.

Characteristic of this concern for freedom of access to generic health, education and welfare services for all children in the United States is the growing awareness of the impact of early social and economic disadvantages on intellectual, social and emotional development and the setting up of compensatory education programmes (Head Start) for children of lower socio-economic status, which have had important implications for traditional categories of handicap.

Early identification of handicapping factors with minimal disruption of normal living patterns are looked upon as essential measures in the realization of community care which is now a goal sought for by federal, state and local action throughout the United States.

Uruguay

The report from Uruguay suggests that equality of access to education may be made more readily attainable by ensuring that the entry to life itself is freed from unnecessary hazards and surrounded by as much care as is humanly possible.

By anticipating the incidence of handicapping factors, even *in utero*, steps can be taken to offset, to minimize and even to prevent disabilities. The primary need as seen by the report is early identification of problems and prompt intervention when the infant is most vulnerable. By setting in motion programmes of care for 'at risk' infants, the precarious position of such children can be remedied and initial disabilities can be prevented from becoming permanent handicaps, with an accretion of unfavourable systemic effects which could have been mitigated by appropriate treatment at the right time. The principal factors found in association with the incidence of handicapping conditions in early life and generally assumed to be causal in effect are simple inheritance, chromosomal abnormalities, external injury, and unfavourable environments such as are found in unsatisfactory homes or in poor socio-economic conditions. Some of these factors may operate on their own to retard development but more often one initial handicap is reinforced by subsequent handicaps which act upon the child even if these consist solely of those unfavourable attitudes which disabilities themselves sometimes engender. Whereas we cannot easily make radical physical changes for the better in constitutional handicaps such as blindness, deafness or severe brain damage, it is possible to modify the environments of many individuals so affected and to compensate for the probable bad effects of their physical or mental disability.

The key to most programmes of remediation is early identification. The earlier the detection of disabilities and the quicker the onset of treatment, the better the chance of remission of the consequences and of the progress towards normal functioning. The creation of the Latin American Perinatology and Human Development Centre sponsored by the Pan American Health Organization presents us with a model of how the foregoing aims may be realized where the programme is implemented by multiprofessional research on early stimulation of at risk infants. This type of multidisciplinary approach has been in operation since 1965 at the pre-school rehabilitation services which offer a predominately educational approach to the problem. The aim is to teach the correct management of mother, foetus and neonate, with a view to reducing mortality and morbidity of mother and child and thus fostering the latter's normal mental and physical development. A corollary to early identification of the handicapped is multidisciplinarian interaction in their treatment. Recognition of the disability is of little avail without consistent maternal care and the immediate institution of appropriate medical and remedial measures. The courses at the centre are at post-graduate level and are open to obstetricians, paediatricians, anaesthesiologists, physiologists, specialists in public health and teachers. This appears to be one method of bridging the gap which so often exists between the delivery of the infant and his first enrolment in school as a pupil. The breakdown in communication between the specialists who are involved, sequentially, with the physical, social and educational development of children operates most unfavourably against the handicapped. These proposals appear to be a valid basis for an active public health programme linking with the schools where doctors, nurses and teachers may be trained to identify physical factors, social conditions and family relationships which can substantially influence mental functioning and personality development for good or for bad. Thus the teacher can be involved sequentially in the treatment process and by a better understanding of the effects of initial disabilities he can play a more meaningful and participative role in combating their systemic effects and in setting the scene for positive learning behaviour.

An important feature of the Latin American report is the stress which it lays on research in learning disabilities among schoolchildren, and the complex of factors found in association with specific learning difficulties. The studies reviewed are mainly connected with the detection of correlates of learning disorders, with the prevention of such disabilities and with finding effective remedial measures and teaching techniques for school failure in a specific basic subject.

Here again two principles of operation are important. Psycholinguistic disabilities originate early in language development and become more intractable as development proceeds so that early detection is essential. For prevention and correction of specific learning disabilities a knowledge of the processes, assumed to be causal in their production, is necessary. These processes may involve organic factors and educational or emotional deprivation so that collaboration of neurologists, psychiatrists, psychologists and teachers is most likely to lead to profitable lines of enquiry. The number of children in ordinary schools throughout the world who fall far below their expected levels of achievement and who leave school relatively illiterate or inumerate for no abvious reasons such as poor general intelligence or unfavourable home conditions requires much more sophisticated techniques of investigation than have been used before. In fact research may present more conclusive evidence for either polygenic systems as responsible elements for the variations of performance to be found among schoolchildren or for the hypothesis of a continuum of reproductive casualties. Biological research may yet uncover much of what still remains a mystery. Experience, however, with such handicapped children indicates that whatever may be the causes of their retardation the treatment is ultimately educational and this appears to be the thrust of much of the reported research from Uruguay.

Research on special education in the past decade

Many of the objectives, values and assumptions of special education are implicit in the work reported in the following studies. The Soviet author sees the basic aim of special education as 'the general education of children (consistent with the possibilities for each type of handicap): work and professional training in order to prepare them for their future practical activity, education of children's personalities on the basis of the principles of communist morality and their preparation for life as fully fledged citizens of the country'. The Uruguayan report sees the principal aim as the initiation of 'effective procedures to promote maximum functioning . . . and to prevent a disability from becoming a handicap'. The Swedish author simply states that the aim is 'to develop each handicapped person to the best of his potentialities'. And the American author considers that integration of the handicapped with the community is best achieved by improving the quality of their care in order 'to build confidence, self-sufficiency and feelings of worth and strength in the handicapped'.

To design effective methods of promoting maximum functioning of the handicapped, to improve programme planning techniques and to ensure that they are put into operation, two important ingredients are the teacher and the research worker. From a cursory examination of special educational progress in most countries, however, one could make the generalization that investment in research bears an unfavourable relationship to the amount disbursed for development and delivery of educational services to the consumer. This has been explained by the lack of resources in funds, but generally the relationships between research and the economics of its subvention represent a much more complex problem than simple lack of money.

Some of the difficulties in the funding and application of research are as follows.

In developed countries, selective influences are at work determining the deployment of resources. These influences stem from the values of a society or more particularly from the values of those who control the allotment of resources in a given society and in the institutions where research can be supported; for example, writing about the sixties, the author of the American report remarks that seldom has so much money and manpower been allocated to a previously neglected human handicap (i.e. mental retardation) in such a brief space of time. This must have been due to a change in attitudes and values rather than to a sudden accretion of money for educational research.

23

A second limiting factor in the progress of special education is the gulf which often exists between the scientific and service communities. On the one hand, there are many pieces of fundamental research containing new principles bearing on classroom practice but often their findings are couched in such recondite terms that the possibilities for direct application and experimentation are lost to the teacher. On the other hand, many teachers have not been trained to read appropriate professional journals and are unable to apply scientific methods of analysis to new subject-matter, materials or methods.

Another difficulty inherent in the application of educational research is that in project evaluation procedures, one or more of the factors in the educational situation must be altered for the experimental group. Unless there is co-operation between the research worker and public administrative authorities, the necessity for variation and experimentation may not be fully understood. Administrative systems and parents who seek equality of treatment for their pupils and children must be apprised of the nature of this experimental activity in order to gain their co-operation and understanding.

Another danger inherent in a great deal of empirical research in education lies in the tentative nature of its hypotheses. Some operational research must inevitably lead to blind alleys and hence much time has been lost, possibly to the detriment of the subjects who could have learned better by proven methods and materials. However, as far as the handicapped are concerned, so little has been done in many places and with many handicaps that one would hope that attention of any kind might have a 'Hawthorne' effect and bring about favourable change incidentally.

When funds are available it is often difficult to strike a reasonable balance between what to allocate to basic research (e. g. learning, memory, concept formation, motor and spatial ability, etc.) and what to spend on specific projects. Generic strategies may lead to the establishment of new knowledge but in the absence of a categorical approach to specific projects, handicapping conditions tend to be neglected.

Because of the multiple factors in the causation of handicaps—chemical, biological, psychological and social—many professions are competing for research funds. Again, the shortage of trained professional personnel such as teachers, social workers, speech therapists, psychologists and physicians retards effective basic field work fundamental to research projects.

In the past, a great deal of educational and psychological research has been done in academic isolation as a partial requirement for a degree, or by scholars in their spare time from teaching, with or without funds. Such projects derived from an individual's interest in a special problem or from the availability of subjects for research. As a result, little work was done on broad issues with practical implications requiring investigation for protracted periods of time by members of different professions. This often had the effect of reinforcing inertia and ensuring a kind of built-in conservatism with regard to innovation in educational establishments. People tend to work as they have been trained and it follows that first-hand contact with research during teacher training would constitute a major step towards the realization of educational innovations. The third chapter the Swedish report indicates how a knowledge of research and experience of research techniques can contribute substantially to the training of teachers for special education, resulting in a sense of professional identity which will make them proud of their work.

In the following chapters it is clear that research projects are not developed with equal intensity, by standards of either frequency or severity, among the different types of handicapping conditions. The general tendency to be seen in the four projects is a focusing of interest on the mentally handicapped and on slow learners, with the blind and emotionally and socially disturbed often attracting the least research.

In Sweden most studies in the past have concentrated on the learner rather than on the learning-instructional process. The trend there is towards an increase of interest in the educational process itself, on the development of goal-related evaluation procedures, rather than norm-related tests, the utilization of self-instructional devices and the evaluation of organizational models. This is paralleled by an increased methodological sophistication and the development of techniques of correlational ability analysis with reference to handicapped children. This trend away from focusing on the individual as he is found, towards the educational experiences to which he is exposed, is a step in the evolution of scientific interest in the handicapped. Paradoxically, however, it in no way signifies a diminished interest in the rights of the handicapped to all the benefits which education can bestow upon them.

The Swedish report to some extent reflects this change of focus and it differs in struture from the other reports. Rather than dealing with individual forms of handicap it concerns itself principally with the implications of research for special education practice, analysis of the teaching learning process, organizational models, programmes and systems, the role of research in teacher-training programmes and other such broad issues.

The Soviet report presents us with a model for the co-ordination of research among all the diverse disciplines which may be connected with the study, instruction, education and occupational training of every type of handicapped person. One great advantage of the Institute of Defectology is the rapidity with which the findings of research reach their relevant targets. Programmes and materials which are verified by experiment are introduced into the appropriate schools and textbooks and methodogical manuals for special schools are compiled, published and disseminated, thus ensuring the possibility of the results of research being put into practice without delay.

In the United States, the amount of research relating to the study of the handicapped is so vast that it would not be reasonable to expect a complete coverage of all the available data. The author of the report has selected: (a) research of immediate relevance done by those interested in the education of the handicapped; (b) research where the aims and methods are similar

25

to the aims and methods of education and; (c) knowledge-oriented research in processes basic to learning.

With these criteria of relevance the data is still vast and the layout of the report exemplifies the great advantages accruing from the availability of computer-stored data for easy retrieval, analysis and dissemination.

Who are the handicapped?

In general terms, the handicapped are those who, for physical or psychological reasons, need special help in order to adjust to living: in the absence of appropriate help they will live well below the level of their potential. Every child needs help in order to adjust to life, but some are so obviously deprived of the usual requirements for normal learning that their need for special help is immediately seen. The child who is blind from birth can have help from the start of life; the hearing-impaired child may not be diagnosed as such until the extent of sensory deprivation has incurred irreversible damage; the mildly handicapped or brain-damaged may not be noticed as such until they enter into competition with their schoolmates. The following studies deal with a wide range of conditions: blind, crippled or otherwise health-impaired, deaf, emotionally disturbed, mentally retarded and speech-impaired. Each of these handicaps entails varying degrees of impairment but, whatever the degree of impairment, the developing personality is always involved to some extent and the child is generally unable to profit fully from the education offered to normal children without marked learning difficulties. For this reason, special educational programmes have evolved in many places, with methods and equipment which supply compensatory education for specific defects and which attempt to let the handicapped share in the store of common knowledge so that they can play an independent and participative role in society.

Crippled or otherwise health-impaired children

Studies of the prevalence of health-impaired children, deprived of normal schooling for either short or long periods, would tend to show wide fluctuations in the population comprised by such an all-embracing category. Follow-up studies on children who have been hospitalized for long periods lend strong support to the hypothesis that ruptures of affectional bonds in early childhood have a damaging effect on subsequent development.

To better understand the effects of long-term illness and hospitalization, it is essential to know what capacity children have for realizing the need for separation from home, the precipitating cause of the stay in hospital, and the severity of the rupture in the affectional bonds of family life. The reactions of an infant of a few months to prolonged separation from the routine of family life and to placement in a large hospital are much different from that of, say, a 7-year-old or a 12-year-old child. A wealth of observational studies support the view that the younger the child the greater the probability of emotional upset from prolonged hospitalization and the more irreversible the consequences.

For those children where the basic foundations for healthy development have already been laid and whose condition entails lengthy hospitalization the problem is not one of special education. Since they are generally no different in their range of capacities from normally healthy children, the problem is more one of logistics—supplying the necessary conditions, materials and teaching personnel for ordinary education.

For this reason, the reports, with the exception of those of the United States and Uruguay, have not treated this category extensively. In fact, the American author shows that, by the criterion of federal funds allocated for research in this area, there was a marked decline of interest over the past ten years and a consequent difficulty in finding research relevant to the characteristics or the special educational needs of crippled or health-impaired children. This probably stems from the fact that the educational heterogeneity of the children in this category defies generalization. There is little reason to expect a direct or close relationship between intelligence and learning capacity and physical conditions, unless these conditions include neurological damage or affect visual or auditory channels. Given educational opportunity, crippled or health-impaired pupils will not differ consistently in learning from non-handicapped pupils.

By 1966 the NEA–CEC research review showed little research of consequence relating to such practical aspects of education as curriculum, methodology, special educational provisions or achievement in crippling conditions, and special health problems. There was, however, a noticeable increase of interest in learning disorder. By the end of the decade a new conceptual-clinical educational entity, variously described as learning disorder, severe learning disability, cerebral dysfunction, and minimal brain dysfunction, had entrenched itself upon the category of health-impaired, and in fact the category of crippled or health-impaired was represented solely by learning disabilities in the NEA-CEC research review in 1969. Again, the end of the decade saw the completion of a revision and further standardization of the Illinois Test of Psycholinguistic Abilities (ITPA), which is described in the American report as 'the single most comprehensive instrument for the remediation-oriented diagnosis of children's psycholinguistic abilities and disabilities'. Research in the United States on 'brain-injured' children is reported to have produced varying, sometimes conflicting and equivocal results—possibly, it is suggested, because of the relatively primitive procedures for identifying and assessing brain damage conditions and for distinguishing between the consequences of organic pathology and those attributable to normal developmental variations. Defining and clarifying the concepts, a USOE conference arrived at the following definition: 'Learning disability refers to one or more significant deficits in essential learning processes requiring special education for remediation.'

While the Soviet author does not devote a separate chapter to this category, he describes programmes for children with temporary retardation of development. From among persistently unsuccessful pupils in ordinary schools, groups with temporary retardation of mental development have been singled out in the past decade. Their working capacity, memory, thought processes and perception have now become the main objects of research in specially organized remedial education conditions. Psycho-pedagogical investigations have revealed initial difficulties in language formation and in mathematical conceptual thinking with these pupils.

The Uruguayan report devotes a separate chapter to learning disabilities, giving a careful definition suggesting that there are educational methodologies which will change discrepancies in functioning among children with significant deficits in essential learning processes. The research reported in the Latin American contribution reflects the attitudes of several professions collaborating with educators, and studies have been included because they attempt to answer three major questions, namely: What are the correlates of learning disabilities? What methods will prevent or offset the effects of learning disabilities? What research methodology is required in order to relate effective remedial procedures to correlates of learning disabilities?

It is clear from the contributions which deal with learning disorder that this promises to be one of the most exciting and, from the point of view of the teacher, possibly one of the most fruitful developments of educational psychological research. Here at last may be the explanation for that well-known type of obscure etiology, 'the late developer', the supposed dullard who succeeds remarkably in the more practical and less abstract problems of life after leaving school. They present themselves as a group by their failure to achieve in a specific subject, generally reading, and at the same time it is often felt that they are at least of average ability. The teacher can be involved not only in ascertainment but, with the development of goal-related assessment devices, he can become part-diagnostician, searching for the specific behaviours which are so frequently found in association with learning disability. Among the encouraging aspects of this new concept is the possibility it holds for a genuine link-up between the professions of teaching, psychology, and neurophysiology, and the promise it holds for the solution of one of the great problems of teaching: the failure to inculcate in some pupils the basic tool of learning—a mastery of reading. There are undoubtedly some people who have succeeded in life after an undistinguished school career characterized by underachievement in verbally oriented subjects but how many more intelligent subjects have lived well below the level of their potential as a result of the frustration incurred by an inability to keep abreast of their coevals in reading?

Emotionally disturbed children

In the course of growing up, children are preparing to become adult members of the community, acquiring skills that will help them to earn a living, learning to know and to adjust to others so that they may become responsible adults, adequate marriage partners, parents and citizens and learning an appreciation of the aesthetic and moral products of man's mind. The great influences in this progress towards maturity are the home, the school and the community.

Faulty parent-child relationships and early disruption in the affectional bonds of family life can impair a child's feeling of security and adequacy and make him vulnerable to the extent that he is unable to deal with his aversions and attractions to others. Emotions are important resources of adjustive potential, and consistent and appropriate emotional satisfaction at each stage of growth greatly helps the progress towards maturity. Reactions to unmet psychological needs show themselves in typical ways at different stages of development. Unfavourable interaction with important adult figures in an infant's life may show itself in hyperactivity or apathy and in feeding or sleeping disturbances.

During the early school years, teachers are aware that some children suffer from symptomatic reactions such as stuttering, habit spasms, phobias and lies; some have habitual dispositions towards nailbiting, thumbsucking, tantrums, enuresis and masturbation as emotional outlets; some are given to disruptive behaviour which seems relatively autonomous, involving conduct disorders, stealing, truancy, cruelty and sexual misdemeanours.

The estimates of the incidence of these disorders in the school situation range from 10 to 25 per cent of schoolchildren in the American report, but the category of emotional disturbance has very broad implications, lacks precision in definition and includes many types, some only with reactions to current stresses which are transient phenomena with spontaneous remissions.

With the exception of the American report, there are no specific chapters devoted to emotional disturbance and its treatment in an educational environment. The Soviet report simply mentions that the Ministry of Public Health controls school sanatoria and clinics for children with disturbances in their mental development. However the American author notes that the sixties saw an increased interest in mental health and more provisions in the public school programmes for emotionally disturbed pupils.

Some fundamental questions which are raised directly or by implication in this report are: What is the role of education in this area of handicap? What are the roles of cognitive, emotional and motivational factors in the development of emotional disturbance? What are the conceptual relations between emotional disturbance and delinquent behaviour? What are the relative weights to be assigned to cultural factors and to internal forces within the individual in the etiology of delinquency? How can we frame the problem in educationally significant dimensions?

Reviews indicate that early in the sixties education was becoming increasingly dominant in providing programmes for emotionally disturbed children, and the conviction was growing that helping disturbed pupils to achieve both academic proficiency and social competence was a fundamental part of the educator's role. By the mid-sixties one contemporary professional trend was the dramatic return to learning theory, specifically behaviourism (cited from Balow) in the treatment of emotional disturbance, but by the end of the decade Glavin and Gray discerned a trend away from an individual child focus of operant conditioning to broader classroom applications, using tokens and parental co-operation in positive reinforcement programmes.

It is possible that emotionally disturbed children are falling between not two, but many stools. Teachers who have had little basic training in recognizing or handling emotional problems of childhood may consider themselves well rid of the more serious problems and pass them to psychologists and psychiatrists or to officers who look after juvenile offenders. But there are not enough such trained personnel to look after the needs of those estimated to belong to this category and if the services for them are not located in the mainstream of educational and social services available to all children, parents are sometimes hesitant about taking them to a hospital which might emphasize the child's role as a sick person. No single discipline holds the key to the solution of this problem and genuine joint interprofessional action involving educators, social workers, psychologists and psychiatrists may mean the renunciation of claims to territories which are often regarded as the exclusive preserves of psychology or psychiatry.

Hearing-impaired children

The great difference between man and other organisms who share his environment is the capacity to symbolize and to use symbol relationships for communication. One of the most important factors in the development of social behaviour is the ability to communicate and this is essentially a learning process dependent both on open sensory channels to the central nervous system and on stimulation from other humans in the immediate surroundings of the growing child. Concept formation and the acquisition of knowledge constitute the foremost processes of the child's intellectual development and it is from the adults who surround him that the child acquires the system of symbols and associated meanings by which he comprehends reality. A serious breakdown in channels of communication in early life such as may be involved in hearing impairment can have a lasting effect on the personality and may even be responsible for unfavourable changes in the structural properties of the cortex itself. Since optimal language learning normally takes place before the age of 7, early diagnosis of hearing impairment is essential, so that remedial measures can be instituted as early as possible.

In the main reports, the Soviet and American authors go into detail about research and its applications in the special education of hearing-impaired children. It is of interest to note that in Uruguay special education started with a school for deaf children organized by the National Board of Primary Education in 1910. A table of frequencies of special education studies in Denmark, Norway and Sweden between the years 1963 and 1965 indicates that more attention has been devoted to hearing impairment than to visual and speech deficiencies. In the Soviet Union, over the past ten years a new system of language learning has been developed for deaf children incorporating the organization of a speaking environment and the inclusion of deaf children in collectives of children with normal hearing in order to promote verbal speech. Finger spelling has been utilized as the principal means of communication with deaf children initially but with the intention of turning this into an auxiliary means of developing oral speech, lip-reading and written speech. This is said to ensure consolidation of speech material and, in comparison with lip-reading, a more adequate perception of the process of communication.

A new approach to the diagnosis of hearing impairment, based on evaluation of residual hearing from the point of view of its role in the development of speech in children, can, it is claimed in the Soviet report, more readily distinguish a partial hearing defect from deafness, aphasia, and mental retardation. In this connexion, particular attention is given to studies of pre-school children with defective hearing and special organized instruction has demonstrated the possibilities of dactyl speech as a means of communication at a very early age. As a result, the quality and quantity of vocabulary is improved in deaf children and the active use of words in association with one another and with those who have normal hearing is facilitated and accelerated. Particular attention is paid to the applications of technology in teaching the deaf, and all Soviet classrooms for deaf children are equipped with sound-amplifying apparatus. Electro-accoustical devices, it is hoped, will help to form habits of visual, tactile-vibratory and combined perception of oral speech. As a result of research on the development of auditory perception it is hoped to introduce changes in the initial training and correction of pronunciation in children with defective hearing in the near future.

Among all the categories of handicaps in the United States funded by USOE during the period 1964–69, hearing impairment was the only one where more grants were made available for demonstration projects than for research projects. The American author expresses surprise that such an opportunity for insights and knowledge of human cognitive development and function is neglected by the scientific community and perhaps this is one of the reasons why he believes that no dramatic breakthrough has occurred in the field of the hearing-impaired. Nevertheless old issues have been clarified, concepts and techniques from other disciplines have been assimilated into research and there has been an infusion of highly sophisticated workers, especially in the area of psycholinguistics, which should increase the quality and quantity of research in the coming decade.

Despite this, there are many research projects reported with interesting results. One project makes it clear that etiology is of paramount importance in assessing the educability of deaf children, since genetically determined deafness (as opposed to deafness acquired by prematurity, meningitis, Rhesus factor, rubella, etc.) showed the least evidence of brain damage and maladjustment, and had the highest mean intelligence and highest educational achievement except for speech and speech reading.

The prelingually deaf child is reported to pose the greatest challenge to educational research because of his severe educational retardation though there is evidence to suggest that such children can be the cognitive equals of children with normal hearing and this has given rise to promising and provocative research aimed at the elucidation of cognitive development and educational achievement.

There has been a noticeable increase in pre-school training attributable in part to improved transistorized hearing aids and increased interest in speech and hearing centres. Very little research has been done on the issue of integration of the deaf and the hearing as opposed to early segregation for training and education. One study, comparing pre-school deaf children using hearing aids, in a programme modelled on those for the hearing, with a group trained by formal procedures for the deaf, reports better results from the 'hearing approach'.

Another study concluded that the early acquisition of a manual communication system aided later achievement and adjustment. Increased interest in manual communication in the United States was attributed partially to earlier research by Soviet investigators. The development of a dictionary of sign language and a filmed programme for teaching the manual alphabet was also noted. One project involved the parents of young deaf children and other family members in visits to a hearing clinic for demonstration of home teaching. Language development in children and parental changes in attitude were assessed and the results were sufficiently favourable to cause this approach to be adopted as a permanent procedure.

One important treatise by Lenneberg in 1967 on the biological foundations of language promulgated a theory of significance to psychoeducational theory and practice. It assumes that language is species-specific derived from biologically determined cognitive capacities peculiar to man, and that language development results from the interplay of biologically determined language readiness and environmental experience. Consequently it presupposes cognitive function to be a more basic and primary process than language.

The adaptation of new concepts and methods of psycholingustic theory to the study of the syntax of the deaf promises new knowledge of direct benefit in the education of the deaf and the resolution of theoretical problems surrounding cognition and language. Nevertheless the practical implications of theoretical issues are still revealed in the continuing controversy over oral/aural versus manual training in the early education of the deaf.

Mentally handicapped children

The term 'mental handicap' generally comprises all those whose adaptive behaviour is inadequate by reason of arrested or incomplete development of mind stemming from unfavourable constitutional, social, or educational factors, or from a mixture of these; it is not a clinical, pathological or etiological entity so that a variety of professional workers are engaged in this field, each tending to stress those aspects on which their professional interests are focused. Development may be retarded initially by a single factor but this is generally reinforced by others. We cannot reverse the occurrence of serious physical defects, nor easily make changes for the better in an individual's constitution, but it is possible to modify the environment of many individuals and so enhance the possibility of optimal development or compensate for the unfavourable effects of physical or mental disability. More than any other category of handicapped, the mentally retarded are likely to become more retarded by neglect. Because their specific defect is a marked lack of intelligence, learning difficulties are their chief problem. In the absence of special provisions, they are often excluded from situations where normal social learning would take place and they generally cannot profit from the ordinary facilities for learning offered to children of normal ability. With special education the majority of the retarded can be prepared for integration in society, for a participative role in the community and in many cases can attain a measure of social independence and adaptation. Despite the new tone of optimistic action which characterizes work in this field, there is always a reduced level or ceiling to which the retarded can aspire because of their marked lack of intelligence, and this is not necessarily true of other categories of handicap.

As a result of psychological research, confidence appears to have been shaken in the long-term predictive value of conventional psychometric devices as far as the retarded are concerned. Apart from situational difficulties of eliciting valid responses from young retarded children, other complicating factors such as motor handicaps, sensory defects and cultural impoverishment may also reduce the predictive value of psychological tests. In the case of children with verbal-expressive difficulties, low speech scores are not reliable indices of future performance as these may stem from discrete lesions in the central nervous system, from mild impairment of the peripheral nervous system or from normal inhibition of mental output, which is a characteristic response of children in conditions giving rise to situational anxiety. Again, brain-damaged children with mild to severe neuromuscular, motor-visual or spatial-perceptual impairment often display secondary behaviour difficulties which make them relatively inaccessible at an early age and they thus provoke assumptions about the severity of their retardation which in turn leads to neglect of the systemic consequences of their initial disability. Another type of case which makes prediction hazardous is where mental handicap is complicated by emotional disturbance, for among the mentally retarded we can expect the full range of personality disorders which arise as adjustment reactions to disturbances in early life. Some significant principles which emerge from a reading of all the following reports are as follows:

1. The earlier the detection of basic handicapping factors and the quicker the onset of treatment the better the chance of remedial and educational measures influencing further development.
2. Single genetic factors are reinforced or give rise to other unfavourable factors.
3. Development of cognitive processes and of higher psychological systems may be adversely affected by social-psychological factors.
4. Ascertained subnormality at any level is not necessarily a fixed or irremediable condition.
5. Since there is a variety of causal factors and consequent conditions involving different degrees of intellectual impairment, the retarded are not a homogeneous group and their needs vary.

The reports without exception give more attention to this category of handicap than to any other. This is possibly because mentally handicapped persons present the greatest problem in numerical terms and if adequate provisions are not available in the form of care, education and vocational training programmes, they can become the greatest source of social problems in modern complex urbanized societies.

Sweden

The Swedish author reports that in the past the most common type of research projects have been descriptive studies, comparing deviant pupils with control groups or with population norm values. There appears to be a trend away from concentration on the learner towards a focus on the learning–instructional process. One example of this is reported in an investigation into work training programmes for a wide range of mentally handicapped children. Since psychomotor skills are crucial in the types of work skills involved in training programmes, this study directed special focus on these. As was expected, achievement of the subjects bore a relationship to I.Q. levels. However, there were considerable variations within each group (with I.Q. ranges 25–42, 43–55, 56–75) and even overlap in performance between these groups. The results showed that many handicapped thought to be fit only for custodial care could meet the requirements for successful work training.

There is expressed dissatisfaction with the widespread use of general intelligence measures for placement, and correlational ability analysis with reference to handicapped pupils shows an increased methodological sophistication. One study demonstrated that retarded subjects differed least from ordinary subjects in manual tasks. They fared worse on speed tests, spatial-inductive tests, and verbal tests, in this order. It is of interest that subjective ratings of intelligence correlated most with verbal ability while ratings of working ability correlated most with psychomotor ability.

Differential diagnostic instruments are supplanting general-intelligence tests for placement and training purposes. Batteries of ability tests and rating methods are under development, including motor and spatial ability, memory concept formation, number concepts, interests and work adjustments. New-type diagnostic tests which are goal-related rather than norm-related are being constructed with a view to giving more information about the extent to which pupils can reach instructional objectives. In this respect emphasis on the pupil's standing in relation to other students is minimized.

Mental measurement has convincingly demonstrated considerable individual variation in capacity, personality and motivation, even in groups which have been selected on the basis of a common handicap. The practical implication of this variation among pupils is that instruction should be compatible with the individual's abilities and needs. Nevertheless a large-scale study in Gothenburg demonstrates that individualization is still a desideratum rather than an actuality and that a considerable proportion of instruction is given in the form of collective class teaching in special classes.

An analysis of the concept of individually adapted instruction by Stukát and Engström found that individualization was characterized by: (a) instruction and tasks adapted to the needs and capacities of individual pupils; (b) Allowing pupils to work at their own speed; (c) provision of individual feedback; (d) making the pupil responsible for goal-setting and planning; (e) making the teacher's main function to arrange learning situations rather than to lecture.

The Swedish author exemplifies the interaction of research and educational practice by reference to developments in the differentiation–integration problem as applied to special education. It was not until well into the sixties that the system of special classes for slow learners was challenged. The arguments were not based on social equality which played a major role in the integration of pupils of average and high ability in the same classroom, but on considerations of efficacy. Since development of adjustment in a normal environment is an educational objective for the handicapped, as for other pupils, doubts were raised about the appropriateness of placing the handicapped in a secluded *milieu*. Research projects mounted as a consequence appeared to confirm the main conclusions from American studies, i.e. that the advantages of special class placement were not evident for all categories of slow learners or from all aspects of educational objectives.

This development hastened experimentation with alternative organizational models for special education; in Sweden pupils may be given some hours a week of extra instruction; they may attend a school clinic for remedial sessions, or may be given special self-instructional materials in their own classes. This has not meant elimination of special classes; in fact, in absolute figures their number has increased. Recent expansion of all handicap education, however, has referred to other remedial forms than special classes.

While the differentiation–integration problem is still far from settled, it illustrates the experimentation, the analysis of pupils' needs, and evaluation experiments which characterize the approach to special education in the recent past in Sweden.

Union of Soviet Socialist Republics
In the U.S.S.R. the most characteristic feature of mental handicap is regarded as the underdevelopment and specific nature of the cognitive activity in children who are retarded, and, while special education may lead to considerable personality development, it is not expected to result in normal levels of development in the mentally handicapped. Special education takes place in auxiliary schools, mostly residential, with an eight-year training period, and the majority of pupils consist of handicapped children who have suffered lesions of the central nervous system leading to developmental defects.

Early diagnosis is regarded as an important first step in the amelioration of handicapping conditions, and teachers, psychologists, physicians and neuro-physiologists are deemed necessary for a thorough differential diagnosis. A system of pre-school establishments has recently been developed and although it is the most severely affected children who have been placed in these, they have often proved to be better prepared for school than mildly affected children who remained at home before starting school. When mental handicap is ascertained in the pre-school period, an attempt is made to discuss with the parents the education of the child and its preparation for school. Advice is given about stimulating the child to enter into the active life of the family with programmes of self-help and assistance to adults.

Before placement is effected in a special school, every mentally handicapped child is examined by a special admission committee. These committees are set up in special schools and include the director of the school, an inspector of public education, a paediatrician, a psychoneurologist, a teacher from an ordinary school and one from a special school. The case notes are made available to all members of the committee, each of whom personally examines the child before a decision is reached. No child is placed in a special school without such an examination, with the exception of those who have undergone an examination at the Institute of Defectology.

The principal problems which are the objects of research in special education are: (a) the development of mentally handicapped children in special education programmes; (b) the structure of special educational establishments; (c) special methods of teaching subjects of the general education cycle as well as of occupational training—great importance is given to research with the aim of increasing effectiveness of oral and written speech since this is regarded as a vulnerable area of development in the mentally handicapped; (d) the principles and methods underlying the education of mentally retarded children and their preparation for work and for integration in society; (e) follow-up studies on the development of the retarded after leaving school which not only demonstrate the effectiveness of special education but also suggest improvements in schemes to prepare mentally handicapped pupils for independent living.

United States of America
In the past ten years, promising methods, principles and theories based upon the scientific study of the retarded in the United States began to appear in a field where there was previously a very limited store of scientific knowledge. This category of handicap consistently acquired more financial support for research than any other single handicap and the impact of the recommendations of the President's Panel on Mental Retardation was reckoned to be a potent force throughout the decade.

Other activities which influenced progress in this decade were a symposium on research design and methodology in 1959 and the publication of a manual on terminology, intended to reduce confusion and facilitate uniform reporting. Attention was directed to the conceptualization of mental retardation for purposes of planning research programmes, the role of administration in these programmes and the development and conservation of research talent. The new definition of mental handicap incorporated the concepts of sub-average intellectual functioning originating in the developmental period, and of impairment in one or more of the following: (a) maturation; (b) learning; (c) social adjustment.

A great deal of research was focused on the organizational structure of training provisions, curricular adaptation, post-school adjustment and on efficacy studies of special class placement and procedures. Studies of mildly handicapped children in special classes compared with similar children in regular classes indicated improved scholastic achievements after one year in the special class, but after two years both groups advanced at a similar rate. Many reviews of research, including one by Kirk, arrived at the conclusion that no definitive decisions were possible regarding the efficacy of special classes for educable mentally retarded pupils.

One study, however, on a group of retardates who divided school time between special class and regular class participation (integrated group) and a group in special class full-time (segregated group), compared these groups on measures of self-esteem. The segregated group gave expression to greater feelings of self-derogation and this was interpreted as an indictment of special class placement. On the other hand, slight gains were acknowledged in personal-social adjustment by those in special classes in another study and this was attributed to a mental hygiene approach by special class teachers. Conflicting or negative findings apparently still characterize this area of research.

Research on individual intelligence tests is reported, confirming the validity and reliability of the Wechsler Intelligence Scale for Children (WISC) and Stanford-Binet in moderate, mild and borderline retardation, while research into the relationship between these two tests and the Peabody Picture Vocabulary Test (PPVT) produced conflicting findings as to the equivalency of the three tests. The Syracuse Scales of Social Relations was revised for use with mentally retarded children. Attempts have been made to develop instruments and direct measures of retardates performance which would predict performance in real-life situations. One test which is consistently used as a research instrument is the ITPA and this is characteristic of the trend towards 'goal-directed' rather than 'norm-related' instruments in the assessment of the handicapped.

The applications of learning theory by the use of operant techniques has developed considerably in the last decade. Behaviour modification studies show a trend towards a broader range of behavioural targets and greater complexity of application. Work with pre-school children, with institutionalized children and with children in special classes using behaviour modification procedures is increasing, and primary (e.g. food) reinforcers, secondary (e.g. token economy) reinforcers and social reinforcements are being more systematically applied on the modification of classroom behaviour.

The report distinguishes between developmental, defect, and difference hypotheses, with regard to the basic nature of mental handicap. According to the developmental view, variation in cognitive development is determined largely by polygenic variations and the familialy retarded represent the lower end of the genetic distribution. Hence, in this view, familial retardates are essentially normal. It is assumed that even if environmental factors were held stable for all, major differences in I.Q. would still be produced by variations of the gene pool.

Difference and defect theories assume that one or more factors, over and above those postulated by the developmental view, are responsible for modifying the rate and level of development of cognitive functioning in mentally handicapped individuals. The difference hypothesis assumes that factors which affect intelligence vary continuously with variations in I.Q., whereas the defect hypothesis assumes that these factors operate to affect I.Q. only in the mentally handicapped range of intelligence.

As in other countries pre-school education programmes are being increasingly devised to prevent, or to compensate for, factors which would increase the possibility of intellectual impairment. The length of time required to produce stable cognitive changes, the optimum age for intervention, the roles of auxiliary teachers in the school and of parents in the home are all variables which have been studied. Traditional nursery schools, Montessori programmes, remediation of specific learning disabilities and direct verbal programmes concentrating on skills basic to scholastic achievement exemplify some of the approaches to the provision of learning experiences for disadvantaged children.

Controversy over compensatory education programmes was stimulated towards the end of the decade by Jensen's analysis which asserted that the concept of compensatory education had little theoretical basis, was unwarranted by past research findings that such programmes failed to yield lasting effects, and that such failure was bound to occur since genetic factors are much more important than environmental ones in producing I.Q. differences. Jensen distinguishes between large-scale programmes which did not affect the cultural and cognitive needs of experientally deprived children and programmes which permitted intensive intervention. Available data does suggest, however, that unless intervention programmes are sustained, the measurable gains which do take place are not likely to be consolidated. Large-scale follow-up studies are likely to clarify such issues and more precise theoretical formulations of the nature of mentally handicapped cognitive functioning may become available. The author highlights the necessity for examination of such issues, for he points out that while all educational programmes ultimately rest on our convictions about the relation between learning and intelligence our basic understanding of these relations is still tenuous.

Uruguay

Research in mental handicap reported by the Uruguayan author appears to comprise mainly descriptive studies undertaken by individuals focusing on handicapped learners rather than on the learning–instructional process. Such studies concern themselves with learning characteristics of retardates, socio-economic status, vocabulary and language development, and communication problems.

As in the other reports, early stimulation is being investigated for its effects on subsequent development. One long-term project is designed to determine the consequences of early, consistent, sequential sensory stimulation on the maturation of the central nervous system. This study includes two groups of children, 'high risk' infants and 'ideal' or 'low risk' infants. Applying strict criteria, these groups will present a close congruence with 'normal' and 'mentally deficient' or 'brain-injured' subjects. A follow-up evaluation is expected to supply important information about the value of a sequence of techniques of stimulation and activities which parallel developmental levels in compensatory programmes for handicapped infants.

Another concern of the author is with the proper use of intelligence tests. These results of intelligence scales are held to be meaningful only in interpretation and are helpful under certain conditions. First the results must be interpreted in the context of a broad knowledge of behaviour and the user must have a thorough understanding of their construction, standardization and validity criteria. Studies are reported on the WISC, the PPVT and

Stanford-Binet, and on the adaptation of the Gunzburg sociometric scale to a mentally handicapped population in a vocational centre.

The number of special classes and special schools is reported to be few in relation to the demand. The major focus appears to be in the sphere of primary education and adolescent retardates have as yet received limited attention. Nevertheless, during the past two decades, programmes for handicapped persons have doubled in Uruguay and in several other countries in Latin America. The end of the sixties witnessed a period of ferment in special education both in practical programmes and in research projects which, it is hoped, will promote more effective procedures in the education of the mentally handicapped in the seventies.

Speech handicapped children

Union of Soviet Socialist Republics

The report from the U.S.S.R. notes that in the treatment of speech disorders a symptomatic approach prevailed for a long time. In other words, external signs of speech disorders received attention as independent symptoms without due regard for the psychological aspects of speech development. This narrow approach limited the effectiveness of therapeutic intervention, did not ensure adequate treatment of the defect, and did not prepare children with speech disorders for successful application to schoolwork.

A new theory of speech pathology has recently appeared which embodies a systemic analysis of speech defects and relates the development of speech to other aspects of mental development. Investigations throwing light on the psychological processes underlying the development of speech have helped not only in differential diagnosis of speech defects but also in the production of special methods of remediation.

Early ascertainment of phonetic-phonematic disturbances in pre-school children has proved beneficial in the prevention of reading and writing disorders in the subsequent school years. As a result of this, the number of pre-school establishments for children with special defects is on the increase.

A new approach to the problem of stuttering has appeared; the phenomenon of stuttering in children is being studied from the aspect of the speech characteristics of the defect and from the aspect of analysis of non-verbal processes of communication. Attention is given to the child's general development as well as speech development, the conditions in which the defect emerges, the conditions which reduce or exacerbate the stuttering, and the relationship between active and passive speech. A special system in use with pre-school children and junior pupils involving manual work helps in the elimination of stuttering. This system provides for a gradual transition from situational to contextual speech.

The more severe defects of speech such as aphasic conditions and pseudobulbar dysarthria have remained outside the influence of pedagogy and are regarded as medical problems. However a great deal of attention is being given to the remediation of minor speech disorders in the ordinary school.

United States of America

In this area much of the research in the United States was directed towards articulation disorders, fluency and stuttering, and problems of voice quality. Towards the close of the sixties, theory and investigation included language and communication disorders within their scope.

Research on stuttering concentrated on personality factors, on conditions at the onset of stuttering, and on improved description, analysis and scaling of stuttering behaviour. Some studies focused on the relation of stuttering to other maladaptive behaviour, some on parent-child interactions and some on the personalities of the parents of stutterers, as well as on those of the stutterers themselves. Basal metabolism, brain waves and muscle tension of stutterers were measured. Projects involved a critical appraisal of various approaches towards the treatment of stuttering, and operant studies indicated the potential value of such an approach. One programme demonstrated stuttering therapy based on principles of family therapy and operant conditioning, with the aim of giving the parent the primary responsibility for treatment.

Research on the special disorders associated with mental handicap, childhood aphasia and cerebral palsy was noted. Research on speech therapy with the mentally handicapped was reported as being inadequate. Some of the major issues in childhood aphasia were noted as differential diagnosis, the comparative value of therapeutic and educational approaches to remediation, and problems of nomenclature and conceptualization of aphasia.

One research project demonstrated a specific deficit in auditory learning in aphasic children independent of chronological age (C.A.), mental age (M.A.) and hearing loss: another research project showed a deficiency in visual spatial memory in aphasic children. Sequencing subtests of the ITPA, a tapping test and the Knox Cube Test were used in a study of perception in aphasic children which identified temporal sequencing as a central factor in aphasic disabilities. Principles and techniques of operant conditioning had a considerable impact on the form and direction of research in this area during the sixties. Verbal punishment contingent with disfluencies in speech was found to reduce the frequency of disfluency, whereas the random use of verbal punishment produced no changes in fluency. Operant conditioning procedures were used to develop speech in mute children, by establishing simple auditory-motor associations in mute autistic children, and by instituting in them consistent reponse patterns to verbal commands.

The American author expresses the opinion that practice and research in the field of the speech handicapped is not as well integrated into educational programming as in other areas of handicap.

One important characteristic of the decade was the increasing concern with language development and the growth in several areas of linguistics. The view that verbal behaviour is a terminal response in a large complex of language responses was acknowledged by an increasing number of people. This change can be seen in the NEA–CEC reviews which progressed from a concern with speech handicapped to research on speech, language and communication disorders. Important among the theoretical contributions of the decade are Lenneberg's treatise on the biological foundations of language and Chomsky's view on the internal structure which equips children with the equivalent of a 'universal grammar' or master-template from which they construct their own language from the stimuli of their language environment. These highlight the genetic component of the nature–nurfure equation, but in no sense absolve us from the obligation to seek for further information about the role of experience in language acquisition.

Visually impaired children

Union of Soviet Socialist Republics

In the U.S.S.R. statistics on visually impaired children enrolled in special schools are collected every five years. Pupils with defective vision are then classified according to the causes of their defect, the clinical form of the defect, the state of their vision, any type of concomitant disturbance and their scholastic progress.

It is reported that between 8 and 12 per cent of pupils in such schools are totally blind. A steady decline in total blindness as a result of acquired forms of the defect has been taking place and the percentage of inate anomalies and of intra-uterine visual defects is also showing a steady decline.

Advances in technology have influenced the development of special apparatus for the blind and have been responsible for the use of general 'hardware' in the education of the blind. Devices are used which transform light signals into acoustic and tactile signals accessible to blind pupils. Laboratory work in physics, chemistry, geography and other subjects hitherto not possible for the blind are now available to them. A reading machine has been developed which speeds up the process and facilitates the reading of words and of groups of words rather than first identifying separate letters. Research has provided information about optimal degrees of illumination in work situations for pupils with defective vision.

Again, experiments in this field demonstrate the necessity for early intervention and for the provision of an adequate learning environment for the young blind child. Pre-school programmes involving play activities, creative work and preparatory training make significant contributions towards normal development in the young blind pupil and can prevent or offset systemic and other secondary effects of the child's visual impairment.

In communicating with his environment the child first uses gestures which designate objects and actions. Such communication with blind-deaf children is impossible without first acquiring the language of gestures. Following upon this, verbal speech in dactyl form with a simultaneous use of already acquired gestures is promoted in the young blind-deaf pupil. The next step is to learn the written form of speech by means of the Braille system. This systematic approach enables blind-deaf children to acquire the grammatical principles of oral speech, to accumulate an adequate vocabulary and to prepare for the school programme. Finger speech and the Braille alphabet are noted here as the basic form of communication in such handicapped children and the necessity for commencing the teaching of oral speech at an early age is reiterated.

United States of America

The NEA–CEC research review (1963) of research on visual impairment drew attention to the need for more educationally oriented research in this field. Most of the more sophisticated investigations had apparently been psychological or sociological in nature, while most projects were undertaken by single, isolated investigators and there appeared to be little systematic, sustained, institutionalized support for investigations in this area. The major sources of research and research information throughout the decade continued to be the American Printing House for the Blind, the American Foundation for the Blind and the Massachusetts Institute of Technology (MIT). One review in 1969 made the point that, except for MIT, no university had assembled the 'critical mass' of research resource needed for a sustained programmatic attack on visual handicap.

Nevertheless the decade saw significant advances and increased efforts to understand the unique developmental characteristics of the young blind child. As reported in other studies, there was a dramatic decrease in cases of total blindness principally stemming from the eradication of retrolental fibroplasia. For example, a review in 1963 notes a decrease of 25 per cent in the incidence of blind children during the period 1960–63, as contrasted with a 70 per cent decrease in the preceding three-year period.

Important trends noted were: (a) maximum utilization of residual vision in the education of partially sighted pupils; (b) a growing emphasis on educationally functional criteria in distinguishing blindness and partial sightedness and less reliance upon medical and legal criteria; and (c) the influence of technology on research and on technical devices which permitted more direct approaches to the problem of information access to the blind, such as the conversion of visual into tactile information.

Surveys of visually impaired children in day schools and residential programmes showed that 20 per cent had concomitant handicaps in addition to blindness. The commonest additional handicap was mental retardation and one study reported an incidence of 15 per cent mentally handicapped blind pupils in residential programmes for the visually impaired.

Braille research occupied a considerable number of investigators. Programmed instruction in Braille became available. Discriminability of tactual symbols was studied in relation to progress in Braille reading proficiency and the role of the differential sensitivity of fingers analysed. Studies indicated that superior tactual perception was a major factor among the best Braille readers whereas M.A., C.A. and I.Q. were not significantly correlated with excellence in reading.

A centre for tactile research and for sensory aids was developed at MIT. Sensory aids included high speed electric Braille writers, means of converting Braille typesetting tapes to spoken words, and improved guidance devices to help the blind find their way. Tactile research was aimed at the conversion of visual information into tactile information.

Since in most cases diagnosis of visual impairment is early, intervention can take place almost immediately. One study suggests that opportunities for learning are the most important determinants of the child's functioning. When the cortex is not directly involved in the visual defect there is no limit to the levels of achievement to which blind pupils may aspire provided that the conditions, equipment and personnel appropriate for their needs are adequate. Research on early learning and perception indicates that neonates can 'see' much better than had been assumed and indicates the importance of early intervention in cases of sensory deprivation.

Multiply handicapped children

All handicapped persons have an initial disability—physical, emotional or mental—which acts as an impediment to development in a particular way. Primary handicaps do not operate on their own to retard development: they are always reinforced by other factors, some which may be consequent upon the handicap itself, including personal and social reactions to it, and others which are incidental to the situation where the handicapped person grows and develops. The Soviet author demonstrates from Vygotsky's research that certain defects, innate or acquired during the early years, instigate various interdependent changes in the whole course of mental development. Deafness or blindness, for example, cause a number of secondary deviations in early mental development. Numerous investigations quoted in the Soviet report support the view that a primary defect is complexly interwoven with secondary defects and with many deviations which are occasioned by them. The more complex the forms of mental activity, the more obvious become these defects. Handicaps which provoke unfavourable attitudes on the part of parents or of the public accentuate the handicapped child's difficulties in ways which further compromise his future. Exclusion from social activities and from developmental opportunities available to other children, and lack of cultural stimulation are circumstances which give rise to secondary disorders, jeopardizing still further the handicapped child's opportunities for progressive growth. In this sense, most handicapped children may be regarded as multiply handicapped since the initial defect is inevitably followed by unfavourable consequences of many kinds. Nevertheless, while we cannot annul a primary defect in a handicapped child we can minimize its effects and so modify the environment that the possibilities for adaptation are enhanced.

However, the term 'multiply handicapped' in the following texts refers to those who suffer from two or more severe primary disabilities, which may be any combination of the previously discussed categories of handicap. The American author acknowledges that at the present level of knowledge it is sometimes difficult or impossible to determine whether a given handicap is primary, or secondary to another, but nevertheless assumes that this distinction can be made.

The American report embodies an analysis of the three main lines of research in an approach to the study of multiply handicapping conditions.

The first is a *clinical* approach where the focus is on individuals with two or more primary defects such as blind-mentally retarded, or emotionally disturbed-deaf children. The second is concerned with *cross disability research* where the focus is on the handicapping conditions rather than on the affected individuals and is thus likely to be more theoretical than clinical. This is often directed towards the comparative study of specific variables or educational approaches across several discrete handicapping conditions. The third approach is concerned with *administrative* matters and the focus is on the system wherein development and models of delivery of services to the handicapped takes place.

The demand for services for the multiply handicapped has increased in the sixties principally because of the extended life-span of affected individuals due to advances in medical knowledge. Projects are reported on studies of various combinations of primary defects. One is concerned with the development of residential programmes in order to overcome early experiential deprivation in emotionally disturbed pseudo-mentally retarded blind children. Another deals with characteristic psycholinguistic disabilities of mentally retarded, emotionally disturbed children. The construction and evaluation of new instructional materials and methods in the education of emotionally disturbed children is also reported.

It is noted that such clusters of primary defects precluded the use of conventional psychometric devices in the assessment of affected children. One suggested alternative to the use of tests in assessment was the use of video-taped recordings of behaviour samples in multiply handicapped infants for further study by clinical experts.

It is clear that there is a growing awareness of the necessity for early ascertainment and intervention, especially in multiply handicapping conditions. Pre-school programmes and involvement in the early education of such handicapped children are once more envisaged as necessary prerequisites in effective programmes for their improvement.

The sixties witnessed an increased interest in disability research with a trend towards the support of long-range programmatic projects. For example, one collaborative perinatal study was initiated to examine the relationships of the conditions of pregnancy, birth and infancy to exceptionality in later behaviour and in school performance. The development of about 2,000 kindergarten, first-grade and fourth-grade children was to be followed over a three-year period by means of the ITPA, standard readiness and achievement tests and behaviour ratings. A related study over a ten-year period sought predictors of reading disability from data collected about perinatal, natal and post-natal conditions.

Other studies quoted which show the broad scope of cross disability research, evaluate the effects of different types of environment upon handicapped children and more specifically the effects of architectural design upon the education of the handicapped. A Research and Development Center was established at Columbia University in 1967. This was one of the first to be established following upon a decision of USOE to support such centres on a programmatic basis over extended periods of time. A comprehensive long-range programme of research with all types of handicapped children was projected. Specific goals of this programme were the analysis of instructional systems, the psychological demands of basic school tasks and the development of a psychoeducational taxonomy which elucidates the interdependencies of pupils, tasks and instructional systems.

It is probable that such research and development centres will play a significant part in translating research findings in terms more readily understandable and hence more easily applicable by the teacher-practitioner. They will also, it is expected, play a part in the professional training of those in direct contact with the handicapped.

Administrative research showed a distinct evolution during the last decade. In the 1959 NEA–CEC research review, emphasis was laid on such topics as optimum size of class, selection of teachers, teacher-aides, pre-school programmes, post-school guidance, parent and community involvement in the education of the handicapped.

While these topics remained high on the list of administrative priorities, the 1963 NEA–CEC research review underlined the need for more intensive study into the roles of administrators in service programmes, the educational background and experiences of administrators, and the optimum ratio of teachers to supervisors in special programmes.

In the 1966 NEA–CEC research review evidence was given of the increase in multiply handicapping conditions and the relationship of socio-economic class to handicap was discussed. The need for pre-school programmes was further stressed and the national 'war against poverty' in the United States was credited with giving impetus to the demands for early intervention.

The 1968 CEC review drew attention to the lack of administrative research. The principal factors compounding this deficiency in research were specified as multiply handicapping conditions, involving in their care multiple disciplines being dealt with at multiple levels of responsibility (federal, state, local and facility) and finally, the lack of research 'know-how' among administrators.

However, by the end of the decade, administrative research appeared to have risen in priority and illustrations of this are afforded by the types of projects which were supported by state and federal funds in 1969:

1. Graduate-level training of specialists in the development and operation of pre-school centres.
2. Delivery of services in any areas where the parents had rejected special classes. The alternative model was to institute small classes, incorporating handicaps to the extent of one-third of each class, and the use of teachers, teachers' aides and master-teachers, trained as learning analysts and consultants.
3. Development of evaluation systems to assess the value of programmes, staff-training schemes, demonstration centres and projects.
4. Development of a written resource guide with co-ordinated automated slide-tape for a set of evaluation materials for teachers and other special education personnel.

These trends reflected the growing criticism that research and developments had concentrated too much on the components of services and too little on the problems of delivery of services. The American author outlines a personal effort to systematize existing knowledge of the delivery of health, education and welfare services to handicapped children. He views the goal of administration as the development and maintenance of optimum relationships between a community's needs and its resources. Not only does he assign to administration the obligation to identify needs but also the obligation to develop and deliver services appropriate to those needs. This obligation is fulfilled only with the ultimate delivery of services to the intended consumer. From this point of departure, the author develops an interesting set of principles which provide a foundation for intensive long-range empirical study of delivery systems.

It is possible that the increased growth of research on the multiply handicapped may lead to a new mode of conceptualizing educational handicaps. Should this take place there will of necessity be changes in the formation and certification of personnel dealing with the handicapped and in the organization of the services which at present provide education to handicapped children. In the past, teacher-training programmes in special education tended to focus on specialization in a single area of handicap. This adherence to standards based on traditional areas of handicap in the training of teachers is raising doubts as to the adequacy of such teachers when it is a question of working with multiply handicapped children. It may also go some way to explain why it is so difficult to meet the educational needs of such children and why the multiply handicapped more than any other group seem to strain institutional tolerance to the limits.

A great deal of the momentum for this new approach stems from the emergence of public concern in the past decade for groups of children variously described as 'socially disadvantaged', 'culturally deprived' and 'intellectually deprived'. Many of those who function socially and intellectually at the levels of mild and borderline mental handicap are to be found among the lower status groups of certain societies lacking in the stimulation and learning opportunities for children which most normal families and homes provide. The evidence from many studies indicates that environment, heredity and effective intelligence are in such complex interaction as to be inextricable and typical findings in the area of backwardness indicate that children from poor and illiterate homes are at a great disadvantage with those more fortunately placed, where the parents are attentive, interested and literate. Unfavourable factors—unmet health needs, cultural values antithetical to the values of the system, negative expectations raised both by their own group and the larger society—result in a significantly high prevalence of learning difficulties and in the stunting of intellectual, linguistic and social competency.

As a result of the increased attention directed towards such groups in the last decade the 'nature–nurture' problem became an irrelevant issue. A further direct outcome was increased concern with the delivery of services to the consumer, for apart from the reluctance of some parents to take advantage of existing services, there appeared to be inequities in the distribution of services which worked to the disadvantage of the poor.

The principal indirect outcomes of this increased interest in the multiply handicapped will probably be, the American author predicts, changes in the training of personnel for all types of handicapping conditions and more proficiency in the delivery of health, education and welfare services at all levels.

Predicted future trends
of research

Among the broad purposes of the reports, the following are particularly important: (a) assessment of the current status of research-based knowledge about the education of handicapped children; (b) the selection of research and demonstration projects which might exemplify the achievements of the last decade, and indicate the extent to which these are applied in special education; (c) the elucidation of trends which would identify areas where the expenditure of further research efforts might prove fruitful.

Each of the reports contains a chapter where the authors attempt to identify those trends which they consider are most likely to have a widespread influence on future ways of conceptualizing the problems of the handicapped and on research related to special education. Their predictions are based principally on a selection and analysis of the work in their own countries which gives a sense of the substance of research, development and demonstration relating to each type of handicap.

The material reported is thus a selection of research from several disciplines which exemplifies current methods and strategies in the field of special education and it is on these that predictions are based. Because of the wide range of reported material, any attempt to report and evaluate the most important future trends must be based on a further selection of abstracts. However, it is hoped that from an appraisal of ongoing activities, even where there may be unavoidable subjectivity in the selection, the long-range planning, which is so essential in every educational undertaking, may be rendered more objective.

Sweden

In an analysis of recent empirical educational research, the Swedish author indicates that the emphasis so far has been on measurement of the individual characteristics of learners and teachers, either for prognostic-diagnostic purposes or for evaluating the effects of intrusion. The teaching–learning process itself, which is the central problem of education, has been neglected. As the practical and methodological difficulties involved in the study of educational processes in natural situations are increasingly being overcome, this will change. It is likely that empirical analysis of the learning-instructional processes in special education will become an important field of research in the near future.

Future process analysis studies will not necessarily be limited to established forms of instruction but will also be used in evaluations of new instructional methods or programmes. It is likely that designs of experimental educational studies will include a procedure for scrutiny control, and documentation of observable and recordable characteristics of the teaching methods under study. It is hoped that independent variables in educational research will be as thoroughly defined operationally as dependent variables have been for a long time.

The trend towards individually adapted instruction in special education has created a need for 'objective-related' tests rather than 'norm-related' tests, that is, tests which indicate not so much the extent to which educational objectives have been achieved, but more the individual's deficits, to which educational strategies may then be directed. It can be expected that research will lead to the creation of new instruments for diagnostic information which can be translated readily into educational recommendations.

While the development of self-tutoring devices and self-instructional systems is likely to continue, changes in approach and organization are likely to become more a technical than a research task, taken over by technologists, subject-matter experts and publishing bodies. The main objects for educational research in the future are likely to be basic instructional problems in

the teaching–learning process, such as inductive versus deductive methods
or understanding versus imitation in language instruction.

In the development of instructional programmes for handicapped
students it is probable that there will be greater integration with the construction of more comprehensive systems for the non-handicapped. The basic
material for self-instructional systems for general use will be supplemented
by additional components adapted to students with special learning difficulties.

Judgements about the efficacy of models of delivery of educational services
will no longer be based purely on tradition, 'commonsense', intuition or the
predilections of certain individuals. Existing organizational models and
innovations alike will be submitted to empirical and systematic evaluation of
their effects, and studies related to educational arrangements are likely to
increase in the seventies.

Union of Soviet Socialist Republics

The Soviet author devotes a series of chapters designed to give an account of
the substance, principal achievements and general directions of research on
the mentally retarded, the deaf, the blind, the speech-impaired and on
research in vocational training procedures. However, since some of the
directions of research will be given relatively greater attention than others,
he analyses the specific areas in which he expects research efforts to be appreciably extended:

1. More sophisticated procedures for the diagnosis of defects in children with
   learning disabilities will be developed.
2. Because of the established effectiveness of early intervention in offsetting
   the systemic effects of initial handicaps, greater stress will be laid on
   methods of evaluating handicaps and their effects in the first years of life.
3. Research in early development is likely to lead to more scientifically based
   and differentiated instructional systems in the pre-school period.
4. There will be an expansion of research projects involving the assessment of
   pupils in the ordinary school with mild developmental defects and with
   partial sensory defects, which when neglected have an adverse effect on
   the learning capacities of pupils.
5. An increased concern with the psychological foundations of the instructional–learning process with the multiple handicapped will be more
   evident.
6. Evaluative studies of the vocational and social competency of graduates
   from special educational programmes will be given more attention.
7. It is expected that more investigations aimed at a scientific–technical
   elaboration of devices to compensate for auditory and visual defects will
   be developed in order to improve the educational procedures for pupils
   undergoing instruction in special programmes for the blind and deaf.

United States of America

In attempting to decide research directions and trends, the American author has relied heavily on the NEA–CEC monographs and has made extensive use of these authoritative reviews:

1. The category of 'crippled or otherwise health-impaired' as originally defined was not reviewed in the 1969 NEA–CEC review of research but a new conceptual–clinical–educational entity emerged. This was variously titled 'learning disability', 'learning disorder', 'cerebral dysfunction', 'minimal brain dysfunction', etc. While the original cause of this condition may be organic, major treatment relies on educational strategies. The author predicts a growing absorption in the seventies with research on learning disabilities and their treatment.

2. The role of education is likely to become increasingly dominent in the provision of programmes for the emotionally disturbed. There will be more emphasis on the elimination of disruptive behaviours and on educational remediation, rather than on attempts to restructure the personalities of distrubed pupils, a goal which, in view of the acute shortage of psychologists and psychiatrists, is in any case unrealistic. The growing awareness that most disturbed children suffer from disturbed cognitive as well as affective functions will mean that the educator will not be regarded as a mere substitute for the specialist in psychology or psychiatry but will contribute in his own right to the more effective functioning of emotionally disturbed pupils. There will be a trend towards an ecological approach to behavioural–social events and this will increase our understanding about the adaptive capacities of societies as well as of those of the individual. Cross-cultural studies are likely to provide crucial information about what is programmed in genetic human nature and what is culturally induced.

3. With the hearing-impaired there will be an increased tendency to view them as individuals rather than as a homogeneous group. Utilization of residual hearing will be improved by means of more sophisticated technical devices. Research will be stepped up on the construction of devices to transform acoustic signals of speech into visual or tactile modalities, and of devices to improve or replace speech reading. Interest in the role of manual communication will increase. From the theoretical point of view, outstanding issues will be better explained as new concepts and techniques from psycholinguistics are assimilated into research.

4. The era of intense activity in mental handicap research ushered in by the sixties will continue and increase in the seventies. Research will most probably be focused on: (a) early development and environmental stimulation of the mentally retarded; (b) compensatory programmes and pre-school education; (c) the principles and techniques of operant conditioning in special educational and work/study programmes for retardates; (d) efficacy studies of special classes, special day schools, and integration of the retarded in regular classrooms; (e) curricular orientation—academic

or vocational—in special education for adolescents and organizational schemes aimed at easing the school-to-work transition for its pupils; (f) the prediction of rehabilitation outcomes; (g) the psychological foundations of special education and more precise theoretical foundations of the nature of the retardates' cognitive functioning; (h) the role of the educational systems in the prevention and remediation of behavioural and cognitive deficits due to differences in social, cultural and economic factors in the larger society; (i) efforts to test and implement the findings of research projects and to bridge the gulf between educators and behavioural scientists; (j) model service delivery systems; (k) interagency co-ordination and the training of personnel.

5. In the field of speech impairment, practice and research have not been as well integrated into educational programming as the other areas of handicap. The magnitude of the problem on its own will probably bring about a better utilization of schools and teachers in the amelioration of the milder forms of speech impairment. The principles and techniques of operant condition will influence the form and direction of much of the research in the correction of defective articulation. An increased concern with language development will spring from sophisticated contributions from several areas of linguistics which already have had considerable impact in this area.

6. With the visually impaired, research is likely to lead to an improved understanding and utilization of their unique cognitive and developmental characteristics. An increase in knowledge about the ego development of blind infants will lead to more sophisticated pre-school programmes, including home guidance programmes and more teaching films for professionals and for parents of blind children. The drive to increase the flow of information to the blind will be further assisted by technological advances and by more complex transformation of information, e. g. visual to tactile, and the direct conversion of print to Braille is a possibility at present being explored.

7. In an analysis of the dramatic increase in support of studies involving multiple handicap, the American author indicates that this may be attributed to a strong trend towards the organization of research and related activities around problems encountered in educational settings, instead of around classification based on medical, physiological or psychological disciplines. From this trend there may emerge a new mode of conceptualizing educational disabilities. This may lead to educational programmes based on educationally relevant behaviour. Should this take place, major changes in teacher preparation and certification will follow. There will also be changes in the organization of the services which provide special education. At present special education is organized and teachers trained in adherence to standards based on categories of handicap. Changes in the direction of research are likely to be reflected in the professional preparation of personnel and in the organiz-

ation of services. The selection, training and experience of professional personnel may become a major focus in research. Since attitudes and values in respect of their profession, acquired in the course of professional training or by experience, may have profound effects on the 'utilizability' of personnel, it is essential that these processes be submitted to objective evaluation. The impetus for research in the area of multiple handicap has come from a heightened awareness of the effects of early social and economic disadvantage upon the early development of children. One outcome of this concern with disadvantaged children will be an increase in research on the delivery of services, including research on compensatory education and on pre-school programmes.

The trends which promise to have a generic influence on conceptual and methodological considerations important to special education and to research in this field may be summarized as: (a) *educational services*, involving: emphasis on early education; attention to the modes of delivery of services; evaluation of the efficacy of programmes; growth of interest in learning disabilities; and (b) *research related to education*, involving: less emphasis on the physiological aspects of disability and greater interest in the behavioural aspects of exceptionality; a growing awareness of interdependent conditions and of multiple disabilities leading to greater focus of attention on the ecology of behaviour; cross-disability research; behaviour modification, operant conditioning and the functional analysis of behaviour; research on early development of the handicapped; research on early cognitive development; the objective appraisal of adaptive behaviour.

In addition it is likely that there will be a trend away from basic to applied research. While popular indignation against the narrow kind of scholarship which exists for its own sake may be justified, the American report sounds a note of warning. The behavioural sciences, in contrast to the physical and biological sciences, have pitifully small stores of basic knowledge from which education can draw. Any significant reduction in support of knowledge-oriented research would probably result in unfavourable consequences for special education.

Uruguay

The author indicates that ascertainment and diagnosis of the handicapped have in the past been the responsibility of medical specialists, and that placement in special educational facilities has therefore been based on the diagnostic judgements of specialists in medicine and psychology. With the recent expansion of special educational programmes, a marked trend among educationalists has been to seek information and diagnostic data from an increased number of sources, and assessment and placement will probably become increasingly a multidisciplinary approach with the teacher playing a greater part.

A new project with the proposed title CIDERM (centre for investigation, diagnosis and education of the mentally retarded) is in the process of organization. This aims at analysing and classifying educational disabilities in children and implementing appropriate educational strategies to deal with them. Such a project will facilitate collection, storage, retrieval and analysis of data for the evaluation of diagnostic procedures, educational methods and systems of delivery of services in special educational practice.

With the help of CIDERM, the near future will see:

1. Improved methods of dissemination of information and guidance to all those with an interest in the education of children with educational disabilities of all types.
2. More objective evaluation of diagnosis, remedial methods, equipment and materials and systems in special education.
3. Systematic evaluation of the effects of special education on pupils in special programmes for specific defects.

In general this will probably result in an increased emphasis on the applications of research to classroom practice and in a lessening of the gulf between the scientific and service communities in the next five years.

Role of research in the training
of teachers for special education

One of the limiting factors in the progress of special education is the gulf which too often exists between the scientific and service communities. On the one hand there are the results of fundamental research containing new principles with a bearing on classroom practice, but these are often reported in journals available only to other research workers, or couched in such recondite terms that the possibilities for direct application are lost to the teacher. On the other hand, many teachers have not been prepared in the course of their professional formation to read appropriate journals and are unable to apply scientific methods of analysis to new subject-matter, materials or methods. People can work only within the framework of knowledge and theory available to them and, in the absence of efforts to utilize the findings of current research, there can be long delays before valuable concepts are embodied in educational practice.

To accomplish the aims of special education the teacher must be informed and questioning, prepared to examine the efficacy of his own procedures in the class, and ready to evaluate those factors outside the classroom which can best promote effective living and maturity in his pupils. By a knowledge of, and association with, research and research methods, the teacher will be better able to arrange the conditions, the materials, the content of instruction and the setting where optimal learning can best take place. Thus the teacher will become a qualified professional rather than 'a mediator of traditional rules of thumb' (Soukat).

Each of the following reports stresses the fact that teacher training for special education should be founded on a scientific basis and that teachers in training should have direct experience of educational research.

In the Scandinavian countries, training for special education is based on two- to four-year courses. The studies are grouped in (a) educational psychology and sociology; (b) methods of instruction; (c) practice; and (d) subject-matter courses. The educational psychology courses carry the main responsibility for the student teacher's research orientation, and it can be seen from examples of the programmes in the Scandinavian countries outlined in the following reports that the behavioural sciences exert a strong influence upon the teacher in training.

The educational system in the United States is decentralized, with each of the fifty States bearing the responsibility for its own system of public (i.e. tax-supported) education. School attendance is compulsory between the ages of 6 and 16 years, although some states extend this obligation to 18 years.

Beyond the secondary level there are technical institutes, junior and community colleges, training institutions for teachers, professional schools and universities. Most colleges offer a four-year programme for a bachelor's degree; the universities, which usually comprise undergraduate colleges, professional schools and graduate schools, offer courses of study leading to bachelors' degrees and advanced degrees.

While the number of private colleges and universities is greater than those supported by public funds, the number of students at public institutions is greater than those at private institutions.

Because of the variety of teacher training programmes in the United States, their role in the development of research manpower and in influencing teachers attitudes towards research is difficult to characterize. However, a survey of the backgrounds of several thousand educational researchers in 1965 showed that 46 per cent were trained in psychology, 45 per cent in education and 6 per cent in sociology. A further study of 87 eminent educationists showed that 61 designated psychology as their major area of specialization, whereas 17 indicated education and 9 sociology as their special study. This would appear to coincide with the Scandinavian experience and illustrates the influence of the behavioural sciences in the development of special education.

One of the obstacles to the preparation of research personnel lies in the confused conceptual structure of the field of special education. The American author identifies the traditional focus on individual handicapping conditions as being the principal source of this confusion. This creates a demand for specialization at undergraduate level, which is emphasized at graduate level and consolidated in professional practice. Focusing on a specific area of handicap raises problems in the training of researchers. In the absence of a unifying model of training, capable of countering the divisive influences of compartmentalization, paradigms are borrowed from some established fields. While this is not inherently prejudicial to development in a new field, there is the danger that the research specialists will simply be methodologists trained in the techniques of psychology or sociology.

However, one of the developments from which may emerge new modes of conceptualizing educational handicaps is the growth of cross-disability research. Other promising factors are the movement towards the classroom, with increased reliance upon the observation and judgements of teachers and the introduction of an educationally focused ecological point of view.

The Research and Development Center at Columbia University exemplifies one of the contemporary patterns of organization of academic resources, having among its principal objectives the development of a new science of special education and the application of research findings to teaching and practice. The centre is linked with the Special Education Department of the State of Columbia and through the department with schools and facilities for the handicapped. It has on-going research in five areas of handicap and a broad framework of experience and knowledge is encompassed by the composition of the staff. Such co-operative enterprises are likely to sustain the quality of research and to ensure that the findings of research are implemented without delay.

In the U.S.S.R. the uniform system of State supervision makes it possible to ascertain the demand for teacher–defectologists and to organize their professional training in higher colleges. Priorities in research can be determined, the work co-ordinated and the results of scientific research implemented without delay. The system of public education not only creates special schools where needed, but provides textbooks, visual aids and manuals for teachers. The compilation of texts for special schools and their circulation so that they are freely available ensures that curricula and programmes are of a universally high standard and that all teachers in special education are made aware of the most up-to-date findings of research.

One of the significant developments in the co-ordination of research with educational practice is the organization of 'pedagogical readings'. These are arranged by the Institute of Defectology at the U.S.S.R. Academy of Pedagogical Sciences and the participants are advanced school-teachers whose papers are devoted to problems associated with the education of handicapped children.

In Uruguay the training of teachers for special education takes place at the Teachers' College, Montevideo, and practical experience is afforded to the students as the Escuela de Recuperación Psíquica.

It appears that a great deal of current research in Uruguay consists of single-person achievements by individuals who are all engaged in professional work with the handicapped. This double function often results in allegiance divided between professional work and scientific discipline. While this may be a necessary step in the evolution of a newly established field, it generally means that a great deal of energy is being directed towards the preparation of teachers, or of those who will teach teachers.

The next step is the setting up of programmes for those who will express their allegiance to service through research. Special teachers for handicapped pupils, those who prepare them professionally and those who devote their energies to basic research are all essential components for a comprehensive programme of special education. Mutual acceptance between these modes of service can best be acquired early in one's career.

People tend to work as they have been trained so that programmes which aim at decreasing the psychological distance between teachers, those who prepare them, and researchers should produce many gains. Easier access to schools and classrooms and increased possibilities of interactions with teachers should heighten the relevance and improve the quality of research enterprise. This in turn should induce more favourable attitudes on the part of teachers towards the production and conduct of research. In such a climate, the knowledge-to-action cycle is accelerated and handicapped persons reap the benefit of co-operative allegiance to the goal of service.

Organization of research

Research is a vital prerequisite for educational advance and for progress in the behavioural sciences. In special education, research entails a systematic observation of handicapped pupils, description and evaluation of the teacher–learning process, the relation of facts with other facts and the elucidation of functional relations and correlations. Resources in funds and in qualified research personnel are the essential bases for research activities. Since there is no assurance that every research project will result in gains, research is often regarded as a high risk enterprise. Yet policy makers are under many pressures to spend money, and they must seek to spend it wisely. This gives rise to many questions—whether resources should be diversified, or concentrated on a limited number of projects, whether priority should be given to basic research problems (brain function, learning, memory, etc.) or to specific problems related to categorical aspects of handicapping factors, and so on. In the latter case, while a balance ought to be struck between a generic and a categorical approach, in actuality, this often proves difficult because of competing claims. Because of the relationship between the findings of re-search and its organization, it is often difficult to separate these two aspects in any analysis.

The American author gives a detailed account of the complex organi-zation and support of research enterprise in the United States; the Swedish author traces the growth of research in his country in the past three decades with the assumption of governmental responsibility for financing and pro-moting research at a variety of levels; the Soviet author devotes a brief chapter to describing the organization of research in the U.S.S.R. with the assumption of centralized responsibility and direction; and the Uruguayan author demonstrates that while descriptive studies of the work of individuals continue to appear, there is a tendency to move away from such single-person achievements towards large-scale projects where the characterization of handicapped groups is taking its place in broader research programmes.

Sweden

Here research in special education takes place within a framework common to all educational research. Traditionally, research was located in university departments but the establishment of the State Institute of Educational Psychology in 1944 and of the National Council for Social Science Research in 1948 gave new direction and stimulus to educational research in general. These events were followed by orders for special studies emanating from the various governmental commissions of inquiry into Swedish educational practice. For example, the need for professional psychologists and recom-mendations for their training comprised the main terms of reference for a commission of inquiry reporting in 1955. Following upon this, the State Institute of Educational Psychology was dissolved and the staff transferred to the Institute of Educational Research at the School of Education in Stockholm.

Several State committees have engaged research institutes to clarify as-pects of such important problems as streaming, differentiation, integration and empirical curriculum analyses for the new comprehensive schools and gymnasia. Again the National Board of Education awarded substantial grants for large-scale educational research projects directed towards the evaluation of existing programmes, the planning of curricula and the development of assessment techniques and instruments.

The City of Stockholm Educational Board has set up a Pedagogical Centre staffed by qualified researchers who give priority to local regional problems. In special education, for example, there is currently an on-going research project to study the effects of a mental hygiene programme in a Stockholm school district.

Around the country, Educational Development Blocks have been estab-lished by joint State and community resources for the purposes of innovation and implementation of new instructional methods. These also co-operate with the schools of education and with research institutes.

While there are no institutions which deal solely with research in special education, it is estimated from cost surveys that approximately one-third of the money devoted to educational research is earmarked for projects and developments directly related to special education.

The last two decades in Sweden have been characterized by the spirit of reform in education and by a rapid and prodigious expansion of educational research. Developments in education have been closely allied with the progress of the behavioural sciences and reflect to some extent the disciplines of those who took the initiative in this broad advance.

Union of Soviet Socialist Republics

In 1918 a special decree of the Council of People's Commissars placed all the educational establishments for handicapped children, including public and private institutions, under the authority of the People's Commissariat of Education. The State character of the system of special education has exerted influences favourable to the rapid development of uniform structures and patterns of organization in special education.

Research work in the field of special education and in all handicapping conditions is conducted in the U.S.S.R. by a number of scientific establishments. The Institute of Defectology at the U.S.S.R. Academy of Pedagogical Sciences is the principal establishment charged with responsibility for developments in research on handicapping conditions and in special education. In the past decade, the activities and staff have increased dramatically and teachers, psychologists, speech therapists, physiologists, physicians and engineers are currently working on problems related to the development, education and occupational training of all types of handicapped children.

The institute comprises twenty-two laboratories dealing with the problems of hearing impairment, visual impairment, speech impairment, mental handicap, temporary development retardation, motor disturbances and multiple handicaps.

The institute communicates with the Defectological Departments of higher pedagogical colleges in different cities of the U.S.S.R. and with the Defectological Divisions at the scientific-research institutes of pedagogy and psychology in the Union Republics of the U.S.S.R. It co-ordinates all work in the field of defectology: (1) by means of annual conferences with the participation of the defectological divisions of the research institutes of pedagogy and psychology; (b) by mutual exchange of programmes of research work; and (c) by organizing scientific sessions devoted to special problems in defectology where the results of the most important and up-to-date research is reported and discussed.

The single system of State supervision and the centralization of research in one leading institute makes it possible to introduce a uniform pattern of organization and structure in special education and research in the U.S.S.R. Thus the chief problems of organization, those of communication and co-operation, are minimized. Priorities can be established, necessary resources can be brought to bear in an appropriate sequence in order to achieve specific goals and decisions can be more easily implemented. Communication has also been helped by the scientific and methodological journal *Defectology*, founded in 1969.

United States of America

A starting-point for the rapid expansion and increased availability of funds for educational research in the United States was the Co-operative Research Act of 1954 with enabling legislation for funding educational research, surveys and demonstrations. The first major contribution of this century towards the education of the handicapped followed in 1957 when $1 million were appropriated for handicapped persons, two-thirds being earmarked for research on the education of the mentally retarded. The report of the President's Panel in 1962 culminated in an enactment by the eighty-eighth Congress which provided grants for demonstration projects on the education of the handicapped.

As a result of the Elementary and Secondary Education Act 1965, funds were given to local education agencies for work with children in low-income areas and states were given financial aid for the handicapped in state school systems and in residential facilities for handicapped children. In 1966, the Education for Handicapped Children Bill was enacted and this provided for the creation of the Bureau for the Education of the Handicapped and the National Advisory Committee on Handicapped Children which advises the Commissioner of Education and the Congress. Since then, federal legislation has created Regional Resource Centers for the purpose of helping teachers by providing educational evaluation and consultation in developing programmes and strategies for dealing with all handicaps.

While education at state and local government level is supported with minimal federal participation, the reverse is the case with research, where federal aid is the major source of support. USOE is the federal agency with major responsibility for research on education. The proposed strategy proclaimed initially by the Bureau for the Education of the Handicapped of USOE was to accelerate 'the knowledge-to-action cycle', this cycle being conceived as 'research–development–demonstration–implementation–adoption'. Other federal agencies such as the National Institute of Neurological Diseases and Stroke (NINDS), the National Institute of Mental Health (NIMH), and the Rehabilitation Services Administration of the Department of Health, Education and Welfare underwrite research which complements work supported by USOE.

At the state government level, special education units are situated within the state departments of education. In some states these special education units have divisions directly concerned with the stimulation, support and conduct of research. Where these exist, the research orientation is most likely to be towards applied and operational research or towards dissemination and utilization of results.

At the local level, administrative provisions for research tend to be informal except in the case of school systems in large metropolitan areas.

In the latter half of the sixties, more than two-thirds of the funds provided for research on the education of the handicapped were allotted to colleges and universities. Since most universities and colleges operate within the framework of state government, this reveals another facet of state participation in research.

Because of the complexity of intra-university organization for research, it is difficult to exemplify patterns of research operations and organization. A variety of structures known as centres, institutes, laboratories, offices and so on, have been established in the last decade and the American report describes some of these, notably the Institute for Research on Exceptional Children at the University of Illinois, the Research and Development Center at Columbia University and the Departments of Special Education at the Universities of Oregon and Texas.

Another important development in the behavioural sciences is the establishment of independent privately directed research organizations such as the Cybernetics Institute, the Organization for the Study of Technical and Social Innovation and the American Institute for Research. The availability of such organizations for specific projects affords tactical flexibility to agencies such as USOE.

Professional organizations represent another significant resource for special studies and for investigations of specific aspects of handicapping conditions.

Finally, the American report pays tribute to private and volunteer groups for their direct services to handicapped persons, for surveys, research and demonstration, assistance to individuals and agencies, scholarships, fellowships, refresher courses, workshops, internships and for their response to the diversity of needs which are raised by the demands of practical realities in a variety of situations. Parent groups in particular are cited as playing a part in maintaining pressure at all levels of government to ensure that the needs of the handicapped are borne in mind by the policy makers. The Joseph P. Kennedy Foundation is cited as an example of the work which can be achieved by a private foundation: in particular it has helped to narrow the gulf between the scientific and service communities.

Uruguay

During the past two decades, programmes for handicapped children have increased markedly in Uruguay, as they have in most other Latin American countries. Research efforts for the most part have consisted of single projects, representing the work of individuals, and there is still a lack of communication and inadequate exchange of results. The author indicates that there is a widespread failure in applying what is known about special education and that it would be worth while to direct efforts towards the translation of research findings into classroom practice. However, in 1967 the National Board of Education accepted a proposal to set up a centre for the investigation, diagnosis and education of the mentally handicapped (CIDERM). Among the objects of this centre, the establishment of a research arm ranked high. With improved systems of data collection, storage, retrieval and analysis for evaluating intervention procedures, it is most likely that large-scale project research will now be a realizable goal in this decade.

Co-ordination and dissemination of research at a national level

The development and effective delivery of services to the handicapped will depend largely on the extent to which up-to-date research information is implemented in practice. Co-ordination and dissemination of research enterprise ensure that priorities are established, duplication of effort is avoided and that difficult and important problems are not shelved or neglected.

Significant progress in research co-ordination was made in Sweden in 1962 by the establishment of a Special Research Section of the Board of National Education, primarily to initiate and co-ordinate educational research and to disseminate information about on-going projects throughout the country.

Identification of research needs is approached in several ways in Sweden. One important method consists of involving the 'consumers' of research as well as the researchers. This is effected by collecting suggestions at conferences, by questionnaires and by personal contacts. Another way has been to arrange symposia on special topics where research projects are presented, methodological problems considered and trends surveyed.

The National Board of Education and the State Council for Social Research are responsible for the systematic retrieval and dissemination of research information pertaining to education, including that concerning special education. Newsletters on School Research are published by the National Board of Education and versions in both Swedish and English are available. Furthermore there are several journals published in Sweden which present continuous information relevant to special education.

In the U.S.S.R., programmes and methods in special education are initially subjected to trial at the Institute of Defectology and at other research institutions. Under the supervision of scientific research centres, experiments are then conducted in a broader sample of schools. Materials and methods which have been put to the test and approved after experimentation by the Ministry of Education are then introduced in all those schools where they may be appropriately utilized. Similarly textbooks and manuals are approved by the Instruction Methodological Council of the Ministry of Education and are made available to all special schools where their applicability has been verified. Recently, for example, the Institute of Defectology has published special manuals relating to the education of the visually impaired, the hearing impaired and the mentally handicapped.

The Institute of Defectology organizes courses and symposia for teachers in special education where the results of contemporary research are presented and discussed. Seminars are arranged by collectives of auxiliary school-teachers where special programmes and literature on the psychology of the mentally retarded are studied and this collaborative enterprise takes place in more than 300 auxiliary schools.

In the United States, growth rate in research output has been so rapid that the study of the processes and problems of its retrieval, dissemination and utilization can now be designated as 'the science of knowledge-utilization'. From a modest output of 100 studies on information utilization in 1955, the bibliography of similar studies expected by the seventies is over 40,000.

USOE is the principal agency concerned with the retrieval, dissemination and utilization of knowledge in special education. Instructional materials centres, demonstration programmes and projects, and information clearing-houses are the principal means by which it is hoped to accelerate 'the knowledge-to-action' cycle.

There are fourteen Instructional Materials Centers, twelve administered by universities and two by State Departments of Education. These centres carry on research in development and evaluation of methods, materials and manuals, provide instructional materials and information to teachers of the handicapped, and promote materials production by the service community.

Another concept where the accent is more on utilization than on dissemination is that of the Regional Resource Center. The basic purpose is to provide teachers and schools with advice and technical services in order to improve the education of exceptional children.

Demonstration is a form of dissemination and teaching whereby an attempt is made to encourage learning on the part of the student by active participation in new programmes. This type of teaching is sometimes incorporated in the core programme of large-scale research undertakings. Another approach to demonstration is through projects which may have a specific message aimed at particular groups. From 1964 to 1969, 34 per cent of the activities funded by USOE were classified as demonstration undertakings.

Finally, the most direct method of spreading information is by clearing-house activities. The Educational Resources Information Center (ERIC) initiated in 1964 as a national information network is probably the most obvious example of this type of activity. It collects abstracts, summarizes on-going research, indexes documents, evaluates literature and materials, disseminates information and provides a document reproduction service.

The foregoing are some of the principal methods of disseminating and utilizing research knowledge within different areas of the world. There is a growing awareness that development and delivery of educational services depend largely on effective communications with, and transmission of information to, those in a position to implement the findings of research.

International exchange
of research information

In the recent past there has been a remarkable extension of our knowledge in the physical and behavioural sciences relative to the study of the causes, alleviation and remediation of all types of handicapping conditions. Where this has taken place it has generally been accompanied by an increased sophistication in methods of retrieval, storage and dissemination of data and in the development of instructional materials and of methods in special education.

Regrettably, international collaboration is still in an embryonic state and consists in the main either of conferences arranged by international organizations concerned with specific types of handicap or of exchange of information within regional blocks, constituted by neighbouring countries. Research on the education of the handicapped would stand to gain a great deal from the wider range of individual differences, genetic backgrounds, environmental influences and educational practices which would become available for study with increased international interaction and cross-cultural research. Such rich sources of variables could overcome to some extent the restrictions which are placed upon the deliberate manipulation of critical biological, psychological, social and cultural variables in large-scale research projects within single national groups. Again, with inadequate systems of international communication, projects can be initiated in some places in ignorance of similar projects having been undertaken elsewhere.

The essential basis for an effective scheme of international research exchange would appear to rest on a system of national documentation centres, and in most countries tentative beginnings in this direction are being made.

The Swedish report shows how a start has been made in regional co-operation by the Nordic Cultural Commission which stimulates co-operation in educational research in the Scandinavian countries. In the U.S.S.R., the Institute of Defectology accepts the principal responsibility for the dissemination of research knowledge, not only within the Soviet states but also abroad, by publication of research results, by scientific missions to other countries, by promoting attendances at conferences and by sponsoring specialists and workers in the field of special education for short- and long-term visits. The creation of the Latin American Perinatology and Human Development Centre opens up the possibility of a regional centre for communication and dissemination of information about 'at risk' cases of anomalous development and for co-ordinating the activities of those concerned with the early education of the handicapped. In the United States, USOE has assumed the responsibility for dealing with the immense accumulation of knowledge about handicapped persons and for translating this into action programmes, principally through instructional material centres, demonstration projects and information clearing-house services. ERIC co-ordinates the work of documentation sub-centres, or clearing-houses. These clearing-houses each deal with a specific topic, such as reading, adult education, educational media and so on, and one of these, located at CEC in Washington, assumes responsibility for documentation relating to the education of handicapped children.

The Council for Europe has established an educational section for European co-operation, namely the Council for Cultural Co-operation (CCC) which contributes to international interaction by arranging symposia and conferences. Unesco stimulates educational research and development in many ways and in the field of special education, the establishment of the Division of Equality of Access to Education in 1968 was an earnest of its intention to share the common fund of universal knowledge relating to handicapped persons and, where feasible, to help to translate this into action programmes. However, there are differences in the degrees of readiness for the acceptance of new knowledge and its applications in practice in different parts of the world. These differences are determined to some extent by the levels of social, technological and economic progress and by the limitations set by the availability of professional personnel in relation to population size. Furthermore, there is scope for differences in conceptions about helping handicapped children towards a state of physical and mental well-being and towards integration in their communities. The progress towards mature and stable citizenship can take place in different types of social structures and within various systems of values and beliefs.

This volume is the product of co-operative effort and has given the authors an opportunity to describe the different and sometimes conflicting points of view over methods of dealing with the education of handicapped children. It has also served to draw attention to typical lacunae in our pre-school arrangements for the handicapped, to the need for constant re-evaluation of accepted practices in special education and for more intensive development of services. One of the outstanding features of the following studies is the connexion made between research and its applications to instructional programmes in special education. They call attention to the increased social responsibility of teachers and, more especially, to that of the institutions where their professional formation takes place.

The reports provide a source of information about research and activities in special education in four regions of the world. While they elucidate approaches to research and development within specifically national contexts, they may help others to relate these to experiences of special education in their own countries and may serve to underline the universality of problems of existence.

The horizon remains unchanged for those standing at a fixed point: changes are seen only by those who keep on the move. If we are wholly satisfied with what we see in special education we must indeed be fortunate; if not, perhaps the following studies will broaden our perspectives and help us to a vision of new horizons.

Karl-Gustaf Stukát

Sweden and other Scandinavian countries

Research on special education
during the last decade

This review does not attempt to give a complete and detailed account of what has happened within the research field of special education during the sixties. Rather, the purpose is to outline some main trends as the author sees them and to give concrete illustrations of these trends. The emphasis is primarily on Swedish research; only occasional references to the other Scandinavian countries occur.

The first part of the chapter summarizes a 1966 research survey covering recent and on-going Scandinavian investigations in special education. This is followed by a review of research development during recent years, and, finally, some of the effects of research on special education practice are discussed.

A Scandinavian survey

In connexion with a conference on Scandinavian co-operation in special education research, held in Gothenburg in 1966, a survey was made of current research in Denmark, Norway and Sweden. The survey covered investigations reported in 1963–65 as well as studies in progress at the time. Information was gathered from journals, publication indexes, and through personal communication with research institutes. The coverage was probably not complete, but most relevant research was no doubt included.

The investigations were classified according to the kind of handicap studied and Table 1 shows the frequencies within the different categories.

It will be observed that the investigations are unevenly distributed among different groups of handicaps. Not unexpectedly, the highest frequencies are found for general learning disabilities, a category made up of slow learners and mentally retarded students. It is of interest to note that relatively more attention has been devoted to hearing handicaps than to sight and speech

The present situation and trends of research
in the field of special education

TABLE 1   Frequencies of special education studies in Denmark, Nor-
                             way and Sweden, 1963–65, classified according to type of
                             handicap

| Handicap | Number of studies | |
	Reported	In progress
General learning disabilities	16	24
School readiness problems	10	2
Reading and writing handicaps, dyslexia	9	13
Mathematics handicaps, dyscalcylia	2	1
Emotional and social maladjustment	9	10
Deafness and hearing handicaps	3	8
Blindness and sight handicaps	1	0
Brain injuries, cerebral palsy, physical handicaps	14	8
Speech handicaps	0	2

deficiencies. In the same way, many more studies have been directed towards
dyslectic than towards dyscalcylic problems.

The total amount of research on the educational problems of handicapped
students during the three-year period covered by the survey is rather modest
in relation to the importance of the problems, the large number of individuals
involved, and the considerable economic investments in special education.
There was, however, some increase in the number of studies reported between
1963 and 1965, and the proportion of investigations in progress also suggests
a positive trend.

The investigations were also classified in relation to the type of research
involved, as shown in Table 2.

The dominating type of research category is descriptive characterization
of different handicap groups, most often performed by comparing deviating
students with a control group or with population norm values. The majority
of the studies have been focused on the learner rather than on the learning–
instructional process, as can be seen from the high frequencies in the first
three categories compared with the low frequencies in the following cat-

TABLE 2   Frequencies of special education studies in Denmark, Nor-
                             way and Sweden, 1963–65, classified according to type of
                             research involved.

| Type of research | Number of studies | |
	Reported	In progress
Descriptions of handicap groups	23	22
Correlative functional analyses	13	10
Instruments for diagnosis and prognosis	13	13
Learning experiments	2	4
Development and testing of new instructional methods	2	12
Evaluation of special education programmes	0	3
Miscellaneous	11	4

egories which refer to learning, instructional methods, and educational programmes. For the latter types there is, however, a striking difference between the number of reported and on-going studies, indicating a clear trend toward increasing interest in the educational process.

Recent research

No systematic survey has been made of research on special education during the latter part of the sixties. Such a survey is underway with a Scandinavian project group in Gothenburg but is not yet finished. This section outlines some of the more pronounced features of present research development and reviews a number of studies representative of present trends. The examples are with a few exceptions taken from Swedish investigations.

Descriptive studies have continued to appear. There is, however, a tendency to make the characterization of handicapped groups part of broader research programmes rather than to treat description as a more or less isolated task, which has sometimes been the case in previous research. Informative examples of the new role of descriptive studies are investigations by Ahlström and Amcoff[1] in Uppsala. The learner analyses form constituent parts of the total project, the purpose of which is to develop methods and materials for silent reading and speech comprehension suitable for deaf and hard-of-hearing children. In the studies quoted, seven tests measuring different aspects of linguistic ability were given to pupils with hearing handicaps and for comparison to normal hearing pupils in grades 1–2. The investigations showed that the acquisition of reading and writing abilities proceeds extraordinarily slowly in pupils with serious hearing handicaps. At the end of their school years, these students have as a rule only reached ordinary grade 2 or 3 standard in reading and writing. The information gathered from these studies has guided the development of instructional methods, which will be reviewed later in this chapter.

Another illustration of descriptive studies performed within a wider frame of reference is provided by two interrelated investigations by Johansson and Johannesson[2] and by Tilander and Wallgren.[3] The purpose of these

1   K.-G. Ahlström and S. Amcoff, 'Färdigheter i Läsning och Skrivning hos Hörselskadade Elever i Årskurs 5–9 [Reading and Writing Ability of Pupils in Grades 5–9 whose Hearing is Impaired]', *Nordisk Tidskrift för Dövundervisning*, No. 3, 1967. S. Amcoff, *Språktillägnandet hos Elever i Årskurs 1–7 i Specialskolan för Hörselskadade* [Language Acquisition of Pupils in Grades 1–7 in Schools for Hard-of-hearing Pupils], Uppsala, 1968 (Ph. D. thesis).

2   L. Johansson and C. Johannesson, *Motorisk Prestationsförmåga på Lägre IK-nivåer* [Motor Abilities at Lower I.Q.-levels], Ped. Inst., Univ. of Gothenburg, 1967.

3   S. O. Tilander and I. Wallgren, *Motoriska Övningskurvor. En Jämförelse mellan Olika Grupper av Psykiskt Utvecklingsstörda och Normalbegåvade* [Motor Learning Curves. A Comparison between Different Groups of Mentally Retarded and Subjects of Normal Intelligence], Ped. Inst., Univ. of Gothenburg, 1967.

studies was to throw light on the possibility of extending a work training programme to new categories of mentally retarded institute clients. Special focus was on psychomotor abilities, since these play an essential role in the types of work skills that the training programme is expected to establish. Three groups of mentally retarded children within the I.Q. ranges 25–42, 43–55, and 56–75 respectively and (in one of the studies) a normal comparison group made up of students at a vocational school, were tested in a number of psychomotor tasks. These were chosen so as to be as similar as possible to typical job tasks, e.g. mounting a coupling-box, and making a box out of a carton. As expected, the average achievement was lower for the mentally retarded, and especially for the lowest I.Q. groups. There was, however, considerable individual variation within each group and overlap between the different categories, even to some extent between the lowest I.Q. group and the vocational school group. Of particular interest was the overlap found between those mentally retarded who were in the training programme and those who had not been expected to gain from it. The results showed that as far as motor ability goes, a substantial proportion of the retardates who were only given custodial care could meet the requirements for successful work training. Furthermore, it was found that the learning curves for the lowest I.Q. groups were steeper than for the other groups in respect of most motor tasks, which suggests that not only initial scores but also learning characteristics should be taken into account in predictions of work success.

Recent development of correlational ability analysis with reference to handicapped students has been characterized by increased methodological sophistication. Dissatisfaction with too widespread use of a general intelligence measure as the main basis for placement and treatment has challenged researchers to apply modern analytic methods for systematic mapping of the ability structure in deviating students as has already been done in the general field of differential psychology. The most ambitious study of this kind has been performed by Kebbon[1] on mentally retarded subjects. Kebbon makes the pertinent remark that while intelligence tests first were devised for diagnosing intellectual subnormality, paradoxically, little of the following impressive progress in mental measurement has been concerned with the field of mental retardation. The object of his investigation was to determine whether persons of subaverage intelligence are characterized by the same abilities as persons of normal intelligence and, if so, whether their abilities are organized in the same way. A number of tests, chosen for their power to tap well-identified factors in normal subjects, were given to different groups of mentally retarded subjects, ranging in I.Q. from 50 to 90, and to subjects of normal intelligence. In the factor analyses essentially the same factors were found in all groups: verbal, numerical, spatial-inductive, and psychomotor factors. A fifth factor, perceptual speed, was identified with somewhat greater

---

[1]   L. Kebbon, *The Structure of Ability at Lower Levels of Intelligence*, Stockholm, Skandinaviska Testförlaget, 1965 (Ph. D. thesis).

certainty in the normal than in the retarded groups. The proportion of the common variance for which the different factors were responsible differed in a systematic way. The lower the I.Q., the more the psychomotor factor accounted for the common-factor variance; the higher the I.Q., the more the verbal factor accounted for the variance. The retarded subjects differed least from the normal subjects in manual tasks. They did worse on speed tests, spatial-inductive tests, and verbal tests, the difference increasing in that order. An observation of great practical significance was that subjective ratings of intelligence (by physicians and supervisors) were most closely correlated with verbal ability, while ratings of working ability most nearly correlated with psychomotor ability.

In a recent study carried out by R. Kääriäinen[1] within the frame of a Scandinavian research project on special education in Gothenburg, the correlations between seventeen variables were factor analysed. The unique features of the investigation are the low intelligence level of the subjects, the I.Q.s ranging between 25 and 55, and the inclusion of learning achievement variables as well as ability measurements. One intention was to bridge the gap between correlational analysis and instructional application by trying to identify crucial factor components in learning tasks, in this case the task of learning a social sight vocabulary. The following factors were identified: perceptual, memory, psychomotor, and verbal. The results were substantially in harmony with those of Meyers, Dingman, and others on subjects of similar intellectual level, as also with the factors found by Kebbon. Group comparisons showed significant differences in the factor profiles between mongoloid and non-mongoloid subjects, and between males and females. The factors correlating highest with social sight vocabulary learning were the perceptual, memory, and verbal, in that order. Multiple correlation between eight selected tests and the learning variable was significant and accounted for 41 per cent of the variance in the social sight vocabulary gains.

There is a continuity between the factor analytic research described above and present activities within the test construction area. More differentiated diagnostic and prognostic instruments are being substituted for a single general intelligence test. Different basic abilities are related to training and vocations, and adequate prediction instruments are under development. At the psychotechnical institute in Stockholm, batteries of ability tests and rating methods are being constructed, including motor and spatial ability, memory, concept formation, number concepts, interests, and work adjustment. The test constructions are paralleled by work analyses to identify the crucial functions for success in different jobs.

A somewhat different line in test construction in the last few years has consisted of providing instruction with test instruments for continuous edu-

---

1 R. Kääriäinen, *The Factor Structure of Intellectual Abilities and Signal-sight Vocabulary Learning at Preliterate, Moderate, and Severe Level of Mentally Retarded*, Gothenburg, Ped. Inst., School of Educ., 1969.

cational diagnosis. These endeavours have been most obvious within the projects aimed at developing method-material systems for individualized instruction. Examples of such projects will be given in later sections. Characteristic of diagnostic tests of the new type is that they are goal-related rather than norm-related. This means that their primary purpose is to give information showing to what extent the pupil has reached the instructional objectives set up for him, whereas information on the pupil's standing in relation to other students is less strongly emphasized.

Basic learning research on mentally retarded people has been a main area of interest for a research group in Norway, consisting of Björgen,[1] Lie, Neggelund, Andersen and others. Because of the heterogeneity of different types of oligophrenia, the studies have been concentrated on mongoloid subjects. Even with this limitation, wide individual variations prevail. In discrimination learning tasks there are a number of interesting differences between the mongoloid patients and matched normal, e. g. as to the sequences of reaction tendencies, number of response tendencies, and the flexibility of the tendencies. Mongoloids often started with position tendencies, while the controls showed preference for shape. The retarded subjects also had a smaller response repertoire and gave evidence of greater perseverance. Experiments with motor learning, pursuit-rotor and mirror-drawing also revealed striking differences, which referred to qualitative as well as quantitative aspects. The learning curves were more variable for the mongoloids and they showed no recall after a rest period. Whereas the normal controls easily acquired a rhythmic movement, the mongoloid subjects were restless, lacked concentration, and needed constant encouragement. In experiments on 'learning set' acquisition, Harlow's finding of evenly falling error curves was re-examined with mongoloids as subjects. As in the previous experiments, there was great individual variation, the subjects reaching the criterion after trying quite different numbers of problems. However, once the criterion was reached, the error curve dropped to approximately zero, but because the subjects reached the criterion at different times, the average gradient for the group showed, as had been Harlow's experience, an even drop.

Basic research of relevance to special education has also been pursued in Uppsala. Linde[2] has reported learning experiments with frequency transposed speech. The experiments were made in connexion with attempts to develop self-instructional devices for training of speech perception in pupils with different types and different degrees of hearing impairment. New equipment was tested experimentally and conventional speech reinforcement was compared to reinforcement mediated by frequency transposed speech. Among

---

1   T. A. Björgen, 'Some Aspects of the Research on Mental Retardation in Norway', in: N. Ellis (ed.), *International Review of Research in Mental Retardation,* Vol. 2, London, Academic Press, 1966.

2   V. Linde, *Tre Inlärningsförsök med Frekvenstransponerat tal* [Three Learning Experiments with Frequency Transposed Speech], Uppsala, 1968 (Ph. D. thesis).

other experimental research within special education, Nyborg's[1] concept learning and Hesselholdt's[2] on direction orientation in dyslectics may be mentioned.

One of the most striking features in recent special education research has been the effort to develop new training and instructional methods, most often by applying principles of educational technology. Some of these activities will be reviewed here.

Recognizing the need for more effective methods of teaching verbal skills to deaf and hard-of-hearing students, Ahlström and Amcoff[3] and others have initiated the SMID-project (Self-instructional Methods for the Instruction of the Deaf). An essential part of the programme has been the design of mechanical and electronic devices for instructional and research purposes. One machine, called TYLA, is used in silent reading, another is a booster facilitating simultaneous introduction of auditory and visual stimuli, and a third is intended for use in group instruction. The two last-mentioned apparatuses can be used for training of speech perception as well as for silent reading. The basic principle is the same for the three devices. The student matches one of three visual stimuli to a fourth one, which can be visual or auditory, by pushing one of three keys on which the three visual stimuli are projected. If the student selects the right key, new stimuli are presented; if he makes a wrong choice he has to try again. The student's responses are continuously registered on a tape recorder, and the tape data can be analysed in a computer immediately after the instruction session. Self-instructional material for silent reading training with the machines has been constructed and tried out in different versions and variations.

Within the Scandinavian research group in Gothenburg, a self-instructional method has been developed for teaching social sight vocabulary to trainable mentally retarded students.[4] In order to find out what words should be included in the programme, a questionnaire was sent to a large number of institutions for the mentally retarded in Scandinavia. The respon-

1   L. Nyborg, 'Undersökelse av Begrepslaering hos Debile Barn [Investigation of Concept Learning in Morons]', in: K.-G. Stukát and R. Engström (ed.), *Samnordisk Specialpedagogisk Forskning* [Inter-Scandinavian Research in Special Education], Gothenburg, Ped. Inst., School of Educ., 1966.

2   S. Hesselholdt, 'En Sammenligning af Retningsfunktionen hos Dyslektikere og Normale Læsere fra de samme intelligensnivauer [A Comparison of Direction Orientation in Dyslectics and Normal Readers of the Same Intelligence Level]', in: K.-G. Stukát and R. Engström (ed.), ibid.

3   K.-G. Ahlström and S. Amcoff, 'Feedback Functions in Teaching Machines', *Scand. J. Psychol.*, No. 8, 1967; 'Programmed Instruction of a Vocabulary in Silent Reading to Deaf Children', *Nordisk Tidskrift för Dövundervisning*, No. 3, 1966.

4   G. Stangvik and A. Lewerth, *Ett Program för Signal-ordsläsning* [A Programme for Social Sight Vocabulary Training], Gothenburg, Ped. Inst., School of Educ., 1969. Niels Söndergård, *En Enquete Vedrorende Vigtige Signalord for Psykisk Utviklingshemmende* [A Questionnaire on Important Social Sight Words for Mentally Retarded], Gothenburg, Ped. Inst., School of Educ., 1968.

75

dents were asked to list the twenty words and phrases that could be considered most essential for the retardate's orientation in his social environment. The highest frequencies were obtained for such words as 'danger', 'stop', 'poison'; that is, word signals which are related to the individual's safety. The self-instructional programme is based on discrimination learning principles. The learner has to chose the correct picture among several alternatives when presented with a word-stimulus. The reading programme also includes the reverse situation, to find the word that corresponds to a picture stimulus.

Preparatory to the reading material, the student is given concept training material. Since this method for establishing a social sight vocabulary assumes that the student can interpret pictures correctly, a special study was made in order to test the extent to which this assumption was valid.[1] The subjects—trainable mental retardates—were shown sets of miniature objects (a set consisting, e.g., of different pieces of furniture) and together with each set a picture corresponding to one of the objects. The task for the subjects was to find the object that corresponded to the picture. In addition to pictures of concrete objects, representations of human actions were shown and the subjects had to match the picture with real actions. The results suggested that trainable mentally retarded students above the age of 13 are ordinarily able to interpret pictures of concrete objects satisfactorily, the percentage of correct responses being around 90. For pictures representing actions, however, the frequency of right responses was considerably lower, around 70 per cent. These results are informative not only for the social sight vocabulary project but for instruction of trainable mentally retarded people in general.

New reading instruction methods are also being developed for educable mentally retarded. In Uppsala, Witting and Ahlström[2] have designed a method called the psycholinguistic method. The main principle of the method is that training in reading comprehension is not started until purely mechanical articulation techniques of combining sounds have become automatic. To begin with, the pupil learns to articulate nonsense combinations of letters. It is assumed that initial concentration on mechanical articulation separated from comprehension training will make it easier for the pupil to learn the sound quality of the letters. For example by not associating the symbol *m* with words like *mother* or *mouse*, the risk of the pupil's identifying the symbol *m* with these concepts is reduced. In a later step, meaningful words are intermixed with nonsense syllables and the pupil is asked to listen carefully when reading aloud so as to find if there are any words he recognizes. This means that the pupil engages in an active search in his own vocabulary only after the mechanic technique has been established, which is assumed to be a simpler task than reading-and-guessing with the help of pictures. The

1 G. Stangvik, *Billedtolkning hos Psykisk Utviklingshemmede* [Picture Interpretation in Mentally Retarded], Gothenburg, Ped. Inst., School of Educ., 1968.
2 M. Witting and K.-G. Ahlström, 'Methods for Reading Training in Schools for Retarded Children', *Newsletter School Research*, No. 4, 1968 (published by the Swedish National Board of Education, Bureau L4, Stockholm).

effectiveness of the psycholinguistic method is empirically tested in an on-going three-year study in which the new method is compared with conventional reading instruction. In some experimental variants, both methods are also combined with a self-instructional arrangement. With the help of a tape recorder and headphones, the pupil listens to, repeats, and finally reads words from a list. Repetitions and checks of knowledge are also carried out by means of the tape recorder.

An extensive special instruction project has been started in Gothenburg, called the SISU project (Self-instructional Special Education). A rationale for SISU[1] is the experience that pupils with learning difficulties, whether they are taught in special or ordinary classes, need well-structured, systematically built-up and individually adaptable learning material which can be used in a diagnostic teaching setting. The material is intended to be supplementary to ordinary teacher instruction. It covers fundamental parts of the elementary curriculum in Swedish and mathematics, which subjects were rated to be most in need of self-instructional remedial material by 128 special teachers in response to a questionnaire. Associated with the self-instructional material are a number of diagnostic tests. These are of two kinds: a broad battery of tests for screening purposes, given at the beginning of each semester, and a number of special tests intended to give more detailed diagnostic information about individual pupils in such functions where the screening test reveals need for remedial training. Since instructional objectives are stated in relatively vague terms in official curricula, a first step in the construction work has been to perform goal analyses and to express objectives in behavioural terms. Those goal descriptions that have been published recently[2] are relevant not only for the SISU project but can be used as guides for instruction in a wide setting. The SISU project is at present at work on the construction of diagnostic tests and instructional material. The tests and the material are first tested on small groups of pupils. Revisions, new testing and implementation will follow. Some characteristic features of the SISU project should be emphasized. It is mainly self-instructional, but is intended to be used as a supplement to, not as a substitute for, teacher instruction. It is limited to such parts of the mathematics and Swedish curricula as are judged to be fundamental and suitable for individual instruction.

The efforts to develop new instructional methods on a systematic basis have not been limited to school subjects. Attempts have also been made to design training programmes for daily life activities. At the Stretered institute

1   K.-G. Stukát and U.-B. Bladini, 'Självinstruerande Specialundervisning [Self-instructional Special Education]', *Newsletter School Research,* No. 1, 1969 (published by the Swedish National Board of Education, Bureau L4, Stockholm).
2   U.-B. Bladini, *Målbeskrivningar i Ämnet Svenska på Lågstadiet* [Descriptions of Objectives in Swedish at Lower Elementary Level], Gothenburg, Ped. Inst., School of Educ., 1968. H. Olsson and I. Österberg, *Målbeskrivningar i Ämnet Matematik På Lågstadiet* [Descriptions of Objectives in Mathematics at Lower Elementary Levels], Gothenburg, Ped. Inst., School of Educ., 1969.

for the mentally retarded, Juteus and Malmborg[1] have tried out a training schedule according to behaviour modification principles for establishing dishwashing routines. The total task was split up into smaller segments which were at first taught separately and successively combined with larger sequences and finally to the whole chain of behaviours that constituted the task. Reinforcements were given in the form of tokens that could later be exchanged for small presents. Progress was measured by means of a detailed observation schedule. At the end of a week's training the experimental group had made substantial progress, while a control group that received ordinary training had not changed its performance level. In spite of some decline observed at a re-test held five weeks after the training period, the result can be regarded as encouraging and as justifying further attempts. A broader project along similar lines was started in 1968 at the Vipeholm hospital for gravely retarded patients under the direction of T. Liljeroth. Eating, hygiene and clothing procedures have been analysed in the simpler acts that constitute them. Filming of children in action is used to determine the behaviours to be taught and the sequences to be followed.

Extensive programmes for training daily life activity skills have also been developed at other Scandinavian institutes, e.g. at Emma Hjorts Hjem and Trasted in Norway and at Lillemosegard in Denmark.

Only a few (although comprehensive) studies have been made during the last five-year period to evaluate broader educational programmes for handicapped students. One of these effect studies is O. Österling's on the efficacy of special education.[2] The main question dealt with by the investigation was whether special classes further the acquisition of knowledge and the social-emotional adjustment of slow learners more effectively than do regular classes. Attempts were also made to elucidate interactions between differences in efficacy and such variables as intelligence level number of years in special class and class size. From a review of previous efficacy studies it would seem that the general result indicates better attainment of knowledge in regular classes and, for some aspects of adjustment, more favourable environment in special classes. However, because of the lack of adequate control over confounding factors in almost all efficacy studies, no definite conclusions could legitimately be drawn. For this, a more experimental approach is needed. In his main study, Österling attempted to meet the requirements of an experimental design by distributing pupils in special and regular classes randomly. Pupils in grades 2 and 3 who were reported to have school difficulties were followed up during the next two years. Tests in arithmetic and Swedish were given after the first, second and fourth semesters of the investi-

1   B. Juteus and K. Malmborg, *Effekterna av ett Träningsprogram för Uppövande av Färdigheter i Diskning hos ett Vuxet Vårdklientel av Psykiskt Utvecklingsstörda* [Effects of a Programme for Training Dishwashing Skills in Low-level Retardates], Ped. Inst., Univ. of Gothenburg, 1966.

2   O. Österling, *The Efficacy of Special Education*, Stockholm, Svenska Bokförlaget, 1967 (Ph.D. thesis).

gation period. The regular class group showed gradually greater superiority, particularly in arithmetic. An interaction tendency was observed, implying that the superiority of the regular classes was especially pronounced when the comparisons were made within the borderline sub-group. For the measurement there were two questionnaires, supposed to cover aggressiveness, passivity and anxiety. One of the questionnaires was given to the pupils and the other to the teachers. At the end of the two-year period in different school environments, the special class pupils showed a significantly higher level of aggressiveness than the pupils in regular classes. A supplementary study gave evidence which supported the hypothesis that a reduced outlet of aggression, if prolonged over a period of frustration, leads to increased passivity and anxiety. Analysis of interactions with class-size leads to the practical suggestion that the transfer of slow learners in small regular classes situated in places having a low population density to special classes in congested areas might not be justified.

In recent years, remedial instruction has to an increasing extent been given by means of other educational arrangements than special class placement. In two investigations[1] Malmqvist has studied the effects of a special programme for prevention and remedy of reading difficulties in regular class settings. The experimental group in the first study consisted of two classes which were compared with three different control groups, one of which was matched with the experimental group in intelligence, sex and social background. On the basis of teacher ratings and schools readiness tests, including tests of reading readiness, the pupils within the experimental group who were predicted to have reading difficulties were selected for special reading training. This instruction was given from five to eight hours a week during the first three school years by a reading clinic teacher. Comparisons between the groups in a number of reading and spelling tests given in grades 1, 2, and 3 showed superiority for the experimental group in most tests, although no increasing trend in the differences through the grades was observed. In order to test the validity of the results Malmqvist performed a more extensive study including forty-eight classes, each of which was divided into two equivalent halves. In one half, pupils with predicted reading difficulties received special instruction in grades 1–3, the other half constituting the control group. This study also gave evidence of the positive effects of the special remedial reading programme. Although conclusions must be subject to reservations because of a substantial drop out of classes, the results can be regarded as encouraging as regards the possibility of preventing reading failures. It should be noted that similar previous studies by Larsen gave somewhat more ambiguous results.[2]

1   E. Malmqvist, *Studies on Reading Disabilities in the Elementary School*, Linköping, 1968 (report from Statens Försökskola).
2   C.A. Larsen, 'Om Undervisning af Børn med Læse- og Stavevanskeligheter i de Førsto Skoleaar [Instruction of Children with Reading and Writing Difficulties in the First Grade]', *Dansk Pædagogisk Tidskrift*, No. 8, 1960.

An evaluation study that will be reported shortly[1] has been performed by G. Stangvik. It refers to a Norwegian investigation of different organizational models for the special education of slow learners. Besides special classes and homogenous grouping of the pupils in core subjects, a third model has been introduced. In this arrangement a remedial teacher works together with the class teacher in regular classes, and a high degree of integration of the remedial instruction with ordinary instruction is pursued. In his report, Stangvik also presents a methodological scrutiny of previous Scandinavian and international evaluation studies, classified according to organizational models investigated as well as the ability level of the pupils involved.

Experiments with remedial mathematics training were carried out during the sixties at several places. No systematic evaluation study has been reported so far, but Magne, who conducted pioneer research work in the field of mathematics difficulties, has published a comprehensive survey[2] that describes the rationale of the remedial teaching in the mathematics clinics. For identification of pupils who are under-achieving in mathematics, Ljung and others[3] have constructed an extensive battery of tests with high discrimination power, particularly at lower achievement levels.

The handicap categories that have been given most research attention during the last few years are those with general learning disability and, through the Uppsala research group, those with hearing handicaps. Studies on other groups of exceptional children and young people are more sparse. Sigrell[4] has analysed behaviour characteristics of emotionally disturbed students and described educational-therapeutic arrangements. In a on-going study, U. Atterström is making systematic behaviour observations of maladjusted students in different educational settings during an extended time period. A thorough analysis of self-confidence, social contacts, and mental disorders in adolescent students with cerebral palsy has been made by Olofsson.[5] An extensive long-term research project that analyses factors related to social adjustment and maladjustment is being conducted in Örebro under the leadership of D. Magnusson. By a follow-up of all pupils who were in grades 3, 6, and 8 in 1965, attempts are made to analyse factors that determine adjustment and school achievement. In addition to prediction possi-

---

1   *Effekter av Specialundervisning. En Kritisk Oversikt og et Empirisk Bidrag* [Effects of Special Education. A Critical Survey and an Empirical Contribution], Preliminary title; Ped. Inst., Univ. of Gothenburg.

2   O. Magne, *Matematiksvårigheter hos Barn i Åldern 7–13 År* [Mathematics Difficulties in Children 7–13 Years of Age], Stockholm, Svensk Lärarlidnings Förlag, 1967 (Pedagogiska Skrifter, 241).

3   E. Lang, B. O. Ljung and U.-B. Palmblad, *Underprestation i Matematik* [Underachievement in Mathematics], Stockholm, Ped. Psyk. Inst., School of Educ., 1969.

4   B. Sigrell, *Skolans Problembarn* [School's Problem Children], Stockholm, Liber, 1966.

5   K. Olofsson, *Självkänsla, Kontakt-förhållande och Psykisk Störning hos CP-handikappade Skolelever i Årskurs 6–10* [Self-confidence, Social Contacts, and Mental Disorders in Cerebral Palsy Students in Grades 6–10], Ped. Inst., Univ. of Gothenburg, 1967.

bilities, the data will also be used for differential diagnosis as a basis for habilitation programmes for youngsters with bad prognosis.

The Scandinavian survey of special education research 1963–65 revealed that sight handicaps had been almost completely neglected by educational research. This is also true for the later period reviewed here. It is to be hoped that awareness of this neglect will challenge researchers in the near future.

Implications for research for special education practice

Before presenting the following comments on practical applications of research results, a few qualifying statements should be made. For one thing, although it may seem clear from the illustrations below that there is a cause–effect relationship between research and application, this relation is far from simple. Research has no doubt been influencing educational practice, but it has in no instance been the single influencing factor. In all cases, research results have contributed to a practical educational development that has also been stimulated by several other agents. This state of affairs is not peculiar to special education. Research by itself seldom if ever produces changes in educational practice. To be effective, research evidence must be 'timed' with other determining factors, such as political and ideological structure, economical situation, teacher opinions, and so forth.

Another point is that research influence on special education practice has been limited by the relatively small-scale nature of many studies. As can be seen from the preceding review, it is only in the last few years that large-scale projects have been started in any number. Since most of these projects are directed toward practical problems, they may be expected to have important and radical implications for special education in the near future; but almost all of them are still uncompleted. Subject to these reservations, a number of substantial contributions by research activities can none the less be identified in respect of special education over the last decade.

As an initial illustration of how research has contributed to changed educational practice, we may take the differentiation–integration problem. The development in this field throws light upon the intricate interaction that are typical of educational research–practice interplay in general.

In the investigations and discussions that preceded the Swedish school reform, resulting in a nine years' comprehensive school without strict streaming before grade 9, the main question concerned the differentiation problem, i.e. whether and when pupils in the compulsory school should be referred to different streams or lines. The decision reached in 1962 meant a principally non-differentiated system: the adjustment of instruction to individual differences in ability and interests is supposed to be solved within the framework of heterogenous classes. It should be observed, however, that the discussion that took place during the fifties was largely limited to pupils of normal or above-normal intelligence. For these categories it was concluded, from equality ideology arguments complemented by research results that gave no clear evidence of superior effectiveness of homogenous classes, that a non-differentiated system was to be preferred.

During the period previous to the school reform there was not much mention in the differentiation discussion of pupils on the lower end of the intelligence scale, the slow learners and the mentally retarded pupils, nor of other groups of handicapped students. During the same period, as provisions were made for bringing pupils of normal and high ability together in the same classes, the number of special classes for slow learners was increasing. It was not until well into the sixties that the system of special classes for slow learners—and other categories of pupils with learning difficulties—was challenged. An 'integration' discussion was also begun in respect of these groups. The arguments were not primarily those of social equality (which had played a major role in the earlier differentiation discussion) but rather of efficacy. Since the objectives for the education of handicapped children are the same as for other students, and thus do not only include the acquisition of knowledge and skills but also development of adjustment in a normal social environment, the appropriateness of placing handicapped children in a secluded school *milieu* was questioned. Doubt was expressed whether the environment of the special class—and special school—was optimal for the attainment of the basic objectives of handicap education.

In order to elucidate the issue, research results were brought into the discussion. The information that could be extracted from international investigations (mainly in the United States) did not afford any definite answers. On the whole, the results indicated better school subject achievement for retarded pupils and slow learners who were taught in ordinary classes than for those who were transferred to special classes. On the other hand, pupil adjustment seemed to be somewhat better in special classes, although the results from different studies were often ambiguous. It was against this background that the previously reviewed Swedish study by Österling was carried out. The results of the extensive investigation seemed to confirm the main conclusions from the American studies, i.e. that the advantages of special class placement were not evident for all categories of slow learners or for all aspects of educational objectives. It is probable that the outcome of the evaluation studies strengthened a development that was already in progress. This development meant that new arrangements for special education, alternative to special classes, were being tried. For an increasing number of slow learners, pupils with special reading and writing difficulties, emotional disturbances and I.Q. handicaps, remedial instruction is given while the pupils remain in their regular classes. The organization of the remedial instruction varies; the pupil may be given a few hours a week of extra training in addition to the ordinary instruction, may substitute a number of remedial sessions at a school clinic for regular hours, or may be given special self-instructional material within his own class. The introduction of new arrangements for special education has not meant the elimination of special classes; rather, in absolute figures their number has continued to increase, but most recent expansion of handicap education has involved other remedial forms than special classes.

It is impossible to say how much research has contributed to this development, so interwoven is its contribution with other factors and forces. Still the development described here well illustrates how decisions in a practical educational problem situation would have been founded on less rational ground, had there not been available a body of research information. It should be emphasized that the differentiation–integration problem is still far from definitely solved. A great deal more practical experimenting with alternative arrangements, need analyses, and evaluation experiments are required.

Another illustration of the influence of research on educational practice with regard to handicapped students may be found in the psychometric field. For placement and prediction purposes it has long been a widespread practice to use a single measure of intellectual capacity, usually I.A. or I.Q. A multitude of research evidence from the last three or four decades has, however, proved the simple I.Q. characterization of a pupil to be all too rough and misleadingly simple. Correlational and factor analytic studies have shown that the total intellectual capacity of an individual is made up of a number of different, although often interrelated, functions. That this is also true for mentally retarded people was, as already noted, shown by Kebbon, and in other investigations. Findings of this kind have made it more and more customary in educational practice to use multifactor test instruments for pupil diagnosis and prognosis. In Sweden, Härnquist's multifactor Differential Ability Analysis (DBA) test is at present in wide use as a basis for study and vocational guidance, and it also belongs to the core battery of tests used by the school psychologist for diagnosis of disturbed children. Since the DBA test has also been shown (e.g. in Kebbon's study) to discriminate at low levels of intelligence, it is frequently used with the mentally retarded.

A further example of practical research consequences is the growing realization that more can be done in preventing learning failures than has so far been attempted. Malmqvist's investigations, referred to previously, suggest, for example, that an adequate reading instruction programme introduced early and based on continuous diagnosis and individual treatment, can substantially reduce the number of dyslectic students. Several investigations on school readiness, e.g. by Johansson[1] and Ljungblad,[2] have clearly shown that the intellectual stimulation, or lack of it, given to the children before beginning school, is of fundamental importance for their success, or failure, in later school work. As a consequence, various educational measures are at present taken to reach children with handicaps or potential deficiencies at an early age in order to provide them with a stimulating and enriching environment. Thus organized and purposeful pre-school activities for mentally

1   B. Johansson, *School Readiness,* Stockholm, Almqvist & Wiksell, 1966.
2   T. Ljungblad, *Skolmognad* [School Readiness], Lund, Uniskol, 1965.

retarded, cerebral-palsied, hard of hearing, and sight handicapped children have been introduced at a rapidly increasing rate during recent years.

In addition to the examples given above, attention should be directed toward an issue where research evidence has not yet been taken into due consideration, namely the realization of adequate individualization of instruction. Nothing has been more convincingly demonstrated by the large body of mental measurement results than the considerable individual variation in capacity, personality, motivation, etc., that exists among human beings. Such differences have also been shown to characterize pupils in groups selected on the basis of a common handicap as much as non-selected groups. A natural practical pedagogical implication of the great variation among students is that there should be a close congruence between instruction and the individual student's abilities and needs. No doubt, there is now general recognition of the need for individually prescribed instruction, and particularly so within the field of special education. Nevertheless, a full step towards the actualization of truly individual instruction does not yet seem to have been taken. Preliminary analyses of observation material from eighty classes, among them twenty special classes, gathered within a research project in Gothenburg, suggest that a considerable proportion of the instruction is given in the form of collective class teaching with the teacher lecturing, and this is so both in regular and special classes. Thus, individualization to a large degree still seems to be something wished for rather than something actually practised. A primary and quite natural reason for such a state of affairs is undoubtedly the difficulty of conducting and arranging instruction adapted to individual pupils. In an attempt to analyse the concept of individually adapted instruction, Stukát and Engström found the following criteria of individualization:[1]

1. The pupil is given instruction and tasks that are adapted to his needs and capacity.
2. The pupil works at his own speed.
3. Feedback is given individually.
4. The pupil is given responsibility in goal setting and work planning.
5. The teacher's main function is to arrange learning situations, not to lecture.

When one bears in mind the multifarious nature of individual instruction and how much it requires of the teacher, it is understandable that true individualization is seldom found. In fact, it can be considered almost impossible for a teacher to realize high-degree individualization without the support of a rich supply of self-instructional material. The strong emphasis on the development of method-material systems in research projects started during the last few years should be seen against this background. It is probable that such activities will continue and expand, although perhaps in somewhat different organizational forms than hitherto.

---

1 K.-G. Stukát and R. Engström, 'TV-observations of Teachers in Natural Classroom Situations', *Pedagogisk Forskning*, 1966.

Predicted future trends
of research

It is always a hazardous and difficult undertaking to predict the future development of research. Unforeseen factors may come into play and there is
always a subjective element in such prognosis, the prediction inevitably
being a mixture of what can on objective grounds be expected to happen
and what the predictor hopes will happen. None the less, attempts to make
a prognosis of future tendencies are well worth while, and a grain of wishful
thinking is not necessarily a bad thing. The time perspective is an important
factor for the reliability of predictions. The nearer the future, the higher the
chances for an accurate prognosis. When one tries to predict the main developmental directions within the next five years in research on the educational
problems of handicapped students, certain extrapolations can be made from
activities already going on, particularly as regards the large, long-range
projects that have been started recently and are to continue for a number of
years.

Analysis of the teaching–learning process
in special education

The outcome of the already mentioned evaluation investigations on the
effects of different organizational forms of special education has raised the
question: 'What is special about special education?' To ask this is the same
as asking what characterizes the teaching–learning process in instructional
situations known as 'special education' in comparison with the instructional
process in other, 'ordinary', education. A survey of the main objects of
interest for empirical educational research so far shows that the emphasis
has hitherto been on measurement of individual characteristics of learners
and teachers, either for prognostic–diagnostic purposes or for the purpose of
evaluating the effects of instruction, whereas the process of instruction, in
other words what goes on when teachers teach and pupils learn, has been
largely neglected by educational research. This may seem surprising and
paradoxical, since the teaching–learning process can rightly be regarded as
the central problem for educational research. The relative neglect can, however, be partly explained by the methodological and practical difficulties
involved when one attempts to study the educational process in natural
situations. As these difficulties are increasingly being overcome, there is strong
reason to believe that empirical analyses of instructional processes in special
education will become an important field of research in the period ahead.

An example of process analysis in a special education context is provided by a study under way within the Gothenburg project: 'Didactic Process and Product Analysis'. The purpose of the study is to compare instructional procedures and interaction patterns in special classes with corresponding processes in ordinary classes. Television recordings of the ten lessons in each of eighty classes have been video-taped and are now being analysed. The basis for choosing the behaviour categories to be observed is a list of hypotheses about what differences may be expected between 'special' and 'ordinary' instruction. The main sources for hypothesis formulations have been questionnaires to special teachers, literature studies and theoretical considerations. To mention a few of the hypotheses to be tested, it is assumed that the frequency of individual contacts between teacher and pupil is higher in special classes, that ampler and more varied instructional material is used and that positive reinforcements are more often given to pupils in the special classes. It is hoped that the information gained from this analysis will, among other things, throw light on factors behind the results found in evaluation studies of special education.

It is likely that future process analysis studies will not be limited to established forms of instruction but will also become frequent concomitants to evaluations of new instructional methods or programmes. There are already numerous questions concerning which systematic process observation would be of benefit, such as: What happens, in objective terms, to a handicapped student when 'integrated' with other pupils in a regular class? What is the typical pattern of behaviour and interaction in a remedial clinic situation? How do pupils behave when working with self-instructional materials? Often there are intuitive expectations about the answers to questions like these, and the expectations may be taken for proof. But it would be a sound practice to use process observation for providing objective answers.

It also seems reasonable to predict that the designs of experimental educational studies in which, for instance, different instructional methods are compared will include a procedure of scrutiny, control, and documentation of observable and recordable characteristics of the teaching methods under study. All too often it is assumed that the actual instructional process characterizing the methods investigated will be identical with the methods as they have been designed and described. It is highly desirable that the independent variables in didactic research should be as thoroughly defined operationally as has for a long time been the case regarding the dependent variables.

*A changed role for educational diagnosis
and new diagnostic methods*

As pointed out earlier, the need for continuous educational diagnosis and individually adapted instruction has been particularly emphasized in special education. At the same time, lack of adequate instruments, aids and methods has impeded the realization of these principles in practice.

It we first consider diagnosis, the traditional emphasis has been on developing instruments for the purpose of basing selection and school placement decisions on objective data about the individual student. Most diagnostic instruments in use are handled by school psychologists, who apply them on rare occasions, often separated by considerable time intervals. The increasing emphasis on individually adapted instruction and training of handicapped pupils has created a strong need for somewhat different types of diagnostic instruments. It is not enough to have ability tests or achievement tests that cover broad curriculum content; what is most needed are tests (and other measurement devices) for continuous and detailed dignosis of the pupil's present state, usable by the teacher in an instructional approach that is flexibly and continously adjusted to the pupil's needs. The demand for measuring instruments of this type makes necessary a new orientation of psychometric development. As noted previously, classic test theory refers to 'norm-related' tests, i. e. tests that provide information about an individual's standing in relation to a representative group of other pupils. The diagnostic instruments referred to here should be primarily 'objectives-related', in other words they should measure the extent to which the pupil has acquired the knowledge, skills and attitudes which constitute the educational objectives and also reveal where there are still learning deficits. It seems to be a relatively reliable prediction that theory and techniques for the construction of this kind of diagnostic instruments will be the object of substantial research efforts in the near future.

The diagnostic tests discussed so far are such as to measure achievements and deficits in a direct and straightforward way. In recent years, increasing attention has been devoted to diagnostic instruments of a somewhat different kind. The most significant feature of these tests is that they are aimed at measuring fundamental functions on which success or failure in different school subjects or skills depends. It is also characteristic that the tests refer to dynamic, modifiable functions, rather than to static 'factors of mind', and so are intended to bridge the gap between diagnosis and educational treatment. In particular, basic functions related to verbal skills have been the object of substantial research which has resulted in new types of diagnostic tests, e. g. the Illinois Test of Psycholinguistic Abilities. The possibilities that are opening up here for diagnostic information that can be transformed into educational recommendations have begun to attract the attention of Scandinavian researchers, and it can be expected that this line of research will be followed in the next few years.

*Programmes and systems
for individually prescribed instruction*

It has already been mentioned that a considerable proportion of present research and development activities in special education is devoted to the design and construction of self-instructional materials and systems of such materials. It may be anticipated that this trend will continue, since the need for instructional devices that allow individualization is still very strong. It seems probable, however, that certain changes in approach and organization will occur.

So far, research institutes have engaged themselves in the whole process of method-material development: analysis of objectives, determination of prerequisites, construction of learning material, evaluation, revision and even implementation. As procedures for these steps have been established, the need for research contributions diminishes. Methods construction will become a technical rather than a research task. Educational technologists, subject-matter experts and publishing bodies will take over the main responsibilities in the developmental work. When new educational areas are entered, there will still be a demand for research contributions, but these will be limited to the construction of models or prototypes of instructional systems that will then be extended and implemented by other functionaries. Research related to the development of new instructional devices will, however, have another key task. Although effective routines for the construction of teaching systems have no doubt been found, there is still a considerable lack of knowledge as to the fundamental teaching–learning mechanisms. It seems a fair prediction that problems which refer to basic instructional questions, e.g. inductive versus deductive method in science, or understanding versus imitation in language instruction, will be the main objects for educational research in the years to come.

Another trend that can be expected in the development of instructional programmes for handicapped students is a higher degree of co-ordination and integration with the construction of more comprehensive systems for non-handicapped people. So far, independent projects have been set up for different handicapped groups, and the total procedure from goal analysis to evaluation refers exclusively to a special handicap category. Such concentration and specialization will certainly be a frequent approach in the future, due to the unique needs of different handicapped groups; but, in addition, attempts will probably be made to take advantage of the resources of extensive projects aiming at a wider range of students. As an illustration of this tendency, mention may be made of the IMU (Individual Mathematics Instruction) project. The original target group for the self-instructional material developed within this project was a non-selected sample of students in grades 7–9 of the comprehensive school. The basic material is now being supplemented with additional components adapted to students with learning difficulties. There seem to be definite advantages with co-ordination of the kind described. The cost and the amount of work necessary for the development of high-quality instructional material are considerable, and there is always a risk that groups of handicapped students (especially small groups) will be neglected. If analyses of instructional objectives—which are basically the same for handicapped and non-handicapped students—and parts of the learning material construction, as well as production facilities, can be co-ordinated, economical and qualitative gains can be expected.

Identification and development of potential abilities in handicapped students

Further research on the ability structure in handicapped students, and efforts to substitute a multifaceted pattern of ability components for an over-all measure of intelligence, can be expected. There are reasons to believe that research attention will be particularly directed towards questions of what factors or functions are called for in different work or training tasks, and towards problems involved in predicting job success from the relation between individual ability profiles and the factor structure of work tasks.

It is also probable that research will continue to be focused relatively more on what the handicapped individual *can* do than on what he cannot. The studies of psychomotor abilities in retardates demonstrated that important functions for work success were intact in a considerable proportion of these individuals. A great deal more analysis of this kind is needed, and can be regarded as a natural concomitant to the active approach that characterizes present-day special education, the aim of which is to develop each handicapped person to the limit of his potentialities.

Development and evaluation of new organization models for special education

The efficacy in all circumstances of traditional organization forms for handicap education, i.e. special classes and special schools, has been challenged. The alternatives to organizational differentiations are various arrangements of 'integration', a term not wholly free of ambiguity. Sometimes it means placement of handicapped students in ordinary schools though still in special classes; sometimes it is used when handicapped students are placed in regular classes; it may also, in other connexions, refer to residence or working conditions. Setting aside the lack of terminologic clarity, the various forms of integration in special education imply new developments of great interest. So far, these innovations have only to a limited extent been submitted to objective evaluation. One can, however, foresee a growing number of evaluation studies related to these questions. It is now generally acknowledged that the introduction of new educational arrangements should be accompanied by an empirical and systematic evaluation of their effects. It seems to be a reasonable prediction that the realization of this sound principle will occur more frequently in the period to come. Such evaluations should not be limited to organizational models already developed but should be extended to new experimental forms. Organization innovations within ordinary education such as team teaching and non-graded units can also be expected in special education (as a matter of fact, activities along these lines are already in progress), and it may then be expected that judgments about efficacy will not rely on intuition and common sense only, but will also and mainly be based on results of studies in which available techniques for educational evaluation have been applied.

Role of research in the training
of teachers for special education

The teacher plays a key role in the realization of educational innovations. If new instructional possibilities are not known or accepted by teachers, the impact of innovations upon educational practice will be negligible. Since teachers acquire their basic pedagogic knowledge and attitudes during their professional training, it is essential that the teacher-training programme should provide the students with the necessary tools for utilizing educational inventions and stimulate open-mindedness toward developments within their professional field. The most important vehicle for development within education, as in other areas of human activities, is research, and teacher training should therefore include enough information about scientific approach, research methodology and research results to give an understanding of the rationale behind accepted practices of teaching. It is only by being closely associated with research activities that teacher training becomes a qualified professional preparation rather than an inculcation of traditional rules of thumb.

Research is of particular importance in the training of teachers for special education. In the instruction of handicapped pupils the teacher is continuously brought up against problems for which no ready-made solutions are available. He must consider the individual characteristics of the pupil, analyse the components of the learning task, and adapt instruction to the conclusions of such analysis. It is also necessary to follow up and evaluate the results of the approach chosen and, if need be, try alternative ways. Successful work along these lines presupposes a substantial knowledge of research-derived laws and principles, along with work habits that in many ways are similar to work procedures in educational research and development activities. In the training of special teachers these objectives can be mainly attained in two ways: by founding teacher training on a scientific basis and by giving the teacher students some first-hand experience of educational research.

*Research-founded curriculum content in the training
of special teachers*

Special teacher training in the Scandinavian countries is based upon two to four years' regular teacher training, which means that general topics can be treated in a repetitious way and emphasis placed on special or advanced issues. The studies, of one or two years' length, are grouped in four main areas: educational psychology and sociology, methods of instruction,practice and subject-matter courses. Of these, the educational psychology course has so far mainly governed the student teacher's research orientation. This is apparent, at least indirectly, in present curricula, as the following extracts from Sweden and Norway show.

An extract from an educational psychology curriculum in Sweden is broken down as follows:
1. The psychological basis of education: development and developmental handicaps; learning principles and their application; differential psychology and psychometrics; social psychology and its application; mental hygiene.
2. Different student handicaps and the application of psychology principles in special education: immaturity; retardation; reading and writing difficulties; mathematics difficulties; emotional disturbances; sight handicaps; hearing handicaps; speech handicaps; motor handicaps.
3. Research and development in special education: information about special educational research problems; introduction to research methodology; statistics.

A similar curriculum extract from Norway shows the following breakdown:
1. Psychology: emphasis on learning and developmental psychology; particular attention to retardation problems.
2. Hearing, sight, and emotional handicaps.
3. Speech and language problems, cerebral palsy: survey of speech and language development; speech correction; psycholinguistics; learning difficulties related to cerebral palsy and brain injuries; special instructional aids.
4. Psychology, diagnosis, and didactics of reading: development of the reading process; definitions; frequency of reading difficulties; causes and theories of dyslexia; diagnosis; instructional methods related to diagnosis; reading psychology with emphasis on readiness, eye movements and vocalization.
5. Emotional and social disturbances in children with special emphasis on the learning situation.
6. Educational evaluation: test theory; training in the use of tests.
7. Special task: material from different sources is gathered, organized and discussed.

The above excerpts demonstrate that present-day programmes for the training of special teachers are well anchored in the behavioural sciences. This conclusion is further confirmed by the character of the textbooks used in the courses. The texts are, with few exceptions, research-oriented, as exemplified by such internationally known handbooks as S.A. Kirk's *Educating Exceptional Children* and P.M. Mussen's *Child Development*. A good deal of the literature overlaps with university requirements and can be counted as units for the basic academic degree.

The research aspect of the curriculum content in the training of teachers for special education has traditionally been more apparent in the diagnostic sections than in those which deal with instructional methods. This has probably been because more extensive supply of applicable information is available from mental measurement research than from research on instructional process and methods. A change seems, however, to be under way. This can be observed most clearly in those parts of the teacher-training curriculum that refer to remedial reading instruction, a problem area that has received considerable research attention during recent years.

Research experience as a part of the teacher-training programme

The emphasis in teacher training should of course be on the teacher's primary function, which is to teach. There are, however, good reasons for including some research experience in the training programme. For one thing, research and development is increasingly becoming an integrated part of the educational system, and it is highly probable that a teacher today will be involved in developmental projects as part of his teaching duties. For another thing, optimal teaching has a good deal in common with research activities. Just as an investigator sets up hypotheses based on available information, arranges experimental situations, tests the hypotheses and possibly revises them, a teacher is expected to use diagnostic data for setting up a tentative learning programme, which is followed up by testing its effects and, if necessary, by modifying it.

Present training programmes for special teachers include a certain amount of research orientation. The Swedish programme, for instance, includes a mainly informative course about on-going research in special education, complemented by courses in statistics and research methodology. In addition, five to six weeks of the training period are devoted to a special task within a chosen area of interest. This task can be related to research, either in the form of an independent investigation of moderate scope, or in the form of participation in an extensive research project. As regards of the latter type, a considerable number of special teacher students have been involved in the SISU project (see page 77), the aim of which is to develop self-instructional methods and materials for students with learning handicaps. Other students have conducted and reported their own studies on various problems relevant to special education. The experience of these activities has so far been positive, and it seems safe to conclude that first-hand contact with research and development during teacher training can contribute substantially to the special teacher's professional insight.

Organization of research

No sharp line of demarcation can be drawn between the organization of research in special education and that of educational research in general. Educational research planning, at least in Sweden, is carried out within a common framework.

General structure of research organization in Sweden

The bulk of educational research has traditionally been located in university departments. In recent years, research institutes have also been established at the larger schools of education. Together with a substantial increase in research funds, this expansion has meant a quite substantial increase of the research potential in education.

The basic resources of research, as to staff and funds, come from ordinary budgets. During the fifties and still more in the sixties, however, a considerable proportion of educational research has been initiated and supported from other sources, although performed within the university or schools of education organizations. Several State committees working with school reform problems during the last few decades have engaged research institutes to elucidate different decision problems. One such example is the differentiation problem, i.e. whether and when students within the nine-year comprehensive school should be referred to different streams or lines. This question was submitted to extensive research projects, including correlational and factor analytic investigations as well as comparisons of pupil adjustment and achievements in homogenous and heterogenous grouping systems. Several studies were directed toward empirical curriculum analyses for the new comprehensive school and the new gymnasium. By means of questionnaires, information was gathered from employers and from representatives of higher education on the question of what were particularly important or necessary knowledge and skills for future work or study success. The data were later used in designing curricula intended as a basis for different occupations or more advanced studies.

For committee research of this kind, the institutes engaged were allotted extra grants which in most cases were appreciable in relation to the basic resources available for research.

Another development that has strongly increased educational research resources during the sixties has been the initiation of large-scale project research. Traditionally, the typical educational investigation has been carried out within an academic career framework as a single-person achievement. As a consequence, broad educational problems with practical implications have often been outside the reach of research. In order to create conditions for such research, different granting bodies have begun to fund larger projects within which a number of specialists co-operate over an extended period with a view to solving problems of great practical pedagogical significance. The most substantial project research grants come from the National Board of Education through its research bureau. Other granting bodies for large-scale educational research are the Tri-Centennial Fund of the Bank of Sweden and the Office of the University Chancellor. Support to more basic research is given mainly by the State Council for Social Research.

Project research includes varying kinds of problems, such as surveys of present conditions, development of instruments for selection purposes, evaluation of existing educational programmes, educational planning, etc. The predominant type of project has so far been the development of instructional systems, and number of such projects with relevance to special education were cited in the section 'Role of Research in the Training of Teachers for Special Education', above. Typically, such projects include a number of different tasks, and consequently a division of functions among different experts is the rule. A report[1] issued by the Committee of Education (Pedagogikutredningen) gives the following example of staff composition in a typical project:

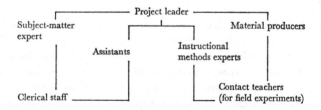

The number of persons involved (contact teachers excluded) is thirteen, most of them on a half- or part-time basis.

The expenditures for project research have increased exponentially during the sixties. This can be illustrated by the curves in Figure 1 which shows the

1   *Pedagogisk Utbildning och Forskning* [Educational Training and Research], SOU (in press).

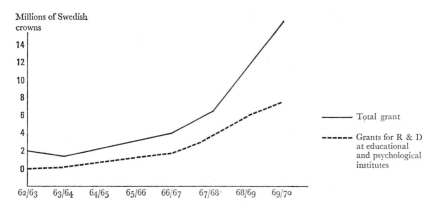

FIG. 1. Grants from the Swedish National Board of Education to educational development, 1962–70.

grants for educational developmental work from the National Board of Education, the main funder of educational research. The data in this figure and the two following tables are from the above-mentioned committee report.

In addition to the grants from the National Board of Education, economic support comes from the other sources mentioned previously as shown in Table 3.

The rapid growth of research funds and research volume has produced a strong demand on personnel resources. The situation, detailed in the same report, regarding the financing of personnel with mainly research responsibilities can be summarized as follows: at the 'Fil. dr. Fil. lic. (Ph. D.)' academic level, 20 persons were being financed from the regular budget and 16 from special grants; at the 'Fil. kand. (B.A.)' level, 11 were being financed from the regular budget and 59 from special grants; furthermore, 15 persons at the 'expert' level were being financed from special grants.

As can be seen, a larger proportion of the total number of persons actively engaged in educational research are paid by special research grants than from the regular budget of the institutes. Only on the highest academic level is the relation reversed, which indicates that most project leaders keep permanent positions. Although the number of researchers has increased con-

TABLE 3	Grants (in millions of Swedish crowns) to educational research 1966–70			
Source	1966/67	1967/68	1968/69	1969/70
National Board of Education	1.7	2.9	5.8	6.4
University Chancellor	0.3	0.5	0.6	1.2
State Council	0.7	0.5	(information not available)	
Tri-Centennial Fund	0.4	0.1	0.9	0.4

siderably, there is a strong need for more manpower to meet the demands of education research. In order to fulfil this need, part of the research resources have been used in recent years for behavioural science training of research personnel. Future project leaders and other functionaries are being trained within current projects. Another personnel category needed in research and development projects and for instructional material production are individuals, predominantly teachers, who already have a basic academic subject-matter training. For this category, a newly designed one-year training course in 'educational technology' was started a year ago at the University of Gothenburg.

Most educational research takes place within, or is associated with, universities and schools of education, but there are also a number of extra-mural organizations of research and development where the emphasis is on applied research. In 1958, a state Experimental School was established in Linköping. It has been organized as a regular public school to which has been linked a research institute with a director and a research staff. A good deal of the research activities at this school have been devoted to special education problems, particularly to psychological analysis of dyslectic children and to the development of instructional methods for this group. School readiness problems have also been the subject of extensive research. The experimental school recently ceased to be a separate institute and is now integrated with the pedagogical department of the school of education in Linköping.

Among the educational research organizations outside the universities and schools of education is the Pedagogical Centre, set up by the Stockholm Board of Education and staffed by a number of qualified researchers. The research programme gives priority to local educational problems, but most projects planned so far have a general applicability. From the point of view of special education, the centre plans to study the effects of an optimized mental hygiene programme in a Stockholm school district and is of particular interest.

Similar to the Pedagogical Centre in purpose, but without research-trained personnel, are the so-called Educational Development Blocks that have been established in different school areas in the country by joint State and community resources. They are intended to serve the combined purpose of innovation and implementation of new instructional methods and educational programmes. Some developmental blocks co-operate with the research institutes of the schools of education.

Organization of research in special education

There are few formal organs in Scandinavia particularly designed for research on the educational problems of handicapped students. The only institute set up for this purpose is the department of special education at the University of Jyväskylä in Finland which has been in existence for twenty years. In

Sweden, plans for establishing a counterpart to this department ended in a compromise whereby special education became part of the responsibilities of the educational institute at the School of Education in Gothenburg.

The Nordic Culture Commission has initiated an inter-Scandinavian project for research in special education. The guidelines for its activities were discussed at a Scandinavian conference in 1966 and were summarized as follows:[1]

1. The project should be directed toward an essential and neglected area of special education.
2. The problems chosen should be of practical importance and the results have potential consequences for special education in the field.
3. The project should be of *inter*-Scandinavian relevance, i. e. meet demands and be applicable in all Scandinavian countries.

The project has by now been in operation for three years and has received a grant from the Nordic Cultural Fund. The research field chosen is the educational problems of trainable mentally retarded subjects (certain of the studies are mentioned in the section 'Research on Special Education During the Last Decade', above). In a report from an *ad hoc* committee within the Nordic Culture Commission,[2] it was proposed in 1968 that the project activities should be transformed into a permanent research centre. The proposal was not adopted completely, but a recommendation was issued that the project activities should continue, supported economically from the national budgets.

In spite of the relative absence of separate institutes for special education research, a respectable proportion of the total research effort has been devoted to the problems of handicapped students. From a cost survey of current school research projects supported by the National Board of Education[3] it is estimated that roughly one-third of the total cumulative expenditures up till 1968/69 for projects in progress have been attributed to research and development programmes with clear significance for special education.

Current interest in the handicap field is also reflected by the fact that special educational investigations are in progress at most institutes engaged in educational research.

1   K.-G. Stukát and R. Engström (ed.), *Samnordisk Specialpedagogisk Forskning* [Inter-Scandinavian Research in Special Education], Gothenburg, Ped. Inst., School of Educ., 1966.
2   T. Lie *et al.*, *Instilling om Samnordisk Specialpedagogisk Forskning* [Report on Inter-Scandinavian Research in Special Education], Oslo, 1968.
3   *Newsletter School Research*, No. 9, 1969 (published by the Swedish National Board of Education).

Research co-ordination and dissemination
at a national level

The total efficiency of research efforts is not only a function of the number and quality of the investigations performed but is also to a great extent dependent upon an adequate co-ordination of different contributions. Lack of co-ordination may cause much research to become a patchwork, with important problems neglected, and unnecessary duplication of effort. At the same time, co-ordination must be a straitjacket; there should always be room for creative individual initiatives even if they do not quite fit in with an over-all scheme.

The impact of research on society is also largely dependent on how effectively research information is spread and to what extent it reaches relevant social targets. At present, much interest is focused on problems concerning the efficient dissemination of research information.

Educational research co-ordination

In 1962, a special section within the Swedish National Board of Education was established, its main task being to initiate and co-ordinate educational research and to distribute information on research and development activities of particular interest. A distinctive feature of the planning activities of this section, Bureau L4, is that opinions as to what constitutes the most important research and development tasks are gathered both from researchers and from the 'consumers' of educational research information, i.e. representatives of schools and of society in general. Suggestions for research problems that should be given priority are taken up at conferences, by questionnaires, personal contacts, etc. Proposals are discussed with researchers at different institutions and promising and feasible ideas for investigation are transformed into research plans. The latter are screened at informal meetings with institute directors, and by the Counselling Committee, whose members represent educational administration, research and society in general. Project schemes that have passed the screening procedure successfully are taken up in the budget plan of the National Board of Education. The time lapse between initiation and start of a project is about one to one and a half years. This may seem a long time but the advantage of the screening period is that it affords some guarantee against premature and incompletely planned projects.

Another way to identify research needs and to co-ordinate research is to arrange symposia (e.g. on adult education, vocational training, future research) at which recent research findings are presented, methodological problems discussed and developmental trends surveyed. From the point of view of special education, two such conferences are of special interest, the Gothenburg conference in 1966[1] on which occasion co-ordination of Scandinavian research in the handicap field in general was discussed, and a symposium on mental retardation in 1969.

Dissemination of research results

The effects of research upon education practice are largely dependent on the extent to which research results become known among those involved in the many different branches of the educational enterprise. The media used at present for dissemination are manifold but somewhat disunited. In addition to the information that is furnished by personal communication at lectures, conferences, etc., various journals present continuous information on research activities. As to special education, articles from various parts of the field, with emphasis on general learning disabilities, are found in *Nordisk Tidskrift för Specialpedagogik*, whereas more topic-centred information is given in specialized journals such as *Psykisk Utvecklingshämning, Nordisk Tidskrift för Dövundervisningen*, and others. Research is not, however, the primary concern of these journals and the coverage is therefore somewhat incomplete. More systematic information about current educational research, including special education, has been issued in the last few years by the National Board of Education and the State Council for Social Research. The former compiles and distributes a yearly catalogue on research in progress. Information is gathered from institutes engaged in educational research and a summary of each project or investigation is usually provided. The catalogue describes, *inter alia*, the background, purpose, design, instruments and time-schedule of the study. A similar catalogue on research reported during the year is sent out by the State Council for Social Research. More detailed information on current research is given in *Newsletter School Research* available in Swedish and English versions. The *Newsletter* is issued by the National Board of Education and covers projects supported by the Board.

Although the dissemination problem has been recognized as a fundamental one—and recent years have seen a noteworthy intensification of efforts—much remains to be done. Aware of this need, the educational committee (*Pedagogikutredningen*) has stressed that a continued increase of the resources for educational research and development should be combined with more efficient dissemination of research results.

1 K.-G. Stukát and R. Engström, *Samnordisk Specialpedagogisk Forskning,* op. cit.

International exchange
of research information

Although there are certain educational problems specific to each country, most subjects of educational research have international relevance. A necessary condition if effective use is to be made of the total research information is that adequate communication channels should be available for research exchange. The following section surveys some of the attempts that have so far been made to organize research information and documentation on an international basis.

Present organs for international research communication

Within the Nordic Cultural Commission different sections are concerned with co-ordination and research information problems. The section for higher education and research has appointed a committee to investigate the needs of inter-Scandinavian co-operation in research on academic instruction. In the school section, a committee devotes special attention to research co-ordination questions and has initiated symposia on common problems, e.g. on educational technology. As mentioned earlier, the Nordic Cultural Commission has also taken the initiative of a Scandinavian research project in special education in Gothenburg.

In the Organisation for Economic Co-operation and Development (OECD), and particularly within its Centre for Educational Research and Innovation (CERI), Sweden is engaged in a co-ordinated project concerning socially and culturally handicapped children of pre-school age. Other project participants are research institutes in Ireland, the Netherlands and Norway. The Swedish project, located in Gothenburg, is directed toward new methods and materials for intellectual and social stimulation. Part of the research programme includes experimental evaluation of the new methods employed with handicapped and deprived children. The co-ordination between the participating institutes has so far been limited to conferences and exchange of written documents, but is intended to include mutual use of instructional material and evaluation instruments.

The Council of Europe has a special organ for European co-operation and co-ordination, the Council for Cultural Co-operation (CCC). This organ has contributed to educational research and development by arranging symposia and conferences. One conference (held in Oslo in 1967) discussed the topic of the school as a system and the applicability of operations analysis.

The council has also a special Division for Educational Documentation and Research.

Unesco stimulates educational research and development in different ways. Of special interest from a Scandinavian point of view is the Unesco Institute in Hamburg which has arranged several conferences with Scandinavian participation and contributions. In the summer of 1968, Unesco sponsored an international symposium on 'Learning and Education' at Skepparholmen, near Stockholm, for advanced students in the behavioural sciences. Unesco is also involved in the International Association for the Evaluation of Educational Achievement (IEA) which is pursuing empirical comparative educational research on a world-wide scale. Its administrative centre is at present in Stockholm.

Scandinavian research also has continuous contacts with such internationally oriented institutes as the Pädagogisches Zentrum and the Max-Planck-Institut in Berlin, the Deutsches Institut für Internationale Pädagogische Forschung in Frankfurt, as well as different national institutes. Of particular interest from the point of view of handicap education is the considerable research exchange that has taken place between Scandinavian researchers and American research centres in special education, e. g. those at the University of Illinois and at Yeshiva University.

International documentation centres

One important aspect of international research information exchange concerns documentation problems. As a general judgement, present forms and organs for educational documentation must be regarded as rather disparate and unco-ordinated. The development of international exchange centres is restrained by the fact that documentation at a national level is still rudimentary in most places, although efforts are being made to improve the situation. As emphasized by both Unesco and the Council of Europe, well-organized documentation centres must be the basis for an international documentation system.

In the United States, the Educational Resources Information Center (ERIC) has been established as a co-ordinating body for decentralized documentation sub-centres, or clearing-houses, each of which covers a special topic, e. g. adult education, educational media and technology, reading, etc. One of the clearing-houses, located at the Council for Exceptional Children in Washington, D.C., specializes in documents on the education of handicapped children. Research reports, to a large extent mimeographed institute documents, are sifted at the clearing-houses. The accepted material, classified and coded by the ERIC thesaurus, indexed by title, institute, etc., and provided with a brief summary, is issued in a monthly publication, *Research in Education*. Individual retrievals are not performed by ERIC, but the reports indexed in *Research in Education* can be ordered in microfiche. It is also possible to subscribe for the whole series of microfiches in a special field. The ERIC services are being used to an increasing extent at Scandinavian institutes, and the complete series of microfiches is available at the Swedish State Library of Education and Psychology.

Another documentation organization used in Scandinavia is *Bibliographic Pädagogik*, published monthly in West Germany. Its main scope is German literature, but some non-German material is included. The number of titles per year is at present in the neighbourhood of 10,000.

The Cultural Committee of the Council of Europe has recently established a working group for investigating the use of computer techniques in educational documentation. The group recommends a successive expansion of information exchange, based upon a simultaneous development of national centres. For the present, a co-ordination centre under the direction of the Council of Europe is envisaged, but activities may later be transferred to the Unesco International Bureau of Education (IBE) in Geneva. IBE is at present working on an international system for the exchange of educational documentation and information, based upon national centres.

Urgent needs

In spite of the many initiatives and activities over recent years, the state of research information exchange on an international level is far from satisfactory, in special education as in other fields. The channels of communication are incomplete and the information exchange irregular. New projects are sometimes started without taking account of similar activities in other countries. Substantial gains would no doubt be made if the efficiency of communication could be increased. As a complement to surveys of research in the whole field of special education, there is a need for surveys specializing in different handicap areas. Such surveys should be made at reasonably frequent intervals. In addition to written research information of this kind, intensified personal contacts between researchers in the same field of special education at international seminars, symposia and conferences are desirable. Research communication efficiency would also increase if national journals regularly contained summaries in one or two international languages of investigation reports. Other urgent needs concern documentation services. Development of effective national systems for information retrieval is a basic prerequisite for co-ordination with international documentation centres. Some of the above desiderata are already being met to a certain extent, but a good deal remains to be done, at both national and international levels.

T. A. Vlasova and V. I. Lubovsky

Union of Soviet
Socialist Republics

The instruction and education of handicapped children in the U.S.S.R., like the whole public education system, are entirely the responsibility of the State. As early as 5 June 1918, a special decree of the Council of People's Commissars, signed by V. I. Lenin, placed all educational establishments for handicapped children—public and private—under the authority of the People's Commissariat of Education. State direction has exerted a beneficent influence on the system of special instruction and ensured its rapid development. It has made it possible to introduce a uniform structure and organization in special schools throughout the country, to establish uniform curricula and programmes, to implement universal education of handicapped children and to provide all types of schools with special textbooks, visual aids and teachers' manuals. Without such control, the compilation of textbooks for special schools would be altogether impracticable owing to the absence of any organized arrangements for their preparation and the substantial economic obstacle represented by the very limited circulation.

A uniform level of special education, which in the case of schools for physically handicapped children is equal to that of ordinary schools, makes possible the integration of these children in society. In particular, after leaving school they are able to continue their education along with ordinary adolescents in the general system of higher or secondary special schools.

The State system of supervision makes it possible to ascertain the demand for teacher–defectologists and to organize their training in higher schools; to concentrate research work in the field of defectology on the most important problems; to co-ordinate investigations; and to put into practice the latest scientific achievements. The system also allows the establishment of uniform standards with regard to the selection of children and the staffing of schools; this in turn creates favourable conditions for the introduction of uniform curricula and programmes in schools of every type, for better utilization of textbooks and for organizing the vocational education and training of handicapped children.

One of the most essential features of the special education system in the U.S.S.R. is a multi-faceted approach to the solution of all problems. The organization and structure of the educational establishments, the selection of children for these establishments and the instructional and corrective-educational activities provided are carried out with due regard for the findings of medical, pedagogical and psychological research and with the participation of various specialists—physicians, teachers and psychologists, as well as engineers for the construction of special equipment and instruments.

Present system of
special education

The main trend underlying special education in the U.S.S.R. is perhaps the more extensive involvement of handicapped children in the process of differential education based on analyses of the action-pathogenesis of the defect and of its structure.

The care of handicapped children is the responsibility of three ministries: the Ministry of Education, the Ministry of Public Health and the Ministry of Social Security.

The Ministry of Education is in charge of kindergartens for deaf children, kindergartens for blind children, kindergartens for mentally retarded children, secondary schools for blind children, secondary schools for partially sighted children, secondary schools for hard of hearing children and for children with a late loss of hearing, incomplete secondary schools for deaf children, auxiliary schools (for mentally retarded children), schools for children with speech disorders, schools for children with disturbances of the supporting-motor apparatus (consequences of cerebral paralyses, poliomyelitis and other diseases), schools for mentally retarded blind children, secondary evening schools for blind adults, secondary evening schools for deaf adults.

The Ministry of Public Health is responsible for school-sanatoriums for children suffering from a disturbed mental development, clinics for children with similar disturbances, clinics for children and adults with speech disorders, speech therapy rooms at polyclinics, crèches for children up to 3 years of age suffering from disturbances of physical development.

The Ministry of Social Security is in charge of all establishments for seriously retarded children and adolescents, as well as instructional workshops for mentally retarded adults.

The system operated by the Central Board of Industrial and Technical Education of the Ministry of Labour Reserves include special schools for vocational training and technical schools for the deaf. Finally, the All-Russian Society of the Deaf and the All-Russian Society of the Blind have special instructional enterprises where vocational training of the deaf and the blind is conducted.

The basic tasks of special schools of all types are general education of the child (in line with the possibilities of each type of anomalous development), work and vocational training in order to prepare the child for future practical occupations, development of the child's personality in accordance with the principles of communist morality and in preparation for an independent life in society as a fully fledged citizen of the country. Another important task is to improve the child's physical (and in the case of mentally retarded children, spiritual) health through complex medical and pedagogical work appropriate to each type of defect.

Different special schools also have their own particular tasks. For example, one of the most important tasks of schools for deaf children is to form and develop verbal speech, one of the key aims of schools for the blind children is to develop an accurate idea of the surrounding world, etc.

Organization of
research

Scientific research work in the field of defectology is conducted by a number of scientific establishments. The most important is the Scientific Research Institute of Defectology at the U.S.S.R. Academy of Pedagogical Sciences. In the course of the last ten to fifteen years, this institute has almost doubled in size, and is now a large scientific establishment employing representatives of highly diverse specialities—teachers, psychologists, speech therapists, physiologists, physicians and engineers thus ensuring a multidisciplinary solution of various problems connected with the study, instruction, education and occupational training of children with different defects and pathological deviations in their development.

The institute has twenty-two laboratories which are concerned with the following defects: deafness and defective hearing, blindness and defective vision, mental backwardness and temporary retardation of mental development, speech disorders, motor disturbances, combined defects (e.g. blindness-deafness-dumbness). The institute deals with children of different ages (beginning with those of pre-school age) as well as with adults suffering from defects of hearing and vision. Defectological departments of higher pedagogical schools in different towns and defectological divisions in the scientific research institutes of pedagogics and psychology in the union republics of the U.S.S.R. take part in this research.

The institute co-ordinates all work in the field of defectology by convening annual co-ordination conferences with the participation of all the defectological departments of the pedagogical institutes and the defectological divisions of the scientific research institutes; by conducting a mutual exchange of programmes of research work; and by organizing every three or four years scientific sessions devoted to different problems of defectology where the results of the most important investigations are reported and an exchange of opinions concerning basic scientific problems takes place. An important role is played by the scientific and methodological journal *Defectology*, founded in 1969.

Of great significance for the development of scientific research among the mass of teachers are the so-called 'Pedagogical Readings', organized by the institute with the participation of advanced school-teachers whose papers are devoted to various problems connected with the instruction and education of handicapped children.

The following basic trends are evident in the development of special education in the U.S.S.R.:

1. The process of differentiation within the system of instruction and education of handicapped children becomes more and more complex. This differentiation is accomplished in the following ways: (a) special schools are created for children with partial defects (for example, schools for partially sighted children have been isolated from schools for blind children); (b) special sections are organized within schools of different types according to the specific features of the children (for example, within schools for children with defective hearing two sections have been formed according to the age at which the hearing defect emerged, a factor which determines different levels of development of the children's independent speech; within schools for children suffering from speech defects special groups have been formed for stammering children); (c) an ever-increasing individualization of the process of instruction takes place within each class (depending on the degree of hearing or vision remaining, and on the level of mental development), this individualization is made possible by a special study of the psychological and clinical peculiarities of variants of a given defect; (d) special schools are founded for children with multiple handicaps (for blind deaf-and-dumb children, for mentally retarded blind children, etc.).

2. Research work aimed at implementing the possibility of starting the education of handicapped children at an earlier age is being extended; this manifests itself in the creation of a system of pre-school establishments (crèches and kindergartens) for children with defects of hearing, vision or speech, as well as for mentally retarded children.

3. The level of general education in all special schools is steadily raised with due regard for the abilities of the children; this reflects the general trend of the development of public education in the U.S.S.R.—the transition to universal secondary education.

4. The trade and industrial education of handicapped children is continuously perfected. In this connexion, it must be pointed out that: (a) the

range of occupations in which handicapped children and adolescents are trained is being greatly extended and now includes metal-working, electro- and radio-engineering, and many others; (b) much attention is paid to agricultural labour which is not only a new kind of vocational training for some categories of handicapped children (blind, visually impaired, etc.), but has proved to be of great corrective significance; (c) the duration of vocational training is increasing as a result of the increased demand of modern industry for trained workers.

5. The problem of utilizing the occupational and entire practical activity of children with the aim of developing their cognitive activity (thinking, speech, etc.) is thoroughly appreciated.

6. The system of selecting children for special schools is constantly perfected. This is above all due to the growing differentiation of the special establishments, and leads in turn to the development of clinical, physiological and psychological investigations, the results of which are of importance for the selection process. The development of complex (medico-pedagogical and clinico-physiological) investigations ensures a more comprehensive solution of various practical problems connected not only with the selection of children, but also with the improvement of the system of educational establishments and of teaching methods and individualization.

7. The methods of teaching are steadily improved. This work includes: (a) elaboration of special methods of instruction (for example, application of the dactylic form of speech which in the initial stage of teaching language to deaf children is the basic method and subsequently plays an auxiliary role) and investigations of specific features and development of the children's cognitive activity; (b) elaboration and utilization of special technical equipment (for example, sound-amplifying apparatus and 'visible-speech' appliances for teaching children with defective hearing, special apparatus transforming optic signals into acoustic and tactile signals for teaching blind children, optic instruments for children with defective vision, teaching machines); (c) introduction of programmed teaching in special schools, etc.

8. Extensive research work is carried out in the study of relatively minor defects of development (temporary retardations of development in children with psychophysical infantilism, cerebro-asthenic states, inconsiderable loss of vision or hearing, speech defects) and corresponding ways of compensating for these defects are elaborated.

Research on the education
of the mentally retarded

Oligophrenopedagogy (special education for mentally handicapped) as a branch of defectology concerned with the specific laws of instruction and education of mentally retarded children is based on the same didactic principles which govern Soviet pedagogy as a whole.

The practical implementation of these principles, the specific character of the education process and its content are determined by the particular development of the mentally retarded child before school and in the course of school education.

The following main problems are studied by oligophrenopedagogy: the pedagogical aspect of mental backwardness; pedagogic and psycho-pedagogic research into the characteristic development of mentally handicapped children under the influence of special corrective instruction and education in auxiliary schools offering an eight-year training period (most are boarding schools); the principles and methods which must govern the instruction and education of mentally retarded children and their preparation for work and an independent life in society on the basis of communist morality; special methods of teaching the subjects which enter the general educational cycle, as well as of occupational training; the structure of special educational establishments for mentally retarded children, and a number of other problems.

The auxiliary schools are concerned with the instruction and education of children whose mentality manifests a steady decline and whose psychophysical development is of a unique character. In these schools the children receive not only a general education, but also adequate vocational training which results in their mastery of certain specialities and in their subsequent assignment to work positions.

The main symptom of mental backwardness is the underdevelopment and specific nature of the cognitive activity which makes impossible the instruction and education of such children in ordinary schools. Additionally, such children exhibit an underdevelopment of the emotional and volitional processes and of speech, as well as a decline in, or limitation of, their interests.

The bulk of pupils in these auxiliary schools are mentally handicapped children who in the past suffered lesions of the central nervous system leading to the above-mentioned characteristics in further development. Many years' experience and scientific research showed that, with specially organized instruction, such mentally retarded children develop and acquire a definite minimum of general educational knowledge and skills, and acquire the habit of working. Under the influence of the special educational system the personality develops to such a degree that, after leaving the auxiliary schools, most children prove to be adequately prepared for work and independent life in society even though they do not reach the normal level of development.

A wide network of children's medical consultation centres which ensures a systematic control, prophylactic service and prompt medical aid to children all over the country, helps to reduce cases of extreme mental backwardness, on the one hand, and, on the other, facilitates early diagnosis.

One of the principles of special pedagogy is to start purposive corrective work with children suffering from certain defects of development as early as possible. In accordance with this principle, a system of pre-school establishments for mentally retarded children is now being experimentally elaborated. The experience already accumulated shows that although the children placed in these establishments suffer from strongly pronounced mental backwardness, they often prove to be better prepared for school studies than children with milder defects who remained at home before entering school. One of the immediate tasks is therefore to extend the network of special kindergartens for mentally retarded children. The work of such kindergartens is in the main directed at all-round development of the children (including initial aesthetic and moral education, physical development, stimulation of curiosity and interests, development of the observation faculty, sustained attention, speech, thinking, habits of self-help, association with other people, mutual assistance, etc.). The work of the special kindergartens is also aimed at a possibly earlier partial elimination or alleviation of the defects in the child's development (such as negativism, passivity, sluggishness or, conversely, excessive excitability, etc.).

Where mental backwardness is detected in the pre-school period, the child receives special attention and the parents receive expert advice on the education of the child and its preparation for school. In particular, they are advised to draw the child into the family's active life (self-help, assistance to the adults) and to contribute to its general development.

Where mental backwardness is less pronounced, it may only manifest itself clearly when the child begins to study at an ordinary school. In such cases, after one or two years at school the child is transferred to an auxiliary school.

Investigations jointly carried out by teachers, psychologists, physicians and neurophysiologists made it possible to elaborate the scientific principles on which the differential diagnosis of mental backwardness of children is based, i.e. to distinguish it from other states which are similar in their external manifestations (temporary retardations of mental development, pedagogical neglect, underdevelopment of the cognitive activity as a result of speech disorders, early loss of hearing or vision, etc.).

Such differential diagnosis is applied in the process of selecting children for auxiliary schools. This contributes to a better psycho-pedagogical study of mentally retarded children of different ages and to a wider utilization of the available clinical, physiological and psychological data.

Before being placed in an auxiliary school, a mentally retarded child must undergo an examination by a special admission committee. All children with suspected mental backwardness are subject to such an examination, no matter whether they were previously brought up at home, were placed in kindergartens (both ordinary kindergartens and those for the mentally retarded), or studied in ordinary schools.

Admission committees are set up in each auxiliary school. They include the director of the auxiliary school (who is chairman of the committee), an inspector of the town or district department of public education, the paediatrician of the auxiliary school, a psychoneurologist (from a local polyclinic or hospital), a teacher from an ordinary school and a teacher from an auxiliary school.

The members of the admission committee personally examine each child and thoroughly study all the relevant documents and materials (medical records kept by the polyclinic since birth, conclusions of the physicians by whom the child was previously examined, pedagogical character references supplied by teachers, the child's notebooks, drawings, etc.). They also analyse measures previously taken to help the child, such as additional individual or group lessons and different forms of medical treatment. On the basis of this thorough study, the committee decides whether it is expedient to place the child in an auxiliary school or not.[1]

The data of differential diagnosis are utilized not only in the process of selecting mentally retarded children for auxiliary schools, but also in the approach to their school education. The composition of the pupils in these schools is not uniform as regards the degree of mental decline and certain other features of their psychophysical development. On the basis of clinical, physiological and psycho-pedagogical investigations, several groups are usually isolated even within the main mass of the pupils (whose mental backwardness is at the stage of debility). This heterogeneity is taken scrupulously into account in the instructional and educational work. It is evident, for example, in the establishment of several levels of occupational training (in particular, in the process of training for agricultural specialities, or in the process of elaborating new variants of syllabuses in the general educational cycle, as well as corresponding methodological aids and textbooks).

The auxiliary schools work on the basis of their own special curricula, programmes and textbooks. At present there are thirty-three special textbooks for mentally retarded pupils, including a number of handwork manuals (for joinery, fitting, needlework, home-craft, etc.). Another leading principle of defectology is widely and diversely applied in the auxiliary schools, namely the principle of correcting the defects of the child's development. During the last ten to twelve years much attention has been devoted by psycho-pedagogical research to a scientific substantiation of different branches of corrective work

1 No child may be placed in an auxiliary school unless the admission committee so decides with the exception of those children who have undergone an examination at the Institute of Defectology whose decision is as valid as that of the admission committee.

with mentally retarded children in conditions of specially organized instruction, taking into account the potential development of their cognitive activities and of their personalities as a whole.

Numerous investigations of this problem include, among other tasks, the elaboration of concrete methods of ensuring a possibly quicker and more effective assimilation by the pupils of accessible knowledge and skills. The problems of corrective work in the field of occupational training, and the general as well as moral education of mentally retarded children, were the first to be subjected to experimental elaboration, generalization and theoretical substantiation. The perfection of the methods of corrective work has made it possible somewhat to extend and deepen the general education and occupational training of mentally retarded pupils (by adding some data concerning modern achievements in the development of science, technology and social life, by introducing into the syllabuses of occupational training accessible information about the technology of production of certain articles, the material used, etc.). Another indispensable condition for such an extension of general education and occupational training is a propedeutic period and its effective utilization.

Psycho-pedagogical investigations showed that, at the very beginning of systematic studies at auxiliary schools, children often experience difficulties due to an insufficient mastery of the various ways and means of cognition which most normal children are able to utilize properly even before school. In order to help mentally retarded children in this respect, particular attention is paid in the curricula, methodological manuals and textbooks to special work aimed at preparing the children for systematic learning. Different directions of such work are provided for (intensification of the pupils' interest in school activity, their many-sided sensory development, stimulation of their speech and thinking, development of the ability to generalize, compare, establish cause and effect dependences, etc.). Of great importance also is the development of the span of attention, the faculty of observation, purposiveness of activity, graphic habits, etc. This period is called 'propedeutic' and is regarded in the system of auxiliary instruction and education as a period which must necessarily precede the teaching of each subject.

Experimental pre-school education of mentally retarded children convincingly shows that the propedeutic school period is considerably shorter in the case of children who have, to some extent, received the corresponding preparatory training in special kindergartens. The development of such establishments is therefore highly promising.

An important place in research work is occupied by investigations aimed at scientifically substantiating and increasing the effectiveness of the development of written and oral speech in mentally retarded pupils. This is one of the weakest aspects of their mentality and much attention is therefore paid to the elaboration of methods aimed at developing speech (its communicative function, correctness, expressiveness, etc.). Investigations in this direction are closely bound up with corresponding psychological, clinical and logopedic researches. The 'work and speech' problem has been specially singled out and is being investigated in line with the instruction of mentally retarded children.

Investigations showed that occupational training creates favourable conditions not only for the development of speech but also for a partial elimination of the defects peculiar to mental back wardness, namely of defects in spatial orientation, purposiveness and motivation of activity, volitional processes, and above all, thinking.

The corrective role of properly organized work, especially agricultural work, is of ever-increasing significance.

One of the essential principles which underlie auxiliary education is a firm connexion between different forms of instruction and education (for example, a connexion between the study of geography and natural science, on the one hand, and training in agricultural works, on the other, between moral and aesthetic education, between musical and physical training, between the study of arithmetics and manual work, etc.). This ensures uniformity in the demands made on pupils by the whole body of educators and creates conditions for a many-sided development of personality.

A definite and reasonable correlation between pedagogical assistance and the pupil's independent work is taken into consideration in the process of elaborating actual teaching methods.

The systemic character of mental backwardness was established by special investigations. Its basic symptoms are often accompanied by a deterioration of sensory functions and by retarded physical development. This is taken into account when methods for ensuring pupils' active acquaintance with objects in the surrounding world are worked out. Such methods involve an all-round study of a wide range of objects and are applied in practice at object lessons or at handwork lessons which to some extent represent a propedeutic period preceding vocational training. Research into the specific features of colour-discrimination and spatial orientation in conjunction with a psycho-pedagogical analysis of drawing lessons has made it possible to utilize the latter more effectively for improving the pupil's knowledge of the colours and spatial properties of objects.

Much attention is devoted to a scientific substantiation of various undertakings aimed at the pupils' physical development and at correcting defects in that development. For example, special methods of combining corrective gymnastics and medical treatment are being worked out with the aim of overcoming muscular insufficiency (not infrequently accompanying oligophrenia). Physical training and sports activities are also combined for the purpose of correcting faults in posture and certain defects of spatial orientation.

A scientific generalization of the experience of musical work in auxiliary schools and experimental investigations of this process has shown that here, too, the available potentialities of development have not yet been fully utilized. It proved, for example, that mentally retarded children show a definite ability when engaged in a directed process of listening to accessible musical compositions) to discern the pitch of sounds, to understand the rhythm and emotional character of music, etc. In some cases this work is combined with the study of works of literature.

Another vital branch of research is a catamnestic study of the subsequent life and development of auxiliary school graduates. In recent years certain results have been obtained in this area which not only demonstrate the achievements of the auxiliary schools, but also help to improve the preparation of mentally retarded pupils for independent life.

Mentally retarded pupils are able to develop aptitudes which manifest themselves during their studies at auxiliary schools. In particular, it has been demonstrated that the interest of the pupils in literature and theatrical work can be markedly strengthened. Various out-of-school groups work in the schools and the pupils learn modelling, drawing, music, choreography, agricultural specialities, etc. Numerous activities, such as excursions, tourist hikes, amateur art performances, pioneer public works, meetings with Heroes of Labour, artists and members of the defence forces widen the outlook of mentally retarded children and favourably influence their development and moral education. A study has shown that it is of great importance for the mentally retarded children to develop a sense of their own usefulness, and a cheerful, positive attitude towards people around them.

The study of various problems in the special teaching of the retarded and in related psychology is carried out not only by scientific workers who are experts in the field, but also by numerous teacher–defectologists, educators, school physicians and other practical workers.

Research on the education
of the deaf

Teaching deaf children to speak is the major concern of surdopedagogy. Eliminating the consequences of deafness and developing the ability of deaf children to master the fundamentals of science and become socially involved depend to a considerable degree on mastery of language.

During the last ten years, a new system of language training has been developed for these children. This system is based on the principle of communication. The children's urge for communication at a given stage of development is carefully considered when verbal material and grammatical forms are selected. The language training of deaf children is always connected with the development of diverse forms of activity. In order to encourage verbal speech as a means of communication a verbal environment must be provided which ensures speech practice throughout the day (both in classes and during out-of-school hours) and to mix deaf children with pupils with normal hearing.

The application of the dactyl form of speech (finger-spelling) is of essential significance for the realization of this new approach. The principal means of communication for these children during the initial stage of education, the dactyl form of speech gradually turns into an auxiliary means with the development of speaking, lip-reading and writing; it ensures a firm consolidation of the speech material, as well as its more adequate perception (as compared to lip-reading) in the process of communication.

Soviet special education for children with hearing defects is based on the principles of differentiated instruction. Research carried out on numerous deaf and hard-of-hearing children has revealed the specific speech features and allowed the elaboration of a new criterion for evaluating their residual hearing. In children, as distinct from adults, such residual hearing is evaluated from the point of view of its role in speech development.

In this connexion, a group of hard-of-hearing children was singled out and described; owing to early acquired hearing defects, the possibility of their speech developing independently was greatly limited.

This new approach to the diagnosis of the abnormal development of hard-of-hearing children permitted the distinction of partial hearing defects, deafness, aphasia and mental subnormality.

The principal task of research in the field of educating children with defective hearing is to create conditions for a maximum expansion of their limited speech practice. Special programmes and language training methods in schools for hard-of-hearing children provide for systematic work aimed at the practical mastery of basic speech regularities (lexical, phonetic and grammatical). The school curricula for these pupils include special lessons aimed at developing pronunciation habits and lip-reading, at correcting grammatical speech defects, at mastering the sound and letter composition of the words and at cultivating oral communication habits. The development of auditory perception is particularly important. All the classrooms of schools for pupils with defective hearing are equipped with sound amplifying apparatus which contribute to a more effective perception of the study material and to a better pronunciation.

The problem of extensive utilization of object-oriented activity in these schools has been thoroughly elaborated in recent years. This activity contributes to the children's specific development and leads to improvement in the quality of the instructional and educational process. A study showed that utilization of different kinds of visual and practical work during lessons is an important condition for extending the pupils' activity and self-reliance.

The object-oriented activity of the pupils is now being investigated as a means of acquiring the so-called 'everyday' ideas, i.e. ideas which are assimilated by children with normal hearing prior to school and without any special instruction. The object activity contributes to the pupils' development and to the implementation of the leading principle of language training—formation of speech in close connexion with activity.

Pre-school training and education present an indispensable link in the work of correcting and compensating for defects in the development of these children. Early instruction achieves appreciable results in the elimination and prevention of secondary disturbances.

A series of experimental-pedagogical investigations was carried out during the last decade into the application of dactylology in pre-school establishments as means of organizing and expanding verbal communication, helping the children master language in the course of everyday life and activity. Specially organized instruction showed that in the case of a deaf child dactyl speech may become a means of communication at a very early age. Any work in this case is accessible to the child, which permits the selection of study material based not on its pronunciation facility, but on relative importance in terms of the child's communication and cognitive activity. As a result, the accumulation of the vocabulary is facilitated and accelerated. The children can make an earlier and more active use of the words in their association both with one another and with others who have a normal hearing and know the dactyl alphabet.

Deaf pre-school children assimilate verbal speech both in its oral and written forms. In the course of oral speech training they master lip-reading and articulatory habits. As a result of their mastery of speech in the dactyl and written forms, they acquire early habits of reading (at the age of 3 or 4) and later of writing (typewriting).

Particular attention is now devoted to studies of pre-school children with defective hearing for the purpose of elaborating methods of early diagnosis. The investigators take into account the state of the child's hearing, and the characteristics of its visual perception, spatial notions, thinking, behaviour and personality.

Investigations of deaf and hard-of-hearing pre-school children also reveal the specific features of their physical development and locomotor functions (gait, posture, respiration, co-ordination of movements, balance, etc.). A special system of corrective exercises is being worked out in this connexion.

Interesting researches have been carried out in recent years in respect of the musical education of children with defective hearing. Experiments showed that almost all children perceive the musical rhythm, tempo, measure, vibration, rests and chords. A certain combination of chords and rests creates 'music' which is accessible to deaf children and allows them to organize their movements. Even their peculiar singing gives these children great aesthetic pleasure. As a result of research, a special programme and a manual of musical education were devised for children with defective hearing.

Soviet defectologists are also concerned with stimulating the interest of deaf children in various forms of activity, as well as with the formation of a system of pedagogical work in the field of vocational education.

On the basis of research into the auditory function of pupils in special schools and inmates of kindergartens for deaf and hard-of-hearing children, a classification of auditory disturbances has been established. This is aimed at solving important practical problems connected with the staffing of children's establishments and with auditory prosthetics. Proceeding from the data of tonal audiometry, the classification distinguishes three degrees of loss of hearing in hard-of-hearing children and four such degrees in deaf children. Motor conditioned-reflex methods of tonal audiometry with an orienting reinforcement have been elaborated as a result of studying the auditory function in such children and have proved to be an effective and reliable means of measuring the auditory function, especially in children of pre-school age.

In recent years, the study of the auditory function in deaf and hard-of-hearing children has shown a further advance due to the application of verbal and supra-threshold tonal audiometry.

A study of the auditory function in correlation with the character and localization of the lesion of the organ of hearing has been started. Particular attention is paid to the study of the auditory function in conditions of an elective amplification of the frequencies.

These investigations will create a scientific basis for a differential approach to children in their instruction and education, especially in that sphere of pedagogical work connected with the development and utilization of the residual auditory function and with the formation of oral speech. The particular significance of these investigations will consist in the establishment of definite medico-pedagogical demands on which the elaboration of new models of sound-amplifying apparatus should be based.

A number of investigations have been devoted to the regularities of children's perception of oral speech and of its diverse phonetic elements with the help of the auditory, visual and cutaneous sense organs in conditions of normal and defective hearing. The data obtained from these investigations form an adequate basis for the theoretical and practical solution of problems concerning the limits within which different sense organs can be utilized, and their mutual compensation during the reception of verbal information. These data also ensure a deeper study of the mechanism of auditory and visual perception of oral speech in conditions of hearing disorders; they allow an elaboration of scientifically grounded ways of developing auditory speech perception and lip-reading, as well as effective methods of a combined reception of verbal information by means of a simultaneous use of different sense organs. The results obtained from previous investigations provided a basis for special programmes and methodological guides in training lip-reading, as well as developing and utilizing auditory perception in schools and kindergartens for deaf and hard-of-hearing children. The task of further investigations will be to elaborate adequate methods of expanding the system of acoupedic work, and forming habits of visual, tactile-vibratory and combined perception of oral speech. Particular attention will be paid to the application of technical means, namely various electro-acoustical devices.

Special investigations are concerned with the development of pronunciation habits in deaf and hard-of-hearing children. These investigations established the state of pronunciation of pupils in special schools and the degree of its distinctness, and revealed the phonetic factors which exert the greatest influence. This made it possible to work out a concentric method for the initial teaching of oral speech to deaf children.

This concentric method consists of a physiologically and phonetically substantiated regulation of an approximate pronunciation which facilitates the verbal communication of the children on the basis of a temporary application of a reduced system of phonemes. This regulation makes it possible to avoid rough pronunciation defects during the subsequent correction of the approximate word reproduction.

Special mention must be made of a series of investigations which promoted the development of methods for a rational utilization of different sense organs and application of corresponding technical means in the process of training deaf and hard-of-hearing children in pronunciation. They included investigations of the role of auditory perception and of the application of technical devices for an auditory, visual and tactile-vibratory control over pronunciation.

One of the most important problems to be studied in the near future relates to specific features in the formation of pronunciation in deaf and hard-of-hearing children. It may be expected that, as a result of these investigations, essential changes will be introduced in the methods of initial training and correction of pronunciation in children with defective hearing.

The basic task of research in the field of surdotechnique is to create a complex of technical means for training deaf school and pre-school children in oral speech. Modern surdotechnique is based on the utilization of the intact sense organs of the deaf—namely, the residual hearing, vision and the sense of touch—for transmiting verbal information.

In order to utilize the residual hearing of the deaf, various sound-amplifying devices are employed, their technical characteristics making it possible to take into account the degree and nature of each hearing defect. The application of these devices involves providing the corresponding acoustic equipment in the classrooms of special schools and should result in more articulate speech.

Special equipment for the visual presentation of speech helps to correct defects in the speech of deaf pupils and pre-school children in cases where these defects are not perceived by ear. Such equipment has proved useful both in teaching correct pronunciation of individual sounds and during work on speech rhythmics and intonation.

The difficulties experienced by deaf children during the perception of oral speech through lip-reading can to a considerable degree be surmounted with the help of equipment for tactile speech transmission. New models of tactile devices are being developed which permit differentiation on an acoustic basis of sounds and sound combinations, which prove to be indistinguishable in the course of lip-reading. It is hoped that within the next few years all the above-mentioned technical means will form a new complex of standard equipment in schools and pre-school establishments for deaf and hard-of-hearing children.

Soviet surdopedagogy is also concerned with the general education of deaf adults. Research in this respect is devoted to the characteristic features of deaf adults and to determining the content, methods and organization of their instruction. An outstanding place in this research belongs to studies connected with the assimilation of the language by deaf adults, and with the elaboration of the most effective methods of forming oral and written speech. Special attention is given to the utilization of the available practical knowledge of deaf students, as well as their industrial activity, for the formation of speech.

Research on the education
of the blind

The content of research work in the field of typhlopedagogy is determined by the most urgent problems which arise before the instruction and education of children with defective vision.

The initial theoretical conception of this research is the proposition that the characteristics of anomalous development depend on the structure of the defect.

Studies of the features of total enrolment in schools for blind and visually handicapped children, which are undertaken every five years with the help of the questionnaire-statistical and clinical methods, have made it possible to classify the children according to the state of their vision, the clinical forms of the visual defects, the causes of blindness and defective vision, the character of the concomitant disturbances and the progress made in study. The results of investigations have shown that 8 to 12 per cent of all pupils in schools for blind children suffer from absolute blindness. The remaining children possess some residual vision (up to 0.04 in the eye which sees better when usual means of correction [spectacles] are applied). The principal clinical forms are: cataract, microophthalmia and optic atrophy.

The visual acuity of most pupils in schools for children with defective vision ranges from 0.09 to 0.2. The principal clinical forms in schools for visually handicapped children are refraction anomalies and partial optic atrophy. Investigations demonstrated that against the background of a general decrease in cases of absolute blindness resulting from acquired forms of disturbances, the percentage of innate anomalies and of intra-uterine visual disturbances shows a steady decline from year to year.

The accumulated statistical data make it possible to substantiate the prospects of further development of a differentiated school network for children with defective vision.

Compensation is of the greatest importance in the system of typhlopedagogical research. The study of this problem helps to establish the principles of compensatory development of blind and visually handicapped pupils in conditions of special instruction, and to determine ways and means of correcting and compensating for the disturbed functions at the expense of the auditory, cutaneous, motor and other kinds of perception.

It has proved possible to reveal the tremendous potentialities of sensory development of blind children and to establish its dependence on the content, methods and typhlotechnical means of instruction and vocational training. It was found that in different clinical forms the process of compensation of the disturbed functions is not similar and depends on the degree of the visual disturbance, on the composition and structure of the primarily and secondarily disturbed functions, on the disturbances of the central nervous system which accompany blindness and visual deficiency, as well as on the conditions of instruction.

Research into the problem of compensation, and strict attention to the dynamic changes taking place in the enrolment of schools for children with defective vision, as well as to the children's specific development, allowed the elaboration of ways and forms of differential instruction, and curricula and programmes of schools for blind and visually handicapped children. These curricula and programmes provide for special classes aimed at correcting the sensory, speech and motor functions of children with defective vision.

A study of the perception of graphic images by blind children served as a scientific basis for working out a special system of teaching the blind to read and for creating adequate visual means.

With due regard for the specific process of compensation and cognitive activity of blind and visually handicapped pupils, special apparatus and devices are designed for transforming light signals into acoustic and tactile ones which are accessible to the blind. These apparatus and devices make possible diverse laboratory work in physics, geography, chemistry and other subjects previously inaccessible to children with deficient vision.

A new model of a reading machine is now being elaborated on the above-mentioned principle of transformation of light signals into tactile ones; this machine allows the blind pupils to read books in normal flat print which is transformed into a conventional code according to the Braille system. Since this machine makes it possible to read whole lines, instead of separate letters, the rate of reading proves to be considerably higher.

In order to raise the effectiveness of the instructional process, programmed teaching of the blind and visually handicapped pupils is being introduced. Of great practical significance in this respect are various technical means which help the pupils to study certain parts of the programme independently. This is also achieved by the application of special punch cards, typhlo-coaches, and typhlo-examiners, resulting in a better check on the pupils' knowledge.

An appreciable role is also played by optic means of visual correction for people with weak or partial eyesight, namely line-covering optical glasses of different magnification. They accelerate the reading process of pupils with deficient vision between one and five times and increase the distance between the eyes and the book from 15–18 to 25–30 cm, the normal distance being 35 cm. This is highly important for the protection of the pupils' deficient vision; it contributes to the normalization of the pupils' posture in the course of reading, and prevents the emergence of secondary deviations in the physical development of children with defective vision (violation of the normal posture, curvature of the spine). Much attention is now paid to the protection and hygiene of deficient vision.

Experiments were carried out for the purpose of studying the influence of different levels of illumination on the change of visual functions in pupils suffering from complicated short-sightedness, strong far-sightedness or optic atrophy. It was found that when the intensity of the illumination equals 1,000–1,500 lux, the pupils' vision greatly improves, their visual fatigue declines and their working capacity increases.

Luminescent sources of light likewise contribute to a reduction of visual fatigue. On the basis of these experimental data, definite standards of artificial illumination for pupils with deficient vision were elaborated. Suggestions were also made concerning classroom furniture for such children.

The principal task of further research is to investigate the typology of the abnormal development of children with defective vision, ways and conditions of compensation in various forms of visual disturbances, the peculiarities of pupils' cognitive activity, and development in connexion with changes in the content, methods and organization of general and vocational instruction.

As a result of experimental investigations in perception, formation of object and spatial notions, development of thinking and speech in blind children at the age of 3 to 6, a pedagogical system of sensory education, as well as of mental and physical development of blind pre-school children was created; in particular, it was shown that play activities, vocational training and aesthetic education are of marked corrective significance for preventing and eliminating secondary deviations in the children's development which are determined by the loss of vision or by innate anomalies in the development of the visual analyser.

A system of instruction and education of blind deaf-and-dumb children and juveniles was organized on the basis of the results of psycho-pedagogical investigations. The task of the first period in the instruction of such children is to form in them certain habits of self-help. The children master ways of satisfying their own requirements with the help of corresponding instruments and objects of work. During this period, images of the surrounding objects are accumulated by the children, who subsequently designate them by gestures and later by words. Of great importance during this period of instruction is the modelling of objects of the surrounding world in plasticine. In this way, the children acquire more profound knowledge of the objects they meet; at the same time such modelling makes it possible to check the adequacy of the images of objects in blind deaf-and-dumb children.

The first special means of the children's communication with the surrounding world are gestures which designate objects and actions. No such communication with blind deaf-and-dumb children is practically possible unless they acquire the language of gestures.

The next stage of their instruction consists in the formation of verbal speech in the dactyl form with a simultaneous use of the already acquired gestures. Subsequently, this dactyl speech turns into a predominant form of communication. When blind deaf-and-dumb children assimilate the dactyl designations of a certain range of objects and actions, they are given the Braille alphabet, i.e. they begin to learn the written form of speech. The mastery of written speech (the Braille system) is highly important for the development of the child's conceptual-logical thinking. It should be noted that the practical mastery of the language precedes the study of grammar.

In the process of language training each word and grammatical category is accompanied by a direct demonstration of the object and action which are designated by them. In order to facilitate the assimilation of the language, a system of 'parallel' texts was worked out; it includes study texts given by the teacher and 'spontaneous' texts composed by the pupils independently. New words and grammatical categories are gradually introduced in the study texts, and the pupils utilize them in their own independent texts, thus assimilating their meanings and memorizing them on the basis of more familiar material.

This system of instruction enables blind deaf-and-dumb children to acquire the grammatical fundamentals of oral speech, to accumulate an adequate vocabulary, and to prepare for assimilating the subjects of the school programme.

Practice has shown that the teaching of oral speech to blind deaf-and-dumb children must be started at an earlier age. However, the assimilation of the language, acquisition of knowledge and development of the children's communication must not be predetermined by the level of development of oral speech. Dactyl speech and the Braille alphabet must be the basic forms of communication with such handicapped children.

Research on speech therapy

The principal purpose of the research work done in the field of speech therapy is to elaborate the scientific principles of a system of instruction aimed at overcoming and preventing speech disorders in children. In this connexion, special attention is paid to the genesis and structure of these disorders. A symptomatic approach to the defects of speech persisted in speech therapy for a very long time; according to this approach, certain manifestations of speech disorders were regarded as independent defects with a heterogeneous pathogenesis. In view of this, the methods of eliminating speech defects were limited to the removal of external manifestations of speech disorders without due regard for the pedagogical and psychological aspects of speech development. Such an approach did not take into consideration the connexion between different components of speech, and this limited the effectiveness of special therapeutic aid, did not ensure an adequate elimination of the defect and did not prepare children with speech disorders for successful studies at school. The correction of the speech deviations was more often accomplished by way of dispensary out-patient treatment.

A new theory of speech disorders in children has been elaborated in recent years. Its methodological foundation consists in the principle of systemic analysis of the speech disorder, as well as in the principle of a connexion between the development of speech and other sides of the child's mental development. A number of investigations revealed the mechanisms of the interaction between disturbances of the auditory perception and the speech motor function, between the pronunciation activity and the formation of phonemes. It was also established that disturbances of the phonetic and semantic aspects of speech are interdependent. Thus, the investigations disclosed the complex and multiform content of the psychological processes which participate in the formation of speech activity. The application of these principles in practice proved to be effective in the ascertainment of the structure of various speech defects, and led to the creation of special methods of corrective teaching.

A systematic study of a large sample of children provided interesting data concerning the incidence of speech and writing disorders in junior pupils of ordinary schools. This material helped to substantiate the necessary extent of logopedic aid in ordinary schools and to determine its most rational forms. As a result of special investigations, it proved possible to establish an interconnexion between disturbances of oral and written speech and to work out methods of eliminating writing disorders. It was found that the mastery of writing and reading habits depends to a considerable degree on the child's preceding speech development, in the course of which practical generalizations of the phonetic and morphological composition of the words are formed. Some speech defects lead to an inadequate mastery of the phonetic composition of the words and, consequently, to disturbances in reading and writing. The establishment of this principle permitted the creation of a uniform system of work directed to the elimination of defects in speech, reading and writing. This system is now widely applied in practice and contributes to a better progress of pupils with speech defects.

Investigations established the incidence of various forms of speech disorders and showed that some pre-school children are not sufficiently prepared for assimilating phonetical analysis. A timely detection of phonetic–phonematic disturbances in pre-school children can prevent manifestations of disgraphia and dislexia in subsequent school years. Thus, it was proved that the creation of special pre-school establishments for children with speech defects is highly expedient; as a result, the number of such establishments in the country is growing from year to year.

The problem of organizing special schools for children with severe speech disorders presents an essentially new branch of logopedic science and practice. During many years logopedic research was confined to elaborating methods of correcting oral speech, and predominantly pronunciation and breath control. One of the most widespread forms of logopedic aid was individual out-patient treatment of children suffering from tongue-tie and stammering. Severe forms of speech disorders (alalia, aphasia, pseudobulbar dysarthria) were within the competence of medicine and remained outside the sphere of pedagogical influence. In approaching the problems of instruction and education of children with severe speech disorders, present-day logopedy proceeds from the theory of the systemic character of the disturbance, from the interaction and interconnexion of different speech functions, as well as from the interdependence of speech and other sides of the child's mentality.

These theoretical premises make it possible to substantiate the differential diagnosis of children with speech disorders (as distinct from mentally retarded and hard-of-hearing children), to elaborate the principles underlying the analysis of such disorders and to reveal the characteristic levels of speech underdevelopment. On each of these levels, the lexical, grammatical and phonetic aspects of speech are studied in detail, and the formation of the syllabic structure of words, as well as of reading and writing, in children with various forms of speech disorders (alalia, dysarthria, dislalia, etc.) is determined.

The results of these investigations are taken into account in staffing the classes of the logopedic schools and in establishing their structure and the content of education.

At present a new approach to the study of stammering in children has been elaborated; it is concentrated on deviations in the formation of the communicative function of speech. The phenomenon of stammering is being studied both from the aspect of the speech characteristics of the defect and from the aspect of the analysis of non-verbal processes which participate in the act of communication. In this connexion, much attention is devoted to investigating the conditions in which the given defect emerges, the child's general and speech development, as well as the relationship between active and passive speech, and the conditions which intensify or weaken the stammering.

The psychological study of the child is directed at determining the peculiarities of voluntary attention, the possibility of switching it over, and the rate and stability of the child's activity. The personality of the child, the conditions of education, and the specific features of the speaking environment are also thoroughly investigated.

Research into the phenomenon of stammering permits the elaboration of methods of correction or prevention of this defect in children. In particular, a special system has been worked out for eliminating stammering in pre-school children and junior pupils in the process of manual work. This system provides for a gradual transition from situational to contextual speech.

The principal task of further research in the field of speech therapy is to investigate the speech of pupils in ordinary and in special speech-corrective schools and pre-school establishments, as well as to elaborate and perfect the methods of corrective instruction of children with speech disorders. Much attention is also devoted to methods of correcting minor speech disorders in pupils of ordinary schools.

Research on vocational training

One of the basic tasks of special schools is to prepare the pupils for practical activity, for their participation in suitable productive labour. This task is to a considerable degree accomplished with the help of a system of vocational training which allows the pupils to learn various trades and which corrects and compensates for the defects of their mental and physical development.

At present the vocational training in all types of schools consists of three stages.

At the first stage (manual work) the pupils acquaint themselves with the simplest materials and instruments and acquire some knowledge and skills. The content of manual labour training is determined by the instructional, educational and corrective tasks of the school. The study programme provides for the development of the children's cognitive activity with due regard to their general development and interests. Special attention is paid during manual labour lessons to the expansion and consolidation of the knowledge acquired at other lessons.

As the second stage (general technical training) the pupils are taught to master elementary processing techniques; they acquire some knowledge of technology and become acquainted with various kinds of labour, including agricultural labour. This reveals the pupils' inclinations towards definite kinds of labour and helps to make a correct choice of profession. General educational tasks corresponding to definite periods of the pupils' studies at school are also taken into account when the content of the general technical training is determined.

The third stage (professional–technical training) consists in the mastery of definite industrial specialities. Much time is allotted to the pupils' work on machine-tools and to their acquaintance with the problems of technology.

Industrial practice takes a prominent place in vocational training; it helps the pupils to acquire the necessary knowledge and skills which sometimes cannot be fully obtained in the school workshops. The defect of each pupil is taken into consideration when a specific production process is chosen for him.

The growing level of the pupils' general education in schools for blind children and for children with defects of hearing and a later start of professional training have made it possible to extend the range of the professions studied.

For the first time in the practice of typhlopedagogy anywhere, pupils of Soviet special schools for the blind acquire high industrial skills, along with a broad general education. Not long ago, the blind could find a very limited application for their capacities in the field of productive labour. It was confined to some handicraft specialities, such as the manufacture of brushes, wicker baskets, etc.; at the best, blind people were able to work on simple punching machines. At present, general and polytechnical education has created an adequate basis for organizing professional training on a sufficiently high level, including activities previously regarded as inaccessible to the blind. The pupils now learn various kinds of metalwork, assembly work at electric and radio enterprises, etc. They successfully master a number of labour processes in which the auditory receptors play the leading role (for example, piano tuning, telephone operation, etc.). They have equally broad opportunities in those fields of labour where the control of the working processes is effected through the combined activity of the auditory, cutaneous and motor sense organs. At the same time, the absence of vision (or a considerable loss of vision) makes it necessary to apply special methods of instruction and to utilize various typhlotechnical means and special teaching aids so as to prepare the children for various kinds of labour in conditions of industrial production.

The absence of hearing is an objective factor which to a certain degree limits the ability of the deaf to master a number of professions and, at the same time, determines the specific character of the content and duration of vocational training.

Soviet surdopedagogy has been able to overcome the excessive emphasis on handicrafts in the vocational training of the deaf. The practice of special schools has shown that deaf children are able to learn a variety of trades and to work efficiently in various branches of modern industrial and agricultural production. At present pupils of schools for deaf children successfully master numerous specialities in metalworking (milling-machine operators, drillers, turners, fitters, etc.) in printing and publishing (type-setters, printers) and many other branches which require secondary technical education. In recent years, deaf pupils have also began to learn such specialities as radio- and electro-assembly work, technical drawing, etc. A considerable number of graduates from schools for deaf children continue their education in higher schools.

Strongly pronounced disturbances in the mental development of auxiliary school pupils and the frequently concomitant disturbances of their general physical development markedly distinguish this group of handicapped children from those who suffer only from disturbances of the peripheral part of the visual or auditory sense organs. In view of this, the problem of the general and special tasks of their vocational training must be solved first of all with due regard for the characteristics of their development.

The auxiliary schools equip their pupils with knowledge and skills in fitting, joinery, cardboard and bookbinding work, sewing and some simple kinds of agricultural work.

In a number of cases, when the children manifest gross disturbances in their psychophysical development, the auxiliary schools confine themselves to teaching a limited number of separate working operations.

The mental and physical development of auxiliary school pupils, the elementary level of general and vocational education and the peculiar personality traits of the pupils demand a thorough study of the latter and the choice of an accessible profession for each pupil. The problem of vocational training of mentally retarded pupils cannot be successfully solved without strict consideration of their individual capacities.

Along with general social tasks, the vocational training in special schools has its own particular tasks connected with the compensation and correction of defects in the development of handicapped children and the whole complex of pedagogical, medical and technical means is utilized for the purpose.

Regular actions with objects at handwork lessons help the visually handicapped pupils to correct their spatial concepts and to develop their cognitive abilities. The perfection of the auditory, cutaneous, motor and other intact sense organs in the process of labour is indissolubly bound up with the perfection of the higher mental functions of the blind. Properly organized vocational training is a powerful beneficial factor in the physical development of blind children.

Vocational training plays a definite role in the system of teaching verbal speech to deaf children. It equips the pupils with concrete concepts, and develops their perception, memory, thinking and other kinds of cognitive activity, expands their stock of words, and stimulates their communication with the environment.

It should also be noted that deafness affects the development of the pupils' motor sphere. The movements of deaf pupils are markedly slower than those of normal pupils of the same age. In the course of vocational training, however, the actions of the deaf become quicker, and this favourably influences their motor activity as a whole.

One of the special tasks of the auxiliary schools is to correct the defects of mental development. All pedagogical means, including vocational training, are directed at the accomplishment of this task. Work activity in its elementary forms (manual labour) is the most easily understood and accessible where mentally retarded children are concerned. Work helps to concretize and correct the pupils' notions and concepts of the surrounding world and contributes to the correction of defects in the physical development of mentally retarded children.

The study of psychological and methodological problems connected with the vocational training of blind and deaf adults has been given much attention in recent years. In particular, it has been established that deaf boys and girls are able to master most professions which are accessible to normal pupils of the same age. Only those kinds of work which cannot be accomplished without the sense of hearing are inaccessible to the deaf. Investigations also showed that it is possible to select for the deaf a number of specialities which involve working with a high level of noise; in these cases the character of the residual hearing is always taken into consideration.

When studying the type of work performed by the deaf and the blind, particular attention is paid to analysing the ways in which the production operations are accomplished and to the organizational and planning problems of working activity. It has been found that the deaf manifest a definite retardation in the pace of their working activity, predominantly because of their inaccurate temporal concepts. Investigations into the formation of spatial concepts in the course of reading drawings, and into the comprehension of graphic images by the deaf and the blind, made it possible to advance a number of suggestions concerning the organization of a course of technical drawing and the methods to be used in teaching this subject.

One of the pressing problems of defectology is to perfect and to elaborate still more thoroughly the content, methods and means of vocational training for each category of handicapped children.

Special psychology

An outstanding place in the research work devoted to the study of handicapped children is assigned to psychological investigations. These are based on the dialectical-materialistic theory of development as the emergence of new properties, which is determinated by the influences of the surrounding social environment.

Diverse forms of experimentation are widely applied in these investigations, including laboratory and educational experiments, as well as different natural experiments. The results of the children's activity (their compositions, drawings, craft work, etc.), are studied, and systematic observations are made.

The psychological investigations established that certain defects, such as deafness or blindness (innate or acquired in early childhood), cause a number of secondary deviations in the child's mental development. They also disclosed the complex structure of psychological characteristics observed in mentally retarded children, in children suffering from disturbances of their speech development (alalia, aphasia, etc.), in children with severe lesions of the supporting-motor apparatus and with some other anomalies of development. A general evaluation of the facts obtained led to the conclusion that certain defects, innate or acquired in early childhood, call forth different interdependent changes in the whole course of mental development (L. S. Vygotsky). In view of this, one of the basic tasks of numerous psychological investigations is to find out the specific features which characterize the psychological processes or different aspects of mental activity in handicapped children.

This research, which has been conducted on a large scale during many years, is necessarily linked with the problems of education. The whole system of education of handicapped children (elaboration of curricula, programmes, general and special methods of teaching) takes into account the characteristics of their mental development as established by the psychological investigations. In this way, more favourable conditions are created for the further mental development of handicapped children.

But the most essential connexion between psychological research and the education of handicapped children consists in the fact that the investigations are aimed at disclosing the potentialities and lines of mental development under the influence of education making for a more complete compensation or correction of the existing defects.

Owing to a more delicate differentiation of the children according to the structure of the primary defect, an ever increasing number of branches of psychology have come into being over recent years in respect of handicapped children. New branches, for example, are now studying the mental development of children with partial defects of hearing or vision. Greater attention is now paid to children suffering from a merely temporary retardation of their mental development, but able to fully compensate their defect and reach the level of normal development. Special scientific branches have been formed by investigations into the mentality of children suffering from combined defects (blind and deaf children, children in whom lesions of certain sensory processes are combined with mental backwardness, etc.).

At the same time, Soviet psychologists attach great importance to comparative investigations in which the characteristics of mental development of children with different anomalies are confronted with one another (for example, of deaf and mentally retarded children, of blind children and partially sighted children, etc.). These investigations yield a deeper understanding not only of the general deviation from the normal level of development which becomes obvious when the results of abnormal and normal children are compared, but also of the deviation which is most significant for each particular defect.

Psychology of mentally retarded children

The psychology of mentally retarded children is one of the most highly developed branches of special psychology. It is essentially an optimistic approach to the decisive role of specially organized education in the development of such children and to their great potentialities in this context. Investigations are predominantly comparative, since the specific nature of the mental development of such children can be revealed and demonstrated only in relation to typical development, i.e. to the development of normal children.

The application of comparative methods is also made necessary by the fact that the research covers a number of problems which remain insufficiently elucidated, including the psychology of observation, problems of general and specific recognition, modifications of concepts in the process of forgetting, modifications of repetitions, processes of comparison, some questions of spatial orientation connected with learning activities, and many others. The elaboration of these problems by means of comparative investigations of mentally retarded and normal children has to some degree enriched the normal child psychology.

In contrast to the proposition that mental backwardness is in the main characterized by a single essential defect (disturbed thinking, or attention, or will) it has been shown that children who suffer diseases at an early age experience functional disturbances of the entire brain activity. This leads to deficiency which unevenly and peculiarly affects their mentality as a whole. Numerous investigations have proved that a primary deficiency is complexly combined with some secondary ones and with all the phenomena provoked by them. The more complex the forms of mental activity, the more manifest become these deficiences.

It has been found that in conditions of special instruction and education, not only do mentally handicapped children acquire elementary skills and habits, but that certain methods of conscious memorization, the power of observation and active attention are also developed along with some use of comparisons and generalizations.

Although these complex processes suffer more than any others in conditions of mental backwardness, owing to the plasticity of the cerebral cortex they readily respond to the corrective influence of instructional and educational work and play a leading role in the development of mentally retarded children, as was demonstrated by investigations of the cognitive activity of such children conducted on a large scale during the post-war years.

In spite of its particular character, the development of mentally retarded children is subordinated to the same general laws as the development of normal children. It has been established, for example, that the perception and memory of these children markedly develop in the course of instruction, but retain their specific character even in older pupils. Their cognitive processes suffer from inadequate generalization and at the same time are insufficiently concrete, even if the conditions of their instruction and education are most favourable. This should be taken into account when the children's preparation for practical labour activity is organized.

The specific features of the development of speech and its influence on the children's mentality have also been subjected to a thorough study. In particular, methods of a highly effective combination of speech with visual means of instruction were elaborated, and the perception, concepts and different thinking processes connected with the children's study activity were investigated (for example, the thinking activity during the process of solving arithmetical problems). The results of these investigations provided a basis for an adequate revision of the school programmes and of the accompanying methodological explanatory notes.

The personality traits of mentally retarded pupils, mainly junior ones, were investigated, along with their cognitive activity, by the method of systematic observations.

A series of investigations were concerned with the practical activity of auxiliary school pupils in the process of solving constructive problems or during the accomplishment of certain tasks connected with handwork or industrial labour in school workshops.

This research into the activity of mentally retarded pupils disclosed some peculiarities of structure and motivation, an insufficiently critical approach by the children to the results obtained the accomplishment of tasks without proper preliminary orientation in their nature, sometimes inadequate self-control in the course of solving a task and 'slide-off' to other activities. The results of these investigations made it possible to elaborate definite methods for organizing the various activities of mentally retarded pupils.

Data obtained from some research helped to create methods of psychological examinations for diagnostic purposes. Soviet defectology applies these methods not for establishing the quantitative index of the level of intellectual development (I.Q.), but for a qualitative analysis of the child's intellectual abilities.

The ascertainment and theoretical interpretation of the basic stages of development of mentally retarded children in conditions of special education present a generalization of research into the cognitive activity of mentally retarded pupils.

In recent years the efforts of researchers have been directed at the examination of psychological problems connected with corrective work in auxiliary schools and have revealed means for activating the children's potentialities at different stages of learning (including the learning of separate subjects) and age development.

In particular, the role of personality factors (such as self-appraisal, appraisal of schoolmates, etc.) in the realization of the potentialities of mentally retarded adolescents is being investigated, as is the formation of inter-subject connexions and the development of incentives towards activation of knowledge acquired.

The aim of further research into the complex interaction of practical and intellectual activity in the development of mentally retarded children is to find effective methods of strengthening the influence of practical activity on the children's mental development.

A differential approach to different groups of mentally retarded children constitutes one of the basic principles underlying the psychological reinforcement of corrective work. The general traits characteristic of all such children as a single clinical group are also taken into account.

The personality of mentally retarded pupils is also studied in relation to their possible aesthetic development. Finally, the research covers a number of more particular problems such as the possibility of correcting defects in the discrimination of colours as well as of spatial attributes and relationships of objects in the course of learning pictorial activity.

The psychology of mentally retarded pre-school children is a new branch of scientific research. It is concerned with the characteristic features of the constructive and play activity of these children, with their speech development, formation of motor activity and a number of other aspects of psychophysical development.

Psychology of children with temporary retardations of development

A group of children with temporary retardations of mental development was singled out from among persistently unsuccessful pupils in ordinary schools. Research into the psychology of such children in the U.S.S.R. has been particularly extensive during the last decade. The children's working capacity, the development of their memory and thinking, as well as of their sensations and perceptions are now the main objects of investigation. Also of great significance are psycho-pedagogical investigations which reveal the difficulties experienced by the children when assimilating initial knowledge in the native language and mathematics. The results of these investigations have shown that the formation of voluntary memory processes in children of this category is delayed, and that their analysis, synthesis and generalization of objects, formation of notions and problem solving are markedly impeded. The investigations are generally conducted in conditions of specially organized corrective instruction, the results of which furnish conclusions concerning the possibility of improving the mental development of these children and of returning them to ordinary schools after appropriate special instruction.

The elaboration of new methods of differential diagnosis is particularly important in the investigations of children with temporary retardation of mental development. Most of the methods now used for determining the level of mental development provide for several stages of assistance to be rendered to the child by the experimenter. This makes it possible to understand better the real difficulties which are experienced by the child when accomplishing experimental tasks, and its potential abilities (the zone of immediate development). Such data are of diagnostic and pedagogical value, since children with temporary retardation of development differ from mentally retarded children in the amount and quality of the help which must be rendered to them: the character and extent of help sufficient to ensure the child's correct solution of a given task form a basis for the elaboration of special methods of instruction.

Psychology of children with hearing defects

The first systematic investigations into the psychology of children who have lost their hearing in early childhood and who can master verbal speech only in conditions of special instruction were carried out by the Scientific Research Institute of Defectology in Moscow in the thirties. The institute is continuing to investigate the mental development of deaf children, whose age varies from 2–3 years to 17–19, i.e. up to the time when they finish school.

In order to establish the special features of the mental development of deaf children, the data obtained from investigations are compared with the results of experiments performed on normal children (pupils of ordinary schools). Similar investigations are conducted in the field of the psychology of deaf adults.

On the basis of the general conception of abnormal development, according to which the primary defect provokes various secondary deviations, the mentality of deaf children has been studied from various aspects. Much attention was devoted to the cognitive activity of the deaf, in particular to peculiarities in the development of their perception, memory and thinking which are most pronounced at the age of 6 to 10 and become less significant at a later age. The investigations showed that it is the verbal logical memory and abstract thinking of the deaf which possess a particularly specific character. At the same time, some less pronounced but essential characteristics of the visual, tactile and kinesthetic perceptions of deaf children have been described (slow perception, impeded recognition of an object by its contour or from an unusual angle, retarded development of the tactile methods of examining an object, etc.). Deaf children also exhibit a certain peculiarity of pictorial memory and thinking. These children, especially of lower school age, experience greater difficulties than normal children when they have to recognize previously seen objects among other similar ones, when they reproduce similar figures, analyse, synthesize and compare objects, or solve problems requiring mental operations with spatial concepts, etc.

An extensive series of researches has been devoted to the laws of the mastery of verbal speech by deaf children, in particular their perception of oral speech with the help of various sense organs by way of lip-reading, tactile-vibratory perception, or residual hearing with the utilization of sound amplifiers. The mastery of pronunciation habits by deaf children is another special object of research and has made it possible to develop a system of teaching pronunciation by means of a transition from approximately correct to fully correct pronunciation (abbreviated system of phonemes). The ways in which children learn to control their pronunciation and to overcome distortions when using devices of the 'visible speech' type are also subjected to investigation.

Research into the mastery of the vocabulary (lexics) by deaf children showed that the word-meanings formed are too narrow in their volume or, on the contrary, too broad in comparison with the word-meanings accepted in the language. Not infrequently there is a confusion of words which are close as regards their meanings, which relate to objects from one and the same life situation, or which denote objects and certain actions performed with them. The retention of the letter composition of words in the memory is also markedly impeded. The children transpose separate letters or syllables; they experience great difficulty when trying to memorize the prefixes and suffixes, which is closely connected with peculiarities in their mastery of the grammatical system of speech. Investigations have shown that this is particularly difficult for the deaf and have also established the ways in which deaf children learn to change the words according to number, gender and case, to master the conjugation of verbs and their tense modifications and to construct their utterances according to the laws of agreement and government of words in the sentence.

Investigations of the vocabulary and grammatical system of deaf children's speech involve both oral and written speech. Characteristic features of the children's independent speech when describing the surroundings, everyday events, pictures, films, books, etc., are of particular interest.

All experimental research into the development of cognitive processes in deaf children and into their mastery of verbal speech is closely bound up with the process of their instruction aimed at overcoming the difficulties of development revealed in the course of the psychological investigations.

Many of these investigations (for example, those devoted to the assimilation of the grammatical system of the language or to the acquisition of knowledge in arithmetic and botany) have exerted direct influence on the methods and content of school teaching. The results of other investigations have led to the elaboration of didactic methods which can be applied in the study of various subjects and which greatly raise the effectiveness of the instruction of deaf children in general (for example, special methods of teaching children to compare objects).

The language of gestures and facial expressions represents a special sphere of research. Soviet defectologists have investigated the meanings of gestures in correlation with word-meanings; they have shown the limited role of the language of gestures and facial expressions in the hierarchical denotation of objects, as well as life phenomena of different degrees of generality; they have disclosed the specific features of the construction of utterances by means of gestures and facial expressions, and their reconstruction as a result of the mastery of verbal speech. Interesting data have been obtained showing how spatial relationships are expressed with the help of the language of gestures.

Ever-increasing attention has been devoted in recent years to studying the activity of the deaf, beginning with the play activity of pre-school children and ending with the production activity of adults. The results of special investigations show that it is expedient to develop in deaf children the ability to play with objects which perform a different role in their games from that in everyday life, i.e. to organize subject games. In order to raise the effectiveness of the pupils' study activity, it is important to stimulate their interest in acquiring knowledge of scientific facts and laws.

Investigations of the labour activity of deaf adults and adolescents are of a many-sided character. They cover the formation of working habits in the deaf, the ways in which their characteristic sluggishness is surmounted (for example, by cultivating in them the sense of time, by teaching more rational methods of work, and developing kinesthetic control), the ability of the deaf to understand their work assignments, to plan their working activity independently, to exercise self-control and to appraise the results obtained. All psychological research into the labour activity of the deaf is conducted in the form of educational experimentation and is directly connected with the organization of their labour training.

Some scientific research in the emotional and volitional spheres is devoted to the specific personality features of the deaf (traits of character, interests, abilities, inclinations).

The point at which the teaching of verbal speech and corrective education begin is of decisive importance to the mental development of deaf children in general as are the pedagogical methods applied. The earlier the deaf child masters verbal speech in its two basic functions—the function of communication and the function of thinking—the more insignificant are their deviations from the normal and the earlier an adequate compensation in their mental development can be achieved.

Investigations of the mental development of children with partial defects of hearing constitute a separate branch of research. It has been established that the retarded development of such children depends not only on the degree of the hearing defect but also on certain other factors—the point at which the defect emerged, educational conditions and the ways in which the child communicates with his environment. The child's individual character traits also exert an influence on the development of speech. The data obtained has made possible a new approach to the diagnosis of the basic defect of the handicapped child. Previously, when examining such children, physicians often underestimated the negative influence of a partial hearing defect on the development of speech and as a result came to erroneous conclusions concerning the existence of lesions in the speech zones of the child's brain.

The new approach to hard-of-hearing children, which takes into account both the degree of the hearing defect and the level of speech development already achieved, has made it possible to elaborate a special diagnostic system, to scientifically substantiate the importance of creating two sections within schools for hard-of-hearing children depending on the level of their speech development, and to build up a new system of instruction.

Numerous psycho-pedagogical investigations have traced the development of speech in hard-of-hearing children (their vocabulary accumulation, formation of the grammatical system of the language, development of skills in auditory speech perception and perception by means of lip-reading—in cases of severe hearing defects—and cultivation of articulate and correct pronunciation).

The development of thinking in the process of learning is also being investigated in hard-of-hearing children (formation of scientific notions, ability to solve arithmetical problems, etc.). At present special attention is being paid to various mental operations performed by hard-of-hearing children entering school; the aim of this study is to work out more effective methods of differential diagnosis of such children and to single out those who suffer from primary disturbances of intellectual development.

Psychology of children with defective vision

All the basic investigations of blind and visually handicapped children are directed towards finding reliable methods of compensating for the affected sense organ. It has been established that blindness leads to a general impoverishment of the child's sensory experience, to a retarded formation of movements, to the development of thinking and speech without any proper reliance on visual–active experience, and to idiosyncrasies in the emotional–volitional sphere. In this connexion, particular importance is attached to studying the cognitive possibilities of the sense of touch and to its development in unity with thinking and speech. Investigations have shown that the disposition of blind children to formalism in knowledge and to verbalism, due to the absence of an adequate support in the sphere of sensory cognition, can to a considerable degree be overcome. For this purpose, it is necessary to teach the children tactile perception of objects and to enrich the sphere of their sensory concepts by means of relief pictures and other methods. Mastery of various kinds of practical activity is especially important for a fully adequate mental development of blind children. At the same time it has been found that when blind children remain outside the system of special instruction, the specific changes of their cognitive activity assume a profound character.

Children with defective vision manifest a particular form of mental development. As a rule, they continue to use the defective vision as a principal source of cognition, while the sense of touch does not play such an important role as in the case of blind children. Multi-faceted investigations into the visual sensations and perceptions of children with defective vision represent one of the main directions of research work which is conducted by psychologists jointly with ophthalmologists and physiologists. Such research combines an exploratory approach with a direct practical approach, since the results of the investigations lie at the base of any conclusion concerning the correct utilization of the vision of a given child, as well as the child's purposive development in the course of education. Systematic clinical observations of the state of vision are conducted in relation to a definite visual régime, and corresponding correctives concerning the utilization and development of the visual perceptions are introduced. The materials of these clinical observations are generalized and thus enrich the theory of the problem as a whole.

At the same time children with defective vision, like other handicapped children, manifest substantial secondary disorders in the development of their cognitive activity which are determined by disturbances of visual perception. Investigations have revealed a retarded and specific development of the children's visual-pictorial thinking and memory. Investigations of the verbal-logical thinking of these children and of its connexion with practical activity are now under way. As a result of this research, psychologists have been able to formulate a number of pedagogical recommendations aimed at improving the development of the cognitive activity of visually handicapped children in the process of education.

Psychological research is also conducted in the field of combined sensory defects, for example, in the psychological development of blind and deaf children in the course of their compensatory education.

The mentality and especially the speech of children who suffer from speech defects (alalia, aphasia, dysarthris, etc.), are studied in close connexion with the corrective-logopedic measures applied.[1]

---

1   The psycho-pedagogical investigations of blind and deaf children, as well as of children with speech disorders, have been discussed in the section devoted to pedagogical research.

Children with disturbances of the motor activity (for example, cases of cerebral paralysis) are subjected to special psycho-pedagogical investigations. It has been established that the object-active experience of these children and their mastery of oral and written speech are retarded. Even corrective education at pre-school age makes it possible to compensate almost wholly for their deficient sensory experience and to prepare them for studying in accordance with the curricula of ordinary schools.

During the last two decades, the results of research in the psychology of handicapped children were published in thirty monographs and twenty-five volumes of collected articles. They were also regularly published in the periodicals *Problems of Psychology*, *Defectology*, *Special School* and others.

Clinical and physiological studies

The scope of clinical and physiological studies of handicapped children has continually expanded in the U.S.S.R.

During the last fifteen years, clinical research was predominantly concentrated on the problem of mental deficiency. This is due both to the great social significance of this defect which characterizes the bulk of mentally retarded children (mentally retarded children form the most numerous category of children with anomalies of development) and to the fact that clinico-pedagogical research into the problem of mental deficiency is of importance for elaborating corrective-educational and medical measures aimed at compensating these states.

Clinical investigations of auxiliary school pupils accompanied by electro-encephalography, studies of the higher nervous activity and psychological experimentation have made possible an exact definition of oligophrenia or mental deficiency as a specific kind of biological insufficiency which is determined by innate or early acquired brain lesions of different aetiology primarily characterized by an underdevelopment of the superficial layers of the cerebral cortex. These investigations also permitted the elaboration of a classification of various forms of mental handicap. It was shown that a definite role in the origin of mental deficiency is played by both exogenic and hereditary genetic factors; in view of this, genetic methods of research are also applied in the study of mental deficiency, along with biochemical, cytogenic and immunologic methods. The structure of the defect and the dynamics of the development of children with anomalies both of the autosome and sex chromosomes are being investigated. In the latter case, comparatively mild forms of mental backwardness or mild retardation of mental development are observed. The relative role of the environmental and hereditary factors in the origin of mental backwardness or retardations of development is ascertained by means of special investigations with the application of the twin method.

Differential-diagnostic studies of mental retardation helped to isolate from among persistently unsuccessful pupils of the ordinary school a group of children suffering from psychophysical or mental infantilism, as well as children with cerebroasthenic states in whom specific features of mental activity led to their being mistaken for mentally retarded (oligophrenic) children. As a result of dynamic clinico-pedagogical investigations of these children, more precise clinical criteria for their diagnosis were elaborated as well as different ways and methods of correcting their pathological states.

Similar clinical investigations were carried out with regard to the structure of the defect in visually handicapped children, especially in cases where the defect was caused by tumorous diseases of the brain.

A special branch of clinico-neurological research is concerned with children suffering from lesions of the motor sphere (spastic paralyses, consequences of poliomyelitis). In the course of investigation and experimental instruction of these children, methods of treatment and rehabilitative work were developed which have proved highly effective as a means of compensating for the disturbed motor functions and the secondary defects of development.

Research work in all the above-mentioned directions will be carried on in the near future, with particular attention to clinical analysis of the children's development.

Neurophysiological research in the field of defectology has mainly consisted of clinico-physiological investigations into the functional state of the brain in various forms of abnormal development. The electrical activity of the brain in mental retardation and in lesions of the visual and auditory organs was studied with the help of the electroencephalographic method (E.E.G.). In order to ensure a more reliable diagnostic utilization of the data obtained, the E.E.G. age norms were established; it was found that a number of symptoms characterizing lesions of the central nervous systems in adults are connected in children with definite stages of the brain maturation and with the dynamic of changes in the cortico-subcortical correlations. These data served as a basis for determining the characteristic features of the brain electrical activity of mentally handicapped (oligophrenic) children, the relationship between the degree of the disturbances and the gravity of retardation and the dependence of the character of the disturbances on the aetiology and pathogenesis.

It was proved that a considerable proportion of children with delayed mental development suffer from organic or functional cerebral disturbances.

Investigations of the brain electrical activity in cases of visual disorders established a direct correlation between visual acuity and the degree of expressiveness of the main cortical rhythm (alpha-rhythm). A shift of the focus of maximal electrical activity to the central areas of the cortex was found in the blind; this phenomenon apparently reflects the processes of compensation connected with the intensified activity of the cutaneous–motor sensory system.

Investigations of the activity of individual neurons have recently been initiated. They have established the intactness of the cortex of the visual sensory system in the blind, which is highly important from the point of view of the possibility of transmitting visual information directly to the cortical centres.

Research in this direction will be continued and extended to other anomalies of development, especially to complex defects when disturbances of vision and hearing are accompanied by lesions of the central nervous system.

A series of investigations also concern the dynamic characteristics of the visual organ in cases of defective vision (rate of perception, temporal contrast, etc.). These investigations are connected with research into the physiology of the sense organs in handicapped children which was conducted earlier, as well as with the elaboration of methods for objective studies of auditory and visual sensitivity. Considerable progress in this respect has been achieved through the use of various components of the orienting reflex (galvanic skin reactions, plethismograms, etc.) as indices of sensitivity. These investigations have disclosed the characteristic features of the dynamic sensitivity range in visual and auditory disturbances and made it possible to work out a number of recommendations concerning the application of certain technical means for compensating the defects.

The problem of the interaction of different functions in the work of the sense organs will be investigated within the next few years.

Studies of the higher nervous activity of handicapped children, and above all of mentally retarded children (pathological inertness, weakness of active inhibition, excessively extensive irradiation of excitation, etc.) have been carried out during recent years. Particular attention was devoted to the development of the verbal system and to its regulatory influence on the direct activity of mentally retarded children. These investigations revealed the peculiarities of the orienting reflex in mentally retarded children which account for the specific characteristics of their attention.

Data concerning the higher nervous activity of mentally retarded children have proved of great importance for the elaboration of a clinical classification and differential diagnosis of various forms of mental retardation.

At present, research work is being carried out on the higher nervous activity of children with temporary retardation of mental development; this research will be continued, and special emphasis will be laid on analysing the dynamics of development of these children.

Main trends

In the near future, the scientific research establishments of the U.S.S.R. will carry on their investigations along the main lines described above. However, some of these lines will be given relatively greater attention. Thus investigations aimed at more refined diagnosis of the structure of the defect in handicapped children will be appreciably extended. It has been established that the earlier the handicapped child begins to undergo corrective influences, the more effective these are. In view of this, investigations whose aim is to elaborate methods of examining handicapped children in their earliest years are of great importance. Psycho-pedagogical investigations of handicapped pre-school children will also be markedly extended, the aim being to create a more rational and differentiated system of instruction and education for such children.

Similar psycho-pedagogical investigations of pupils of ordinary schools show that even a slight defect in development (a slightly pronounced disturbance of hearing or vision, general nervous weakness, etc.) may cause (if special attention is not paid to it) serious difficulties in the child's studies and leave a undesirable imprint on the developing personality. In view of this, the range of psychological and pedagogical research devoted to the study, instruction and education of ordinary school pupils with slightly pronounced defects of development will be extended during the next few years.

Likewise, pedagogical and psychological investigations of children with combined defects will be continued (they include, for example, defective hearing or vision combined with mental backwardness, disturbance of a leading sense organ combined with a general nervous weakness of the organism, disturbances of the motor and speech spheres).

More attention will be paid to studies of the occupational activity and social life of people having graduated from special schools. Finally, still greater importance will be attached to investigations aimed at a scientific–technical elaboration of devices whose application in the process of corrective-pedagogical work may ensure a more complete compensation for auditory or visual defects.

Dissemination of results

The results of scientific research are disseminated and put into special education practice in several ways.

The most important consist of creating new instructional methods, determining the content and volume of general education as well as of vocational training (curricula, programmes), perfecting the structure of special educational establishments, etc. This work begins in experimental groups or classes which have been organized at the Institute of Defectology and some other research institutions with the aim of verifying suggestions advanced by different scientific laboratories. Experimental programmes and methods are worked out on the basis this verification, they are then subjected to a wider test—in several basic schools which conduct experimental education under the guidance of a given scientific-research centre. The materials thus verified are then approved by the Ministry of Education of the U.S.S.R. and, in accordance with its directives, are introduced in all schools (kindergartens) of the appropriate type. Visual aids and special technical means are put into practice in a similar way.

Closely bound up with this work is the compilation by scientific workers (often jointly with teachers of experimental schools and classes) of textbooks and methodological manuals for special schools which are published after their experimental verification and subsequent approval by the Instructional Methodological Council of the Ministry of Education.

A highly important way of introducing scientific achievements into the process of instruction is the publication of monographs and scientific articles on problems connected with the theory and practice of special education.

In this respect, the participation of scientific workers in the training of teachers and in raising their qualification is also of major significance. The workers in scientific research institutions deliver lectures at defectological faculties engaged in the training of teachers, as well as at advanced training courses for workers from special children's establishments. They also compile manuals for students and teachers. In recent years, the Institute of Defectology alone has created special guides for teaching and educating children with defective hearing, manuals concerning the psychology of mentally retarded children, handbooks for teachers in schools for blind children, teachers in auxiliary schools and others.

Scientific conferences and symposia, with the participation of teachers from special schools, are organized by the Institute of Defectology and constitute an effective means of putting the results of research into practice.

Scientific workers also sum up their work in special communications delivered at so-called 'Pedagogical Readings' in which many teachers from special schools take part.

An effective way of disseminating the results of research concerning the psychology of mentally retarded children are seminars organized by collectives of auxiliary school-teachers. The latter study the psychological literature on the basis of special programmes elaborated by the Institute of Defectology and make reports on experimental investigations carried out by themselves. This kind of work is conducted in more than 300 auxiliary schools throughout the country.

The results of research carried out by Soviet defectologists are also disseminated outside the Soviet Union in several ways. The Institute of Defectology conducts an extensive exchange of scientific books with many countries. Institute publications devoted to general and particular problems of defectology are regularly sent to 122 foreign organizations. In 1969, for example, 46 publications representing a total of 6,000 copies were sent to different countries.

It should be noted that in recent years a number of such books have been translated into foreign languages and published abroad—in Bulgaria, the German Democratic Republic, Japan, Poland, the United Kingdom, the United States of America, and other countries.

The workers of the Institute of Defectology take an active part in international scientific congresses and conferences on problems of special education and rehabilitation of handicapped children and adolescents, as well as in international psychological congresses.

An important role in the dissemination of the results of research conducted by Soviet defectologists is played by their scientific missions abroad aimed at exchanging experiences and giving lectures on scientific problems.

At the same time, the Institute of Defectology and other Soviet establishments are often visited by foreign specialists. In the course of such visits, both short-term and long-term, these specialists are able to acquaint themselves with the research work and the activities of the establishments for handicapped children.

Joint investigations, though on a moderate scale, have recently been started by Soviet and foreign defectologists, and there is every reason to believe that in the near future these investigations will be appreciably extended.

SELECT BIBLIOGRAPHY

Boskis, R. M. *Gluhie i slaboslyšaščie deti* [Deaf and hard-of-hearing children]. Moscow, Academy of Pedagogical Sciences of the Russian Soviet Federated Socialist Republic (R.S.F.S.R.), 1963.
Boskis, R. M. (ed.). *Osnovy special'nogo obučenija slaboslyšaščih detej* [Foundations of special education for hard-of-hearing children]. *Prosveščenie* (Moscow), 1968.

DULNEV, G. M.; LURIA, A. R. (eds.). *Principy otbora detej vo vspomogatel'nye školy* [Principles governing the selection of children in special schools]. Moscow, Academy of Pedagogical Sciences of the R. S. F. S. R., 1960.

DYACHKOV, A. I. (ed.). *Surdopedagogika* [Surdopedagogy]. Moscow, Academy of Pedagogical Sciences of the R. S. F. S. R., 1963.

——. *Kratkij defektologičeskij slovar'* [Short defectological dictionary]. *Prosveščenie* (Moscow), 1964.

——. *Osnovy obučenija i vospitanija anomal'nyh detej* [Foundations of training and education of handicapped children]. *Prosveščenie* (Moscow), 1965.

EIDINOVA, M. B.; PRAVDINA-VINARSKAYA, E. N. *Detskie cerebral'nye paraliči i puti ih preodolenija* [Cerebral palsy in children and its treatment]. Moscow, Academy of Pedagogical Sciences of the R. S. F. S. R., 1959. (English edition: Oxford, Pergamon Press, 1963.)

KOSUNKSKAYA, B. D. *Metodika obučenija gluhih doškol'nikov reči* [Methods of teaching deaf pre-school children to speak]. *Prosveščenie* (Moscow), 1969.

KULAGIN, Y. A. et al. *Slabovidjaščie deti* [Visually impaired children]. *Prosveščenie* (Moscow), 1967.

LEVINA, R. E. (ed.). *Osnovy teorii i praktiki logopedii* [Foundation of the theory and practice of logopedics]. *Prosveščenie* (Moscow), 1968.

LURIA, A. R. (ed.). *Problemy vysšej nervnoj dejatel'nosti normal'nogo i anomal'nogo rebenka* [Problems of higher nervous activity in normal and handicapped children). Moscow, Academy of Pedagogical Sciences of the R. S. F. S. R., 1956 (Vol. I), 1958 (Vol. II).

——. *Umstvenno otstalyj rebenok* [The mentally retarded child]. Moscow, Academy of Pedagogical Sciences of the R. S. F. S. R., 1960. (English edition: Oxford, Pergamon Press, 1963.)

MOROZOVA, N. G. *Formirovanie poznavatel'nyh interesov u anomal'nyh detej* [Formation of cognitive interests in handicapped children]. *Prosveščenie* (Moscow), 1969.

NOVIKOVA, L. A. *Vlijanie narušenij zrenija i sluha na funkcional'noe sostojanie mozga* [Influence of visual and hearing disturbances on the functional condition of the brain]. *Prosveščenie* (Moscow), 1966.

PEVZNER, M. S. *Deti-oligofreny* [Oligophrenic children]. Moscow, Academy of Pedagogical Sciences of the R. S. F. S. R., 1959. (American edition: *Oligophrenia. Mental deficiency in children.* New York, N.Y., P. B. Consultants Bureau Inc., 1961.)

PEVZNER, M. S.; LUBOVSKY, V. I. *Dinamika razvitija detej-oligofrenov* [Dynamics of the development of mentally deficient children]. Moscow, Academy of Pedagogical Sciences of the R. S. F. S. R., 1963.

PINSKY, B. I. *Psihologičeskie osobennosti dejatel'nosti umstvenno otstalyh škol'nikov* [Psychological characteristics of the activity of mentally retarded pupils]. Moscow, Academy of Pedagogical Sciences of the R. S. F. S. R., 1962.

RAU, F. F. *Obučenie gluhonemyh proiznošeniju* [Teaching pronunciation to the deaf-and-dumb]. Moscow, Academy of Pedagogical Sciences of the R. S. F. S. R., 1960.

RAU, F. F.; BELTYUKOV, V. I. *Ustnaja reč' gluhih i slaboslyšaščih* [Oral speech of the deaf and hard-of-hearing]. *Proceedings of the Academy of Pedagogical Sciences of the R. S. F. S. R.*, no. 140, 1965.

SHIF, Z. I. *Usvoenie jazika i razvitie myšlenija u gluhih detej* [The mastering of language and development of thinking in deaf children]. *Prosveščenie* (Moscow), 1968.

SHIF, Z. I. (ed.). *Osobennosti umstvennogo razvitija učaščihsja vspomogatel'noj školy* [Specificities of the mental development of the pupils of a special school]. *Prosveščenie* (Moscow), 1966.

SOKOLOV, E. N. (ed.). *Orientirovočnyj refleks i problemy recepcii v norme i patologii* [Orientation reflex and problems of reception—normal and pathological]. *Prosveščenie* (Moscow), 1964.

SOLOVEV, I. M. *Psihologija poznavatel'noj dejatel'nosti normal'nyh i anomal'nyh detej* [Psychology of the cognitive activity of normal and handicapped children]. *Prosveščenie* (Moscow), 1966.

SOLOVEV, I. M. (ed.). *Razvitie poznavatel'noj dejatel'nosti gluhonemyh detej* [Development of cognitive activity in deaf-and-dumb children]. Moscow, Učpedgiz, 1957.

VLASOVA, T.A.; PEVZNER, M. S. *Učitelju o detjah s otklonenijami v razvitii* [For the teacher: on children with defects in their development]. *Prosveščenie* (Moscow), 1968.

ZEMTSOVA, M. I. *Puti kompensacii slepoty* [Ways of compensating blindness]. Moscow, Academy of Pedagogical Sciences of the R.S.F.S.R., 1956.

ZEMTSOVA, M. I. *et al.* (eds.). *Deti s glubokimi narušenijami zrenija* [Children with serious visual disturbances]. *Prosveščenie* (Moscow), 1967.

ZYKOV, S.A. *Obučenie gluhih detej jazyku po principu formirovanija rečevogo obščenija* [Language training of deaf children through the principle of verbal communication]. Moscow, Academy of Pedagogical Sciences of the R.S.F.S.R., 1961.

William P. Hurder

United States
of America

Background, scope
and method of study[1]

Introduction

This report provides a survey of research and research-related activities relevant to the education of handicapped children. The study focuses on the 1960s. Major research developments in this period are examined, culminating with an emphasis upon the current scene. An attempt is made to discern directions that research will take in the seventies. Aspects considered include the substantive nature of research projects and programmes, patterns of organization and support, the disposition and utilization of research results, the relationship between research activities and teacher preparation, and international collaboration.

Many obstacles and hazards await any attempt to supply a representative

---

1 The reader's attention is directed to the following abbreviations used in the text and especially in the footnotes:

CEC: Council on Exceptional Children.
ECEA: *Exceptional Child Education Abstracts.* See page 263. Numbers following ECEA
            in the footnotes refer to accession number in specific issues of the clearing-
            house bulletin.
NEA: National Education Association.
NICHHD: National Institute of Child Health and Human Development.
NIH: National Institutes of Health.
NIMH: National Institute of Mental Health.
NINDB: National Institute of Neurological Diseases and Blindness.
NINDS: National Institute of Neurological Diseases and Stroke (successor to
            NINDB).
RRTC: *Research Relating to Children.* See page 264. Numbers following RRTC in the
            footnotes refer to accession number in specific issues of the clearing-house
            bulletin.
USDHEW: United States Department of Health, Education, and Welfare.
USOE: United States Office of Education. Numbers following USOE in the foot-
            notes are those of contract or grant referred to.

picture of a topic of this scope, depth and complexity. The field of special education is in a state of flux. This is due to sheer growth and to changes in subject-matter and responsibilities. In 1960, the U.S. Office of Education (USOE) had less than $500,000 earmarked to support research on education of the handicapped. By 1969 the figure had risen to $14 million per year. Changes in priorities, in definition of the subject-matter, and in the responsibilities of special education, followed from increases in the prevalence of multiply handicapped children, growing acceptance of emotionally and socially maladjusted children in special classes, and recognition of children with learning disabilities in programmes for the handicapped. At the time of writing, the federal Congress is considering legislation which would provide millions of dollars annually for research, teacher preparation and programme development in the area of learning disabilities.

Major influences of the sixties

Factors outside the sphere of education contributed to this growth and are important to an understanding of the present state of affairs. The 1960s witnessed an upsurge in humanistic concern for the handicapped in the United States. In the late fifties, the Congress of the United States established the Joint Commission on Mental Illness and Health and charged it with responsibility for recommending ways to improve the care of the mentally disordered. This group focused largely on the adult population and made its report to Congress in 1961.[1] The commission strongly recommended that the quality and quantity of services to the mentally ill be increased, and especially that these services be made available to citizens in their home communities. The goal of *community* mental health services was set before the nation, and federal, state and local action was set in motion. The commission's work drew attention to the plight of the abnormal and handicapped, and placed great emphasis upon the need to provide for them early in their illness with minimal disruption of their normal living patterns. The public schools were identified as important in the prevention and detection of behavioural handicaps early in life.

The next significant event was the creation by President John F. Kennedy in 1961 of the President's Panel on Mental Retardation. Following the report of the panel in 1962[2] there came substantial legislative, administrative and professional action at all levels of public and private concern.[3] A major recommendation of the panel was that the nation should invest more heavily

1   *Action for Mental Health: Report of Joint Committee on Mental Illness and Health,* New York, N.Y., Basic Books Inc., 1961.
2   *A Proposed Program for National Action to Combat Mental Retardation,* Washington, D.C., Supt of Doc., U.S. Govt Printing Office, 1962.
3   *Mental Retardation '69. Toward Progress: The Story of a Decade,* Washington D.C., Supt of Doc., U.S. Govt Printing Office, 1969.

in research in child development, and as a partial result the National Institute of Child Health and Human Development (NICHHD) was created within the National Institutes of Health. The President's panel reinforced the recommendation of the joint commission that services be provided in the community. In mental retardation, the balance of resources between community services and residential care was particularly distorted. In 1963 approximately $300 million was spent for care in residential institutions. At the same time $250 million was spent for all community services for the retarded; yet, only 4 per cent of the mentally retarded were in residential institutions. This imbalance led to the recommendation of vastly increased services for the mentally retarded children in public school systems across the land. In addition both the joint commission and the President's panel placed great emphasis upon utilizing the findings of research in practice.

A third focus of activity which promises to be important to provisions for the education of handicapped is quite recent. In 1967 the federal Congress created a task force, the Joint Commission on Mental Health of Children, to study children suffering from emotional disorders. This group made sweeping recommendations regarding the need to ensure that *every* child has access to basic health, education and welfare services, and that special services in any of these areas be available when needed and where needed.[1] Again, emphasis was placed upon community-based service for children, and the role of education in the cognitive, affective and social development of children was spotlighted. This commission also recommended an elaborate mechanism of child advocacy at all levels of government in order to assure that the needs of all children be kept to the forefront.

These three activities, initiated by a major branch of the federal government and relying largely upon the skills of professional and lay leaders from a number of fields, have played (or promise to play) a significant part in focusing attention on problems of handicapped children and adults. In so far as they were concerned with children they pointed to the role of education in the prevention and overcoming of handicap. Inasmuch as all stressed the need to provide services in the community in the form of community mental health or community mental retardation services, they directly or indirectly spotlighted the role that pre-school, elementary and secondary education can play in these and other types of handicap.

The humanistic tenor of these movements of the sixties is illustrated by the prologue of a document,[2] produced by the Commission on Mental Illness of the Southern Regional Education Board[3] as an instrument to help mobilize

1   *Crisis in Child Mental Health: Report of the Joint Commission on Mental Health of Children, 1969,* New York, N.Y., Harper & Row, 1969.
2   *Commitment to Health,* Atlanta, Ga, Southern Regional Education Board.
3   The Southern Regional Education Board is a quasi-governmental body formed by fifteen states of the southern United States which provides a means of pooling resources of higher education of the states in order to attack major social problems through co-operation in planning, training and research.

state-by-state efforts toward the development of community services for mentally ill and mentally retarded children and adults.

From the prologue:

WE CHOSE ATHENS

Over 2,000 years ago Western civilization came to a crossroads—to go the way of Athens or Sparta. We follow those who chose Athens.

We have fallen short of the ideals of the Athenian way many times in many ways. But it is in our treatment of the mentally ill and the mentally retarded that we have come closest to shame. The way of Sparta was to destroy the weak, the sick and handicapped. The way of Athens was to heal, to nurture and to restore.

We have not destroyed; neither have we healed or restored the mentally disordered. Though we did not destroy, we banished. We met the challenge of the Athenian way with mixed feelings. . . .

Two more forces which contributed substantially to action on behalf of the handicapped in this decade were parent's associations and professional associations. The National Association for Retarded Children has been a potent factor in bringing about legislative, administrative and programmatic benefits for the mentally retarded, and indirectly for other handicapped children. This was done through political action, through programmes of public education and information, and in some instances by limited and selective support of research and demonstration efforts in local communities and in various academic settings. Never a massive organization in terms of numbers or finance, it has nevertheless exercised remarkable leverage through the adroit use of its limited resources to the benefit of all handicapped children.

Two professional associations played major roles in developments in education for the handicapped and in research in this decade. The first, the American Association for Mental Deficiency, is an organization of professional workers aimed at improving all phases of the care of the mentally retarded. In the mid 1950s, with the assistance of a special programme grant from the National Institute of Mental Health (NIMH) the association initiated an abstracting service which for the first time sought to keep abreast of relevant research reports in a variety of publications throughout the world. Publication of these abstracts as an integral part of the *Journal of American Association for Mental Deficiency* assured improved access to such reports. This abstracting service was later consolidated into a separate publication by the U.S. Department of Health, Education and Welfare which continues to publish it.

The second association, the Council on Exceptional Children (CEC), is a department of the National Education Association (NEA) and is an organization of professionals whose primary interest is in the education of all handicapped children. This group has contributed to the growth and nurture of research through the publication of periodic reviews of research. The present report has been facilitated by the availability of such NEA–CEC reviews published in Washington, D.C., in 1959, 1963, 1966, 1968 and 1969.[1-6] CEC also publishes *ad hoc* reports of topical conferences, special reviews of research and other valuable items. Most recently CEC initiated publication of the *Exceptional Child Education Abstracts*. These promise to strengthen research.

Another factor which influenced research was growing awareness of the impact of early social and economic disadvantage upon the intellectual, emotional and social development of children. One of the major thrusts of the war on poverty, the Head Start programme for poor children, has had important repercussions on both early childhood education and the education of the handicapped. The results of Head Start converted many who were previously uncommitted to the belief that the I.Q. is much more responsive to environmental influence than previously considered possible, albeit not all agree and conflicting interpretations of the findings have given new vigour to the nature–nurture controversy. Head Start-type activities have had important implications for traditional categories of handicap in that many children in this compensatory education programme might have previously been diagnosed as mentally retarded, emotionally disturbed, or socially maladjusted, and denied special educational opportunity. But the single most significant influence of Head Start may have been to renew enthusiasm for early childhood education.

Criteria for selection of research

In a report of this type the determination of research relevance is critical. Yet, such determination is inescapably arbitrary. The boundaries of education of the handicapped are poorly demarcated and the definitions and designations of handicap are in a state of flux. The potentially significant studies are so numerous that they must be examined and described selectively. No analyst has the prescience to discern the ultimate implications of a given programme, project or piece of research. In recognition of this dilemma three criteria were used to choose 'relevant' research.

The first was that research done by those with an explicit concern for the education of the handicapped is *ipso facto* relevant, e.g. research supported by the Bureau of Education for the Handicapped of USOE, doctoral dissertations in special education and related areas of education, research sponsored or conducted by agencies with a primary responsibility to provide educational services for handicapped children, etc.

1   'Education of Exceptional Children', *Rev. Educ. Res.*, Vol. 29, No. 5, December 1959.
2   'Education of Exceptional Children', *Rev. Educ. Res.*, Vol. 33, No. 1, February 1963.
3   S. Kirk and B. Weiner (eds), *Behavioral Research on Exceptional Children*, Washington D.C., CEC, 1963, 377 p.
4   'Education of Exceptional Children', *Rev. Educ. Res.*, Vol. 36, No. 1, February 1966.
5   O. Johnson and H. Blank (eds), *Exceptional Children Research Review*, Washington D.C., CEC, 1968.
6   'Education of Exceptional Children', *Rev. Educ. Res.*, Vol. 39, No. 1, February 1969.

The second criterion was the degree of correspondence between the aims and methods of the research and the aims and methods of education. The aim of education was considered to be primarily the development of the child's cognitive competencies. The methods were viewed as various means of providing experiences believed essential to the development of cognitive competencies; i.e. educational, training and tutorial experiences. By this criterion, for example, research on the vocational practicability of training in typewriting for the educable mentally retarded high school student is of immediate relevance to the education of the handicapped. Much research is of intermediate relevance by this criterion, i.e. studies aimed at controlling disruptive classroom behaviour by means of behaviour modification techniques or psychotropic drugs, use of compressed speech to increase the input of auditory information in the blind or the mentally retarded, etc. Studies of this kind have in common the aim of improving the conditions which underlie educability.

The third criterion in selection encompassed research in which a theoretical concern with such conditions of cognition as cerebral function, perception, learning, memory, motivation and socialization was predominant. Research of this nature is almost always knowledge-oriented, i.e., the primary goal is to get more information about an underlying concept or phenomenon, whereas research of immediate or intermediate relevance is likely to have the primary goal of acquiring information of immediate utility to the education of the handicapped.

*Method of description and analysis
of substantive research activities*

The following seven sections are designed to give a sense of the direction and the content of research, development and demonstration in this decade. These sections deal with categories currently used by the Bureau of Education for Handicapped of USOE. The categories of handicap are: crippled or otherwise health impaired; emotionally disturbed; hearing-impaired; mentally-retarded; speech-impaired; visually-impaired; multiple or cross-disability research.

These categories were used because the bureau supplied comprehensive and current information used in this report in the form of summary descriptions of research, demonstration and development efforts funded by USOE in the period 1960–69. Since this information was grouped and analysed according to these categories they offered the most efficient mode of organization. Periodic reviews of research sponsored by NEA and CEC in 1959, 1963, 1966, 1968 and 1969 were important sources. They too use these categories. These reviews record the judgement of active dedicated workers as to research which is most relevant, promising, or neglected at given points in time.

The third and largest body of information consisted of original research publications, the proceedings of scientific meetings and reviews of research in specialized technical journals and monographs. These do not, however, encompass the totality of significant activity at any given time and for this reason data from specialized clearing-houses comprise the fourth kind of input to the present study. These services, which are relatively new, hold much promise for the further stimulation and facilitation of research. They are considered further in the section. 'Dissemination and Utilization of Research Findings'.

Whatever the source of information used to prepare substantive descriptions of research, primary emphasis was placed upon stating the aims and the approach of the investigation. Secondary emphasis was put on description of the findings or conclusions of research projects and programmes. This was done in part because in many cases the research was still in progress and in part because only rarely had the completed research been confirmed by replication. The most important consideration, however, was the writer's judgement that the totality of the research enterprise in the course of the decade could best be portrayed by focusing on the directions it took—the stated aims; and the manner in which these aims were pursued—the approach.

Research on the crippled
or otherwise health-impaired

Research in this area of handicap ran a dramatic course over the decade. It declined by the criteria of funds allocated and the amount of attention given in professional reviews. USOE funds dropped from a peak of 15 per cent in 1965 to a low of 1 per cent of the total funds for the handicapped in 1969. The category in its original form was not reviewed in the 1969 NEA–CEC survey of research; but out of the old category emerged a new conceptual–clinical–educational entity. Variously called 'learning disability', 'learning disorder', 'cerebral dysfunction', 'central processing dysfunction' and 'minimum brain dysfunction', the 'new' entity had achieved marked vitality by 1970.

Early developments

At the beginning of the sixties this category encompassed such handicaps as cerebral palsy, orthopaedic handicap, brain injury and chronic medical conditions such as cardiovascular and metabolic disorders. The overlap among these was great and attempts to correct this were generally inadequate but the ground was being prepared for major changes. An influential work was that of Strauss and Lehtinen who attacked problems of educating brain-injured children.[1] Although they focused upon brain injury, their ultimate contribution was to have helped make clear the need to study the behaviour of children irrespective of the presumed etiology or category of the primary disability. An important influence which arose from outside education was increased attention to the etiological relationships between low socio-economic status and this category of handicap as well as others such as mental retardation.[2] This direction of enquiry was to thrive during the decade. The foundation of a significant methodological approach was laid in studies of personality patterns among children with cerebral palsy, muscular dystrophy, etc.[3] This was a precursor of the method of behavioural ecology which proved to be one of the most promising available to research on handicap.

In an educationally oriented review in 1959, Connor and Goldberg noted that the prevalence of these disorders was in flux due to advances in medical care.[4] They called attention to a range of studies such as community recreation, pre-school programmes and research on vocational opportunities but concluded that the research surveyed was deficient in design, theoretically weak and failed to come to grips with fundamental educational problems of the crippled and otherwise health-impaired. Other work of importance included a 1960 treatise by Gallagher which dealt with the tutoring of brain-injured mentally retarded children.[5] In addition to its intrinsic research value, this study contributed to the growing awareness that etiology *per se* and classification as such are not as significant as information about how the child behaves in learning situations. Another valuable contribution was made by Cruickshank who focused on the brain-injured and the emotionally disturbed in a way which stimulated theoretical interest in the education of such children.[6]

A long-range study of the relationship of perinatal factors to later neurological and behaviourial development got well under way in this period.[7]

1   A. Strauss and L. Lehtinen, *Psychopathology and Education of the Brain-Injured Child.* Vol. 1: *Fundamentals and Treatment of Brain-Injured Children,* New York, N.Y., Grune & Stratton, 1947.

2   B. Pasamanick *et al.,* 'Socioeconomic Status and Some Precursors of Neuropsychiatric Disorder', *Am. J. Orthopsychiat.* (Broadway, N.Y.), Vol. 26, July 1956, p. 594–601.

3   R. Barker and H. Wright, *Midwest and Its Children: The Psychological Ecology of an American Town,* Evanston, Ill., Row, Peterson & Co., 1955.

4   F. Connor and I. Goldberg, 'Children with Crippling Conditions', *Rev. Educ. Res.,* Vol. 29, No. 5, December 1959, p. 471–96.

5   J. Gallagher, *The Tutoring of Brain-Injured Mentally Retarded Children: an Experimental Study,* Springfield, Ill., Charles C. Thomas, Publisher, 1960.

6   W. Cruickshank, *A Teaching Method for Brain Injured and Hyperactive Children: a Demonstration—Pilot Study,* Syracuse, N.Y., Syracuse Univ. Press, 1961.

7   B. Heinz, *Collaborative Studies in Cerebral Palsy and Sensory Disorders of Infancy and Childhood,* NINDB, 1956 (RRTC 24 AA 13).

Still in progress, this work joins staff of the National Institute of Neurological Diseases and Stroke (NINDS) with staff of many medical centres in the study of several thousand births each year. The initial aim of following children until age 5 has been extended through USOE participation so that now school progress is also being followed. A technical report by Kirk and McCarthy in 1961 introduced the Illinois Test of Psycholinguistic Abilities (ITPA) which was to play a substantial part in later research and theory regarding learning disabilities.[1] These authors set forth a philosophy of evaluation which purported to go beyond the classification achieved through individual omnibus tests of intelligence and aimed at a type of assessment which pinpoints areas of function needing remediation.

In a 1963 review, Hunt noted that by the measure of number of monographs the brain-injured and the cerebral-palsied got most attention in the period he surveyed.[2] Many efforts to improve the psychological assessment of these children were cited. He pointed to growing concern that central nervous disorders were increasing in the young and speculation as to whether this was due to improved case finding, greater foetal salvage, or both. In 1963 Kirk and Wiener edited a special research review under CEC sponsorship.[3] This review put much emphasis on the behavioural aspects of exceptionality thus serving as a portend of what was to be perhaps the single most significant trend in research. The authors' rationale was that the earlier emphasis in the literature upon the biological aspects of disability, while valuable, had little relevance to problems of school learning and adjustment. They reasoned that responsible instruction, programme development and guidance in education depend upon information about the behavioural aspects of exceptionality.

Another trend manifest in the Kirk–Wiener review was the division of the crippled or otherwise health-impaired category into *orthopaedic handicaps* and *cerebral dysfunction*. Jordan, who reviewed the orthopaedic areas, stressed the scarcity of research relevant to the learning characteristics or the special education needs of such children.[4] Her interpretation of this reflected increasing awareness of the complex make-up of this category of handicap and the imperative need to reorder it on the basis of educational considerations. She wrote:

The most probable answer is hinted in the conclusion drawn almost universally from studies of the orthopedically handicapped—namely, the extreme educational heterogeneity of the children of this classification, a heterogeneity which discourages gener-

1   S. Kirk and J. McCarthy, 'The Illinois Test of Psycholinguistic Abilities: an approach to Differential Diagnosis', *Am. J. Ment. Defic.* (Albany, N.Y.), Vol. 66, No. 3, November 1961, p. 399–412.
2   J. Hunt, 'Children with Crippling Conditions and Special Health Problems', *Rev. Educ. Res.*, Vol. 33, No. 1, February 1963, p. 99–108.
3   Kirk and Weiner (eds), op. cit.
4   L. Jordan, 'Children with Orthopedic Handicaps and Special Health Problems', in: Kirk and Weiner (eds), op. cit., p. 244–58.

alization. Furthermore, physical handicap which does not extend to damage to the visual or auditory channel of learning is not an essentially educational handicap. There is little reason to expect a close relationship between a child's intelligence or learning characteristics and some physical condition which effects his mobility, dexterity, or vigor, unless that condition includes neurological damage. Recent research in this area has tended to focus on cerebral palsy, a type of crippling which unquestionably promotes educational problems . . . When the cerebral palsied are subtracted from their ranks, there is little reason to expect the physically handicapped to differ consistently or extensively from the non-handicapped in the way or in the amount that they will learn, given the opportunity to learn.

The Kirk–Wiener review accorded cerebral dysfunction a separate chapter in which incidence, evaluation and education, perceptual characteristics, psychological appraisal and vocational preparation and placement were of major concern. The reviewer, Reid, commented on the need to distinguish carefully between the syndromes, cerebral dysfunction and cerebral palsy. His rationale was as follows:

. . . a very large number of children reveal syndromes of cerebral dysfunction. The exact number is difficult to estimate. The cerebral palsied constitute only a small portion of the total group. The term *cerebral dysfunction* includes all neuromuscular disorders resulting from brain damage, and many other associated difficulties, such as disorders in language and thought processes, learning disabilities, and certain personality deviations.[1]

Other work of particular interest in this period includes several representative studies supported by major federal agencies or other sources. Two efforts supported by USOE illustrate trends of the time. One project had the aim of determining the relationships among various behavioural tests of perception and measures of hyperactivity.[2] The second was a pioneer enquiry into social disadvantage as a cause of educational retardation through the analysis of auditory skills and reading achievement in culturally disadvantaged retarded readers.[3] The National Heart Institute funded a long-range study of the effect of open heart surgery on development, in which the effect of lowered body temperature, circulation changes, etc., on the maturing central nervous system was the focus of concern.[4] In 1963 a large municipal school system concluded a six-year field study of children with neurological disorders in which the efficacy of regular and special class placement was compared.[5]

1   L. Reid, 'Children with Cerebral Dysfunction', in: Kirk and Weiner (eds), op.cit., p. 226–43.
2   M. Trippe *et al.*, *Relationship Among Visual Perception and Hyperactivity in Elementary Age Children, 1963–1965*, Nashville, Tenn., Peabody College (USOE CSAE 3–10–024).
3   S. Feldman *et al.*, *Effectiveness of Training of Retarded Readers in Auditory Perceptual Skills Underlying Reading, 1963–1965*, New York, N.Y., New York Medical College (USOE G 7-42-0920-220).
4   K. Finley and M. Honzik, *Neuropsychological Development and Open Heart Surgery*, Univ. of California, National Heart Inst. (RRTC 24GE5).
5   'An Exploratory Study of Children with Neurological Handicaps in School Districts of Los Angeles County', *Los Angeles County Supt of Schools Office*, 1963 (ECEA 914).

Middle years

A major review of progress in the treatment crippling conditions and special health problems published in 1966 reported little research directly related to such aspects of education as curriculum, methodology, special educational provisions or achievement.[1] A number of studies were cited which demonstrated the difficulty of ascertaining the precise nature of brain damage in children, particularly when such damage was inferred from behavioural data and growing awareness that the developmental age at which brain damage occurs is an important qualifier of the behavioural consequences of such damage. This reviewer cited a number of investigations which focused on the personality reactions of children suffering various crippling conditions. Other works assessed the attitudes of normal children toward their crippled classmates, the self concept of handicapped students and teachers' attitudes toward handicapped students.

In a 1966 survey of learning disorders, Bateman presented evidence of a marked increase in interest in these disorders.[2] She suggested several possible causes of this interest, including:

... the increased growth of all other areas of special education, which has served to highlight the problem of the 'leftover' child with learning disorders who, after the treatment of the slow learners, the culturally deprived, and the emotionally disturbed, still fails to learn efficiently via regular educational procedures ...

Bateman noted a lack of consensus regarding terminology and incidence of learning disorders and observed that the area was so wide as to perhaps encompass not one but several fields. The scope of the topic is reflected in the range of her review which sampled research in reading disabilities and visuo-motor disabilities, discussed such theories of etiology as cerebral dominance, brain damage or dysfunction, maturational lag, and various multifactor theories, and examined such issues as the question of whether remediation should emphasize a child's assets, his deficiencies, or some combination of these. In an analysis of issues in research on learning disorders, Bateman in the same study suggested that their resolution would benefit the whole of education:

Data from such studies would bear directly on the entire issue of teaching methodology, viz., is there, after all, a single best method of teaching a given task? Also, when educational gains are effected by a given remedial procedure, to what precise factors are those gains related ... to the method itself; e. g., the simultaneous association of visual and auditory cues? ... to other factors such as individual attention, decreased parental anxiety, or a different learning set?

A number of studies supported by USOE are instructive of trends in this period. Efforts to evaluate special programmes were prominent. A four-

---

1   J. Hunt, 'Crippling Conditions and Special Health Problems', *Rev. Educ. Res.*, Vol. 36, No. 1, February 1966, p. 162–75.
2   B. Bateman, 'Learning Disorders', *Rev. Educ. Res.*, Vol. 36, No. 1, February 1966, p. 93–119.

year grant underwrote an attempt to evaluate a special education programme
for crippled children by determining medical, psychological and social functioning of the children before and during special class attendance.[1] A three-
year evaluation of a programme of home-bound instruction compared a
combination of radio broadcasts, group telephone hook-ups and visiting
teachers with more traditional methods.[2] Other USOE studies were directed
toward problems of identification, description, classification and etiology.
A three-year project sought to identify potential learning disabilities among
kindergarten children. High-risk children were defined as those in the lowest
25 per cent in three or more areas of function such as visual perception, eye-
hand co-ordination, and auditory discrimination.[3] Another grant underwrote
a five-year developmental study to determine perceptual, conceptual, motivational and self-concept differences between normal and hyperactive boys
with the aim of improving methods of classification of behaviour disturbances.[4] In a study of children who had suffered viral encephalitis, age of
onset of encephalitis, severity of physical after-effects and type of organic
damage were related to academic achievement, social competence and
measures of intelligence.[5]

Some studies had the goal of making provisions for children with learning
disabilities an integral part of the public school programme. One project,
begun in 1966, aimed at developing a combined diagnostic–remedial–con-
sultative approach within the public school system in order to demonstrate
that the regular classroom teacher can help children with severe learning
disabilities and avoid the need for special class placement.[6] A second grant
enabled a demonstration of techniques of identification, diagnosis and treatment. The focus was the concept of a diagnostic teacher working in a public
school setting. The teacher worked with the child after formal diagnostic
testing in order to extend and refine knowledge of the child's unique deficits
and to devise means of intensive remedial training within the framework of
the public school.[7]

1   L. Kabasakalian, *Evaluation of a Special Education Program for Crippled Children, 1965–68*,
    New York, N.Y., Medical and Health Res. Assoc. (USOE G 32-42-7600-5022).
2   T. Capone, *Home Bound Instruction of Handicapped, Crippled, Other Health Impaired, 1966–68*,
    Albany, N.Y., State Dept Ed. (C6-10-166).
3   N. Haring et al., *A Study of Early Diagnosis and Clinical Education of Children with Learning
    Disabilities, 1964–66*, Lawrence, Kans., Univ. of Kansas Med. Centr. (USOE G 32-26-
    9015-1001).
4   R. Simches, *Study of Perceptual, Conceptual, Motivational, and Self Concept Differences Between
    and Within Hyperactive and Normal Groups of Pre-adolescent Boys, 1965–1969*, Albany, N.Y.,
    State Dept Ed. (USOE G 32-42-6170-5004).
5   K. Finley, *Post-encephalitic Learning in Young Children, 1966–67*, San Francisco, Calif.,
    Presbyterian Med. Centr. (USOE G 4-6-062187-1598).
6   J. McCarthy, *A Public School Program of Remediation for Children with Severe Learning Dis-
    abilities, 1966–68*, Schaumberg, Ill., Schaumberg Community Consolidated School,
    13 Dist. (USOE GEOG 3-6-062003-1583).
7   A. Jacobson, *A Demonstration of Techniques in the Identification, Diagnosis and Treatment of
    Children with Learning Disorders, 1966–69*, Skokie, Ill., Skokie School Dist. No.68 (USOE
    GEOG 3-6-062244-2094).

Two projects with an organic orientation need noting. The first was a long-range project on head injuries which was funded by NINDS. Neurological, psychiatric and psychometric data were to be used to assess short- and long-range effects of head injury in children with the special aim of determining interactions between age at injury and primary effects of the injury.[1] Second was a long-range study of a selected brain potential, the contingent negative variation (CNV), in normal, brain-damaged and culturally deprived children. The CNV is thought by some to be the first reliable and distinctive electrophysiological correlate of higher mental function.[2,3]

Among publications of the period, a major monograph on perception and cerebral palsy should be cited. It gave Cruickshank's findings from a study of visual, tactile, proprioceptive and kinesthetic functioning in over 300 cerebral-palsied and 100 normal children.[4]

A second CEC-sponsored review of research appeared under Johnson and Blank's editorship in 1968.[5] Although they expressed concern about the proliferating terminology of the total field and growing turmoil with respect to classification of handicapping conditions, they spoke of a promising trend:

The trend appears to be in the direction of grouping according to function, insofar as learning is concerned, and away from the physical or medical characteristics which have little or no direct value for education. Further editions of CEC's research review will undoubtedly reflect this change in approach.

Orthopedic disabilities and special health problems were surveyed by Best and Force who presented much material from doctoral dissertations.[6] Research foci included such topics as the meaning of disability as manifest in the child's image of his own body, his self concept, the significance of the 'visibility' of physical defect, educational research which encompassed such matters as education for homebound children, factors in the vocational progress of cerebral-palsied persons, and the work adjustment of young physically handicapped adults. The reviewers' impressions of the field are of interest:

The number, range, and quality of these studies make it certain that progress has been made, but much is yet necessary. While studies of changing incidence may concern the medical profession, it seems clear that of greater importance to psychologists,

1   P. Black, *Child Head Injury Project, 1964–69*, Baltimore, Md., Johns Hopkins Univ. (NINDS RRTC 24GC8).
2   J. Cohen, *Evoked Brain Potentials to Expectancy and Meaning: The Contingent Negative Variation, 1966–1972*, Chicago, Ill., Dept Neurology and Psychiatry Univ. of Illinois Medical School (RRTC 24DA2).
3   H. Myklebust, *Progress in Learning Disabilities*, Vol. I, p. 122, New York, Grune & Stratton, 1968.
4   W. Cruickshank, *Perception and Cerebral Palsy*, Syracuse, N.Y., Syracuse Univ. Press, 1965 (Monograph No. 2).
5   Johnson and Blank (eds), op. cit.
6   G. Best and D. Force, 'Orthopedic Disabilities and Special Health Problems', in: Johnson and Blank (eds), op. cit., p. 210–25.

educators and other behavioral scientists will be studies which are directed at the behavioral consequences of disability as well as toward the use of newer and different teaching and learning strategies.

Work on cerebral dysfunction as of 1968 was reviewed by Meyer who noted a wide range of speculation about the etiology of minimal brain damage.[1] This extended from preoccupation with perinatal anoxia to the assumption that certain cultures may lack the minimum intellectual stimulants required to induce adequate neurophysiological development. Review of research suggested a high probability that anoxia was detrimental to neural and behavioural development but interpretation was hazardous. Existing studies of anoxia confounded such factors as time of onset, degree and duration of anoxia, the post-anoxic interval at which behaviour was assessed, and the differential impact of anoxic insult upon perceptual, intellectual and social development. Identical limitations existed in investigations of other types of insult to the central nervous system.

Other research on the behavioural characteristics of children identified as 'brain-injured' produced varying, often conflicting and equivocal results, suggesting that procedures for identifying and assessing brain injury *per se* were still primitive and that there remained major problems of distinguishing between the consequences of organic pathology and variation due to normal development. Methods of discerning and describing relevant behaviour patterns were tenuous at best. An occasional study indicated the need for caution in equating hyperactivity and distractibility with 'brain injury' and ignoring all other possible antecedents of behaviour abnormality and restricting the range of remedial procedures.[2] A more promising approach appeared to be one in which stress was laid upon determining patterns of behavioural capability and upon the development of remedial procedures keyed to the child's behaviour patterns.[3]

Two USOE-funded projects illustrate continuing effort to identify brain-injured children earlier in life, to describe their behaviour more precisely, and to discover remedial steps. One sought an age specific definition of the structure of the intellect, a description of the patterning of the growth of intellect and knowledge of the relationships of patterns of intellectual ability and patterns of growth to academic achievement. The approach was to gather cross-sectional and longitudinal data about these for three successive years from brain-injured children.[4] Another project proposed to develop diagnostic and remedial materials and methods based on Piaget's theory of intellectual growth. A basic assumption was that Piaget's postulate of an

1   W. Meyer, 'Cerebral Dysfunction', in: Johnson and Blank (eds), op.cit., p. 181–209.
2   H. Birch and S. Chess, 'Behavioral Development in Brain Damaged Children', *Archs. gen. Psychiat.* (Chicago, Ill.), Vol. 11, 1964, p. 596–603.
3   J. Gallagher, 'Children with Developmental Imbalances', in: W. Cruickshank (ed.), *The Teacher of Brain Injured Children*, Syracuse, N.Y., Syracuse Univ. Press, 1966.
4   M. Bortner, *Cognitive Development in Children with Brain Damage, 1968–71*, New York, N.Y., Yeshiva Univ. (USOE GO 8-071272-3317).

invariate progression through stages of cognitive development would facilitate comparison of normal and handicapped children, expedite assessment of the type and degree of learning deficit and guide efforts to develop remedial steps geared to abilities characteristic of each stage of cognitive development.[1]

In 1967 NINDS funded a five-year programme aimed at differentiating children with aphasic disorders from other severely handicapped children. Analysis of neurological status, perceptual functions and psycholinguistic abilities was proposed.[2] The National Institute of Child Health and Human Development (NICHHD) initiated support of a long-range project on hyperactivity. The aims were to develop more objective measures of activity and to study the effects of combinations of drug and behavioural treatments on hyperactivity.[3]

Illustrative publications include two focused on social adjustment; one a post-school follow-up of severely orthopaedically handicapped high school graduates,[4] and a second in which the accuracy of social perception of physically handicapped and non-handicapped college students was studied in experimental social groupings.[5] In a study of perception the eye movements and eye–hand co-ordination of a large number of children with visual perceptual deficits were compared with normal children; the results were interpreted as indicating dysfunction in the oculomotor system.[6] The effect of a brain-stimulating drug was examined in a study of the oral language production of youngsters with cerebral dysfunction. It was reported that the drug increased the quantity but not the abstract quality of speech.[7]

Close of the decade

By the end of the decade, the concept of learning disability and enquiry prompted by this concept was remarkably wide-ranging. The scope achieved was revealed in a comprehensive and systematic survey of pertinent research which appeared in 1969.[8] This breadth is best seen by examining the topical

1   R. Bulgarella, *Facilitation of Cognitive Development among Children with Learning Deficits, 1968*, East Lansing, Mich., Michigan St. Univ. (USOE GO 8-080054-2694).
2   J. Eisenson, *Research Program of Aphasic Involvements in Children, 1967–1972*, Stanford, Calif., Stanford Med. School (NINDS RRTC 24DH3).
3   R. Sprague and J. Werry, *Hyperactivity in children, 1968–1971* (NICHHD RRTC 24BA1).
4   D. Brieland, 'Follow-up Study of Orthopedically Handicapped High School Graduates', *Except. Children Res. Rev.*, Vol. 33, No. 8, 1967, p. 555–62, Washington D.C., NEA.
5   R. Ingwell *et al.*, 'Accuracy of Social Perception of Physically Handicapped Persons', *J. soc. Psychol.* (Provincetown, Mass.), Vol. 72, No. 1, June 1967, p. 107–16.
6   A. Kirshner, 'Comparison of Eye Movement and Eye-hand Coordination Scores between Normal and Handicapped', *Am. optometric Assoc. Journal* (St. Louis, Mo.), Vol. 38, No. 7, July 1967, p. 561–6.
7   R. Creager *et al.*, 'Effect of Menthylphenidate on Verbal Productivity of Children with Cerebral Dysfunction', *J. Speech Hear. Res.* (Washington, D.C.), Vol. 10, 1967, p. 623–8.
8   J. Chalfant *et al.*, *Central Processing Dysfunctions in Children: Review of Research, 1968*, Inst. for Res. on Exceptl Child., Univ. of Ill., 1969.

organization of the report. The authors' chose the phrase 'central processing dysfunction' in lieu of 'learning disability'. The major loci of dysfunction were conceived as in the analysis of sensory information, the synthesis of sensory information, and in symbolic operations. The processes involved in analysis of sensory information were the auditory, the visual and the haptic (combinations of touch and movement). Two processes were seen as underlying the synthesis of sensory information: the integration of stimuli from multiple sensory channels and short-term memory. The symbolic operations examined were auditory language, reading, writing and quantitative language (arithmetical and mathematical operations). The authors' use of task analyses of complex processes such as the acquisition of auditory-receptive language as a means of organizing their survey of research is of special interest. It reflected in part a widely shared concern to subject learning tasks to more intense and precise analysis.

In the 1969 NEA–CEC-sponsored review of research, the category of the crippled or otherwise health impaired child was represented solely by learning disabilities.[1] The reviewer, Kass, noted that the term learning disability had achieved wide acceptance and she called attention to a conference devoted to definition and clarification of the concept.[2] Central to the final position taken by the conference was the statement: 'learning disability refers to one or more significant deficits in essential learning processes requiring special education for remediation'. Appraising the status of the field, Kass offered the opinion that the disciplines seemed to be groping for new theories and research directions and characterized most contemporary writing as being more in the nature of position papers than research reports. She was concerned about the difficulty of adapting traditional research designs to clinical research and cited Kirk's espousal of the case study approach as a possible way of finding common ground between the demands of research and the realities of clinical work with learning disabled children.[3]

Research took many directions. One was the attempt to develop methods of prediction on the basis of patternings of scores derived from various combinations of established tests or on the basis of new patterns of analysis of scores on single tests. Another approach was to compare the judgements made by teachers with predictions made by the use of tests. An important direction was taken in studies which probed learning disabilities along a developmental dimension. Thus analysis of the vocabulary responses of 9-year-old normal and learning disabled children suggested that at age 9 inadequate language function correlated more with reading ability than with perceptual ability.[4] Another study led to the conclusion that poor readers in

1   C. Kass, 'Learning disabilities', *Rev. Educ. Res.*, Vol. 39, No. 1, February 1969, p. 71–82.
2   Northwestern Univ. & USOE, *Proceedings of the Conference on Learning Disabilities and Interrelated Handicaps, 1967*, Evanston, Ill., Northwestern Univ.
3   S. Kirk, *Diagnosis and Remediation of Psycholinguistic Disabilities*, Urbana, Ill., Univ. of Ill. Press, 1966.
4   H. Birch et al., 'Auditory-visual Integration in Normal and Retarded Readers', *Am. J. Orthopsychiat.*, Vol. 34, October 1964, p. 852–61.

the fifth grade had difficulty with the symbolic content of language whereas the first-grade child had trouble with visuo-spatial relations, hence raising doubt as to the validity of comparisons across age groups.[1] The potential scope of enquiry opened through research on learning disabilities was well demonstrated in a study of 400 elementary school children who evidenced behaviour problems.[2] Teachers rated the children's behaviour and the ratings were factor analysed. A factor, disoriented behaviour, was found to be related to the cognitive-motor dysfunction in some children but not in others. The authors' hypothesized that in those children in whom disoriented behaviour and cognitive-motor dysfunction were related, the emotional disturbance was secondary to learning difficulties. It was conjectured that among the remaining children the emotional disturbance was the primary disorder.

It has been noted that USOE support of research on the crippled and otherwise health-impaired child had dropped precipitously by the end of the decade. Two studies can be cited in this period. One explored the value of intensive aural and visual modality stimulation in correcting disturbed speech motor patterns in cerebral palsy.[3] The other focused on personnel utilization in the treatment-training of the cerebral-palsied. The aim was to adapt the method of Peto of Hungary, who advocates that all treatment and training be administered by one professional person, to conditions in the United States where direct services are usually rendered by multiple specialists.[4]

An analysis of learning problems is of interest. In this investigation the habituation of EEG responses to auditory stimuli was taken as a form of learning with the intent to compare the 'learning' of brain-injured, communication-impaired children and that of normal children. These findings were to be complemented by behavioural observations, e.g. tests of auditory memory and receptive language.[5] Several publications are of special import. Extensive revision and standardization of the ITPA was reported. This is perhaps the single most comprehensive instrument for the remediation-oriented diagnosis of children's psycholinguistic abilities and disabilities.[6] United States Senator Yarborough, sponsor of proposed new legislation in the field of learning disabilities, gave a first-hand account of federal legislative action in this and related areas of handicap.[7] Finally, for those concerned with

1   J. Reed, 'Reading Achievement as Related to Differences Between WISC Verbal and Performance I.Q.', *Child Development*, Vol. 38, September 1967, p. 834–40.
2   E. Rubin *et al.*, *Behavioral Learning Disabilities Associated with Cognitive Motor Dysfunction*, Detroit, Mich., Lafayette Clinic, 1967.
3   R. Love, *The Effect of Sensory Modality Stimulation on the Disarthria of the Cerebral Palsied, 1969*, Nashville, Tenn., Vanderbilt Univ., (USOE GO 9-522043-2326).
4   J. House, *An Integrated Treatment and Educational Approach to the Management of Cerebral Palsy, 1969*, Eau Claire, Wis, Wisc. St. Univ. (USOE GO 9-592149-4540).
5   B. Weber, *Habituation of Auditory Evoked Response in Normal and Neurological Impaired Children, 1969–1971*, Child Development and Res. Centr, Univ. of Wash. (RRTC 24CC1).
6.   J. Paraskevopoulos and S. Kirk, *Development and Psychometric Characteristics of Revised Illinois Test of Psycholinguistic Abilities*, Urbana, Ill., Univ. of Ill. Press, 1969.
7.   R. Yarborough, 'Learning Disabilities Act of 1969, a Commentary', *J. learning Disabilities*, (Chicago, Ill.), Vol. 2, No. 9, September 1969.

problems of distinguishing between organic and experiential factors in the etiology of childhood psychopathology, a forthcoming essay is of particular value as an authoritative overview and rigorous critique of current knowledge.[1]

The decade in retrospect: some impressions

Research on the education of the neurologically intact crippled or otherwise health-impaired child decreased markedly. One explanation seems to reside in Jordan's observation that these children differ very little from the non-handicapped in the way or the amount they will learn, given the opportunity to learn.[2] The focus of study has shifted from special education to a concern with the special delivery of education to such children.

Cerebral palsy continued to engage investigators in many disciplines and diverse settings. Most remarkable, however, was the growing absorption in learning disabilities. In 1968 the first of a series, 'Progress in Learning Disabilities', appeared under Myklebust's editorship.[3] Volume III of Hellmuth's *Learning Disorders*, came out in 1968.[4] *The Journal of Learning Disabilities* went into its second volume in 1969 and the Association for Children with Learning Disabilities held its sixth annual international conference.

Why this phenomenal growth? Many factors must be considered. The concept of learning disability is pivotal to many attributes of behaviour and to the interests of many disciplines. The research touches on learning, perception, language and affective processes. It crosses the boundaries of most traditional categories of handicap and challenges neurologists, psychiatrists and psychologists as well as educators. For example, one of the early influential works was by the psychiatrist, Rabinovitch.[5] This plurality of disciplinary interest is reflected in the many terms used to denote the concept of learning disability.

The concept is attractive for methodological reasons. Viewed in a perspective such as that of Kirk, the learning disabilities approach offers promise of significant advances in diagnostic and remedial operations which have their basis in the behaviour of the child. Because of this, practice is easily translated into operations familiar to teachers. Parenthetically, such advances would enhance the value of biologically oriented research which in so far as it aims at the understanding or control of behavioural variables will gain from increases in precision in the description and analysis of behavioural variables. Also, while learning disabilities may be an organic problem in their

1 H. Quay and J. Werry (eds), 'Organic Factors in Childhood Psychopathology', *Children's Behavior Disorders* (in press).
2 L. Jordan, op. cit.
3 Myklebust, op. cit.
4 J. Hellmuth (ed.), *Learning Disorders*, Vol. III, Seattle, Wash., Special Child Publications, 1968.
5 R. Rabinovitch, 'Reading and Learning Disabilities', *American Handbook of Psychiatry*, chap. 43, p. 857–69, New York, N.Y., Basic Books, 1959.

original cause, their major treatment—as of now—rests within the educational sphere.

Another factor is that the *zeitgeist* is favourable to the study of early human development, and confrontation with learning disabilities almost inevitably leads to inquiry into early development. Psycholinguistic disabilities, for example, frequently occur at the rote or automatic-sequential level of language behaviour. These attributes of language are evidently shaped early in language development. Adequate prevention or early correction of such deficits awaits knowledge of the processes involved in their formation. The urgency of the task is evident when one considers the probability that such errors of behavioural development approach irreversibility at a rapid rate and the likelihood that the aberrance they introduce is magnified as development proceeds.

Finally, some very human considerations have undoubtedly played a part in the rapid development of the field of learning disability. The fact that the label, and the concept, 'learning disability', offers much more hope and is eminently less stigmatizing than such labels as 'mental retardation' or 'emotional disturbance' has probably played a part in mobilizing support among both professionals and parents.

Research on the
emotionally disturbed

Although the sixties saw an upsurge of interest in mental health, concern for children came late.[1] The prevailing attitude toward children who suffer emotional disturbance and behaviour disorder was at best one of marked ambivalence. Education did not escape this ambivalence. Whereas public school provisions for such children increased greatly, USOE support for research declined in spite of an increase in requests for such support. The most authoritative explanation of this discrepancy was that very little of the proposed research was educational in nature.[2] At the level of conceptual concern, the role of education in this area of handicap remained an unresolved issue at the close of the decade.

It was urgent that public policy and professional philosophy be clarified. The nation was experiencing a rapid rise in delinquency and anti-social conduct among the young. Public schools were the site of much of this dis-

---

1   *Crisis in Child Mental Health ...*, *op. cit.*
2   M. Mueller, 'Trends in Support of Educational Research for Handicapped', *Except. Children* (Arlington, Va), Vol. 34, No. 7, March 1968, p. 523–30.

order. Surveys by the National Institute of Mental Health (NIMH) revealed
that the rates of first admission and the census of children in mental hospitals
had increased much faster than the number of children in the general population. Projections indicated this trend would accelerate for some time to
come.[1] Clearly both education and the mental health field were confronted
with an enormous challenge.

Early developments

In the late 1950s most educational thinking about emotional disorder was
dominated by psychiatric theory which stressed unconscious motivation and
virtually defied translation into educational procedure. The need for paradigms relevant to education was indicated by the estimated incidence of 10
to 25 per cent emotional disorder among children of school age. It was in
this climate that Bower and Holmes in 1959 prepared the first review of the
literature on the relationship of emotional disorders to academic disabilities.[2]
Noteworthy were attempts to screen children through use of information from
the school setting, such as Bower's index of adjustment,[3] studies of teacher–
pupil and parent–child interactions around school matters, and efforts to
utilize teachers more effectively in detecting, prognosticating and improving
students' mental health. Evidence of significant association between specific
academic ability and emotional factors came largely from the field of reading.
It was claimed that the greater the child's psychopathology the greater the
likelihood of reading disability.[4] A popular but elusive research aim was to
determine if anxiety had differential effects on reading and arithmetic.

The relationship between emotional disturbance and delinquency was the
source of many unresolved theoretical and practical issues throughout the
decade. This was reflected in research reviews some of which treated the two
separately whereas others approached them as components of a common
handicapping condition. Thus in the 1959 NEA research review the two
were handled separately. Kvaraceus characterized movement in the field of
delinquency in the following way:

The last six years have shown significant trends in research on delinquent youth . . .
Delinquents were more precisely defined and differentiated as to types. Validations
of prediction tools and techniques were carried out. Factors generating delinquent
behavior in the culture and the subculture, as well as the psyche, received greater

1   Project Re-ED, *New Concepts for Helping Emotionally Disturbed Children*, Nashville, Tenn.,
    Kennedy Center for Research on Ed. and Human Development, Peabody College, 1969.
2   E. Bower and J. Holmes, 'Emotional Factors and Academic Achievement', *Rev. Educ.
    Res.*, Vol. 29, No. 5, December 1959, p. 529–44.
3   E. Bower, 'A Process for Identifying Disturbed Children', *Children*, Vol. 4, July 1957,
    p. 143–7.
4   A. Fabian, 'Reading Disability: an Index of Pathology', *Am. J. Orthopsychiat.* (Broadway,
    N.Y.), Vol. 25, April 1955, p. 319–29.

emphasis. School-community efforts to prevent and control delinquency were better based on integrated conceptualizations, although evaluations of such efforts appeared crude and subjective.[1]

Significant monographs of the time included the report of a major project by NEA,[2] in which the delinquent was defined as 'the persistent and serious norm violator who has come to the attention of official authority'. A major weakness in this definition was wide variation in laws and norms, and their enforcement, throughout the nation. A pivotal theoretical issue was the relative weight to be assigned to culture and to forces within the individual psyche in the etiology of delinquency, e.g. the NEA project conjectured that 75 per cent of norm violations stem from cultural forces. Illustrative theoretical formulations included the concept of a 'delinquent sub-culture' of boys and gangs described as 'non-utilitarian, malicious and negativistic', a view in which the lower-class *milieu* was seen as a generating norm violating behaviour largely through imitative example and prestige-achieving and status-building conduct, and the concept that deviant behaviour grows out of the discrepancy between values and opportunities provided by social position in American society. Positions in which intra-individual factors were stressed included Erickson's concept of ego identity and psycho-social moratorium (delay in adult commitment) as important to the genesis of delinquent behaviour.

Reviewing efforts at early identification and prediction Kvaraceus noted that few investigators had successfully defined the pre-delinquent and stressed the danger of the self-fulfilling prophecy inherent in the identification and labelling of delinquents.

Research on the emotionally and socially handicapped was surveyed in a single chapter in the 1963 NEA–CEC review.[3] The authors, Morse and Dyer, cited an estimate of 4 to 7 per cent seriously maladjusted children. Bower's use of teacher, peer and self-appraisal was recognized as a most promising approach to identification.[4] The need to define empirically demonstrable traits was stressed and pioneer efforts in this direction by Peterson and Quay noted.[5] Two other studies must be mentioned. A study of superior adult males led to the conclusion that their childhood histories did not differ from those of psychiatric patients on variables traditionally thought to be prognostic of later maladjustment; the authors cautioned that in the absence of a theory of positive adjustment, serious errors are apt to be made in theor-

1 W. Kvaraceus, 'The Delinquent', *Rev. Educ. Res.*, Vol. 29, No. 5, December 1959, p. 545–51.

2 W. Kvaraceus *et al.*, *Delinquent Behavior: Culture and the Individual.*, Washington D.C., NEA Juvenile Delinquency Project, 1959.

3 W. Morse and C. Dyer, 'Emotionally and Socially Handicapped', *Rev. Educ. Res.*, Vol. 33, No. 1, February 1963, p. 109–25.

4 Bower, op. cit.

5 D. Peterson *et al.*, 'Personality and Background Factors in Juvenile Delinquency', *J. consult. Psychol.* (Washington, D.C.), Vol. 23, October 1959, p. 395–9.

izing about pathology.[1] Research on 200 disturbed boys, half of whom had learning problems, suggested that information about family dynamics and socio-economic factors was sufficient to differentiate those with learning problems from the 'normal' learners.[2]

The Joint Commission on Mental Illness and Health[3] had identified the school as a strategic agent in getting at the source of behaviour disorders, but that there was no consensus as to the school's role. Some recommended a therapeutic role, others saw primary prevention and early intervention as strategic, while still others viewed schools in varying degrees as engendering emotional disturbance, particularly where no effort was made to accommodate to differing cultural backgrounds and values of the students.[4] In considering special classes, Morse and Dyer noted that there was no coherent design for appraising classroom procedures or therapies affecting learning. The literature consisted largely of monographs of a general nature among which they characterized Kirk's as especially meritorious.[5] Studies of school consultation and liaison with mental health specialists pointed up the need to find better ways to put mental health expertise at the disposal of teachers and school administrators without expecting them to become mental health experts.[6] Other research foci included exploration of behaviour modification techniques, client-centred therapy, principles of group dynamics, and psychopharmacological agents to improve the school performance of disturbed children. Redl's 'life space interviewing' technique was seen by some as having potential utility in educational settings.[7]

Delinquency and emotional disturbance were treated separately in the 1963 CEC review.[8] Quay examined delinquency and cited definition as a persisting problem.[9] The most popular definition was legal; but it fell short because of differences in the law, and variations in enforcement as a function of locale and socio-economic class of the offender. He expressed the conviction that success in identifying psychological correlates of delinquency depended at least partially upon the ability to group delinquents into homogeneous categories and presented studies in that direction. These took such forms as detailed analyses of the level and nature of perceptual-cognitive development of known delinquents, the measurement of carelessness and impulsivity

1   H. Renaud et al., 'Life History Interviews with One Hundred Normal American Males: Pathogenicity of Childhood', Am. J. Orthopsychiat. (Broadway, N.Y.), Vol. 31, October 1961, p. 786–802.
2   I. Harris, Emotional Blocks to Learning, New York, N.Y., Free Press of Glencoe, 1961.
3   Action for Mental Health . . ., op. cit.
4   F. Riessman, The Culturally Deprived Child, New York, N.Y., Harper Bros, 1962.
5   S. Kirk, 'Behavior Deviations in Children', Educating Exceptional Children, p. 330–64, Boston, Mass., Houghton Mifflin Co., 1962.
6   G. Caplan, 'Mental Health Consultation in Schools', Elements of Community Mental Health Program, 77–85, New York, N.Y., Milbank Memorial Fund, 40 Wall St, 1956.
7   F. Redl, 'Strategy and Technique of Life Space Interview', Am. J. Orthopsychiat (Broadway, N.Y.), Vol. 31, July 1961, p. 584–90.
8   Kirk and Weiner (eds), op. cit.
9   H. Quay, 'The Delinquent', in: Kirk and Weiner (eds), op. cit., p. 318–56.

among delinquents, and analysis of data from police records in search of characteristics which differentiate delinquents who repeat from those who do not. With regard to studies of etiology. Quay was of the opinion that whereas theories of etiology tended to focus on either social or intra-psychic factors, research indicated that combinations of the two accounted for more variance than either alone, and that theorization was more promising when directed at homogeneous groupings of delinquents. Significant theretical and empirical works included Shaw and McKay's exploration of the ecology of delinquency and crime in American cities,[1] and Lander's study, based on 8,000 court hearings, in which census tracts of a large city were described in terms of such variables as residents' education, housing conditions, home ownership patterns, and racial make up; the multiple correlation of these variables with delinquency rate was 0.89.[2] Another project was based on data from 2,000 children who had taken the Minnesota Multiphasic Personality Inventory (MMPI) eight years previously, and about whom follow-up court data was available. Analysis of MMPI scores and data about later delinquent or non-delinquent behaviour revealed that boys with non-delinquent MMPI scores who later became delinquent, differed from boys with similar MMPI scores who did not become delinquent in that they came from economically poorer homes, had parents with poor social adjustment, and suffered poor relationships within the family. In general all boys who became delinquent had parents who were poorer role models and who were less stable.[3]

Haring, who summarized studies of emotional disturbance in the 1963 CEC review, chose a wide range of studies, e.g. research on early infantile autism, the effects of institutionalization on personality, analyses of the parents of severely disturbed children and a number of biologically oriented investigations.[4] Among these, three are of special interest. One undertook to adapt the life space interviewing technique to children in a therapeutic summer camp. In this reality-oriented approach, child care staff utilize real-life personal and social incidents to help children analyse the feelings and the behaviour of themselves and others *at the time* the incidents occur on the fundamental assumption that social behaviour is learned and can be facilitated by immediate guided analysis and evaluation of real-life predicaments.[5] An evaluation of a programme for hyper-aggressive boys who suffered learning disturbances was noteworthy as a pioneer effort to discern and describe pupil, teacher and task characteristics and interactions in a school setting and to

1   C. Shaw et al., *Juvenile Delinquency and Urban Areas; a Study of Rates of Delinquency in American Cities*, Chicago, Ill., Univ. of Chicago Press, 1942.
2   B. Lander, *Towards an Understanding of Juvenile Delinquency*, New York, N.Y., Columbia Univ. Press, 1954.
3   R. Wirt et al., 'Personality and Environmental Factors in the Development of Delinquency', *Psychol. Monogr.*, Vol. 73, No. 485, 1959.
4   N. Haring, 'The Emotionally Disturbed', in: Kirk and Weiner (eds), op. cit., p. 291–317.
5   W. Morse et al., 'Group Life Space Interviewing in a Therapeutic Camp', *Am. J. Orthopsychiat.* (Broadway, N.Y.), Vol. 29, 1959, p. 27–44.

define and refine specific teaching techniques for work with this type of child.[1] In the third study, three methods of teaching disturbed children were compared over a two-year period. Disturbed children in the 7–12 age range were randomly placed in one of three types of classrooms: (a) a structured environment in which each child was programmed in terms of his ability; (b) regular classrooms with the teacher given special assistance by the school social worker and psychologist; or (c) a 'traditional' special class in which the curriculum followed pupils' interests and little structure was imposed upon the class. Reportedly, those in (a) showed greatest academic and social gains, those in (b) produced greater academic gains than those in (c), but children in (c) achieved better social adjustment than those in (b).[2]

Haring's over-all impressions of movement in the field are still relevant:

The role of education is becoming increasingly more dominant in providing programs for emotionally disturbed children . . . it is important to study several methods of teaching, curricula, class size and class-room conditions. Once the most effective combination of techniques and conditions has been determined, it would then be worthwhile to compare results from special classes (including medical and psychological consultation) with other treatment facilities, such as community child guidance clinics and private therapists.

In 1961, Project Re-ED, a long-range developmental programme for emotionally disturbed children, was begun by the states of Tennessee and North Carolina, Peabody College and NIMH. Re-ED was initially conceived as an experiment in manpower conservation in which carefully selected and trained teachers would be used to compensate for an acute shortage of psychiatrists, psychologists, etc. Teachers were used in the conviction that disturbed children suffer disturbed cognitive as well as affective functions and that helping them to gain and keep both or achieve academic proficiency and social competence was fundamental in their remediation. The concept that these children need to 'keep school' as well as 'keep life' was an integral element in the reality-oriented programme.[3]

Middle years

In a 1966 review of research on emotional disturbance and social handicap, Balow called attention to two contemporary movements: one political, the other professional.[4] The political was a national upsurge in interest in prob-

1   R. Newman, 'Assessment of Progress in Treatment of Hyper-aggressive Children with Learning Disabilities', *Am. J. of Orthopsychiatry*, Vol. 29, 1959, p. 633–43.
2   N. Haring *et al.*, *Educating Emotionally Disturbed Children*, New York, N.Y., McGraw-Hill 1962.
3   *Crisis in Child Mental Health* . . ., op. cit., p. 310–12.
4   B. Balow, 'The Emotionally and Socially Handicapped', *Rev. Educ. Res.*, Vol. 36, No. 1, February 1966, p. 120–33.

lems of the poor and the handicapped. The professional was '. . . the dramatic return to learning theory, specifically behaviorism, for the treatment of disturbed behavior'. Work in case finding and prediction produced several studies which confirmed the value of teachers' judgements of maladjustment. A major study indicated below-average I.Q. level in a sample of 50,000 delinquents tested during a thirty-year period.[1] Studies directed at determining the effect of emotional disturbance on academic achievement were inconclusive and Balow declared it a moot question as to whether disturbed children are necessarily academically disabled.

A 1964 study of public school classes for emotionally disturbed and socially handicapped children in the United States revealed that the commonly stated goal of the schools was to foster normal educational development leading to return to regular class; most teachers had no special preparation, the pupils were mostly boys of upper elementary age, behaviour control was the problem cited most by teachers (motivation was next), and group discussion and interaction were seldom used in the classes.[2] A critical review of studies aimed at determining the long-term effects of school-related treatment yielded the conclusion that there was little difference in adulthood between children who applied for treatment and got it, and those who applied, but did not get treatment.[3]

Five studies supported by USOE illustrate the type of work initiated in this period. A project to develop, refine and validate a new system of classifying children with behaviour disorders proposed to make use of pre-school learning experiences, current behaviour patterns, psychological and educational treatment procedures, and the child's level of functioning before and after the therapeutic classroom experience.[4] A five-year follow-up of the academic achievement of emotionally disturbed children who had received clinical treatment utilized children selected so that half of them had been treated alone, and half had been joined by their parents in the treatment programme.[5] Another study hypothesized that consistency between home and school in child management would reduce the incidence of maladaptive classroom behaviours.[6] Support was given to a proposal to develop criteria and procedures for estimating the prevalence of chronic social and emotional problems in public schools, making use of descriptions and classifications of

1   G. Caplan *et al.*, 'Distribution of Juvenile Delinquent Intelligence Test Scores Over 34 Years', *J. clin. Psychol.* (Brandon, Vt), Vol. 20, April 1964, p. 242–7.

2   W. Morse *et al.*, *Public School Classes for Emotionally Handicapped: a Research Analysis*, Washington, D.C., NEA, CEC, 1964.

3   W. Lewis, 'Continuity and Intervention in Emotional Disturbance', *Except. Children* (Arlington, Va), Vol. 31, May 1965, p. 465–75.

4   R. Cromwell, *The Development of Behavior Dimensions for Emotionally Disturbed Children, 1965–1969*, Nashville, Tenn., Vanderbilt Univ. (USOE G 32-52-0450-5001).

5   C. Ashcraft, *School Achievement in Emotionally Handicapped Children Following Clinic Treatment, 1965–1967*, Nashville, Tenn., Peabody College (USOE G 32-52-0120-5026).

6   R. Collins, *Treatment of Classroom Behavior Problems by Employment of a Partial-milieu Consistency Program*, 1966, Eugene, Oreg., Univ. of Oregon (USOE G 4-6-068366-1592).

problem behaviour carried out by public school personnel.[1] A survey-research type activity aimed at determining how academic failure is related to attitudes toward life acquired by children from their parents by inter-viewing parents of children failing in school and parents of those who were academically successful in search of value orientations which correlate with school performance.[2]

In 1964, NIMH funded a five-year study to determine the effect of social isolation on the automatisms, e.g. hand flapping, of autistic children. The child's behaviour was to be observed under varying conditions of social and non-social stimulation so as to analyse automatisms on dimensions such as rhythmicity, patterning, etc.[3] A 1965 grant initiated research on the growth of psychophysiological patterns in infancy. The subjects were normal infants; the approach was to describe and analyse behavioural and physiological (heart rate, etc.), responses of the child from birth to sixteen weeks and to correlate these with maternal and birth history, and with behaviour later in life.[4]

Two psychiatric publications illustrate continued concern with classification problems. A 1964 conference report summarized various experimental and clinical-administrative efforts to improve diagnostic classification in child psychiatry by use of factor analysis, direct clinical observation, etc.[5] Subsequently, a special psychiatric study group reported on its efforts to bring order into classification by striking a balance among psychosomatic, development, psychosocial and pathogenic considerations.[6]

Graubard and Miller, who encompassed both emotional disturbance and delinquency in a 1968 survey of research on behavioural disorders cited an emphasis upon learning theory and technique, sharper focus on the *behaviour* of disturbed children, and a concomitant move away from a speculative psychodynamic tradition as trends of the time.[7] They stressed continuing difficulties of comparison of research method and findings due to the lack of a common base in definition, description or criteria of behaviour disorders. A project of special interest was a pioneer effort to study the interaction of

1   R. Mattson, *Assessment and Treatment of Deviant Behavior, 1966–1969,* Eugene, Oreg., Univ. of Oregon (USOE G 4-6-061308-0571).

2   R. Currie, *Variations in Value Orientations of Parents of Academically Successful and Unsuccessful Children, 1966–1967,* Los Angeles, Calif., Univ. of S. Calif. (USOE G 32-14-1490-6027).

3   A. Sorosky, *Systematic Observation of Autistic Behavior, 1964–1968,* Los Angeles, Calif., Dept of Child Psychiatry, Univ. of Calif. Medical Centr (RRTC 24JE1).

4   W. Bridger et al., *Growth of Psychophysiological Patterns in Infancy, 1966–1969,* Bronx, N.Y., Einstein Medical College, Yeshiva Univ. (RRTC 24AA8).

5   R.Jenkins & J. Cole (ed.), 'Diagnostic Classification in Child Psychiatry', *Psychiatric Research Report,* October 1964, Washington D.C., 1700 Eighteenth St, N.W.

6   Group for Advancement of Psychiatry, *Psychopathological Disorders in Childhood,* 1966, New York, N.Y., Group for Advancement of Psychiatry, 104 E. 25th St.

7   R. Graubard and M. Miller, 'Behavioral Disorders', in: Johnson and Blank (eds), op. cit., p. 262–303.

temperament and environment in normal and disturbed children in which temperament was inferred from such behavioural attributes as activity level, rhythmicity, distractibility and persistence; and environment was defined in terms of the response patterns of parents and other significant persons. Reportedly, temperament–environment interactions were significantly different among the disturbed.[1] Research aimed at better description and analysis of behaviour produced new behaviour rating scales for use with elementary-age children[2] and a broadly based factor analytic study of teacher's ratings in which factors designated as conduct problems, inadequacy-immaturity, and personality problems, accounted for 75 per cent of variance.[3] A growing number of investigations of socio-economic correlates of the management of children's behaviour disorders strongly indicated that patterns of initial referral, diagnosis and disposition of children are very much influenced by the socio-economic level of the family and the biases of professional agencies and staff. Among higher socio-economic groups, the diagnosis tended toward 'anxiety state', obsessive-compulsive or somatic complaint and psychotherapy recommended. Among lower-class children, the diagnosis tended toward personality disorder or borderline psychoses, and psychological therapy much less apt to be recommended. A study of potential delinquents is noteworthy in that it was reported that the Glueck Delinquency Prediction Scale was 80 per cent effective in identifying elementary school children who later showed some type of delinquent behaviour.[4] Among treatment interventions, one offered much methodological promise. The research aim was to identify various dimensions of teaching style which might be related to the behaviour of disturbed children in regular classrooms. Classroom activities were sampled by videotape, and these subjected to intensive systematic analysis. Teachers were said to vary in ability to 'manage' the surface behaviour of disturbed children, to communicate that they knew what was actually going on in the class, and to effect group transition from one activity to another. These abilities were judged to be essential in contending with classroom misbehaviour and maintaining a comfortable 'climate'.[5] In their review,[6] Graubard and Miller observed that the study pointed the way toward the delineation of specific teacher behaviours pertinent to pupil misbehaviour, indicated the possibility that teacher behaviour *per se* may be a source of insights about

1   S. Chess *et al.*, 'Interaction of Temperament and Environment in Production of Behavioral Disturbance in Children', *Am. J. Psychiat.* (Washington, D.C.), Vol. 120, 1963, p. 142–7.
2   G. Spivack, 'Devereux Elementary School Behavior Rating Scale', *J. special Educ.* (Philadelphia, Pa), Vol. 1, 1966, 71–90.
3   H. Quay *et al.*, 'Personality Patterns of Pupils in Special Classes for Emotionally Disturbed', *Except. Children* (Arlington, Va), Vol. 32, 1966, p. 297–301.
4   E. Hodges, 'Follow-up Study of Potential Delinquents', *Am. J. Psychiat.* (Washington, D.C.), Vol. 120, 1963, p. 449–53.
5   J. Kounin, 'Managing Emotionally Disturbed Children in Regular Classrooms', *J. Educ. Psychol.* (Washington, D.C.), Vol. 57, 1966, p. 1–13.
6   See note 7, page 174.

treatment approaches, and suggested that more attention be given to the management styles and techniques of teachers.

Research undertaken with USOE support showed a trend toward the adaptation of new knowledge and techniques into classroom operations or evaluation of these. Thus, one project proposed to evaluate a 'behaviourally engineered' classroom design. The experimenters designed a programme for emotionally disturbed children aimed first at helping children pay attention, follow directions, explore their environment, and get along with others, and then at improving their academic and intellectual performance.[1] An evaluation project aimed to determine the effectiveness of Project Re-ED by comparing Re-ED 'graduates' with untreated controls on specific measures relevant to school and home adjustment.[2] A substantial effort to demonstrate the utility of the functional analysis of the behaviour in the classroom management of elementary-age children with problems in academic learning and social adjustment was begun. The approach was first to train the teachers, then to test the validity of the methods of functional analysis of behaviour, and lastly to evaluate the total operation.[3] Comparison of traditional special class methods, individual centred reinforcement, and group-focused reinforcement techniques, was the object of another grant. Maladjusted boys with serious reading problems were randomly assigned to one of the three groups. One entire group was to contract for rewards, with payoff dependent upon all members reaching a specified level of proficiency in reading.[4]

Three additional projects under differing auspices are pertinent. NIMH initiated support of a five-year study of 'the stress of school'. A specific aim was to find ways in which teachers can become more sensitive to individual differences and intervene when the child's development goes awry. Of administrative interest was the aim to find ways to pass on developmental information gained in one year of the child's school career to the next.[5] State funds enabled evaluation of a major state-supported day and residential programme for the education and treatment of emotionally disturbed children. Data came from parental interviews, behaviour ratings of the children and records of academic achievement.[6] A study which reflected growing interest in ecologically oriented research got under way with university support. The re-

1 F. Hewet et al., Demonstration and Evaluation of an Engineered Classroom Design for Emotionally Disturbed Children in the Public School, 1967, Los Angeles, Calif., Univ. of Calif. (USOE G 4-7-062893-0377).

2 L. Weinstein, Evaluation of a Program for Pre-educating Disturbed Children, 1967, Nashville, Tenn., Peabody College (USOE G 2-7-062474-2207).

3 N. Haring, The Application of Functional Analysis of Behavior by Teachers in a Natural School Setting, 1968, Seattle, Wash., Univ. of Wash. (USOE G 0-8-070376-1857).

4 P. Graubard, The Use of Indigenous Grouping as the Reinforcing Agent in Teaching Maladjusted Boys to Read, 1968, New York, N.Y., Yeshiva Univ. (USOE G 0-8-080174-4383).

5 N. Lambert, The Stress of School, 1968–1972, Berkeley, Calif., Univ. of Calif. (NIMH RRTC 24OG5).

6 H. Hoffman, Evaluation of Selected Aspects of Program for Education and Treatment of Emotionally Disturbed School Age Children, 1968–1969, Waltham, Mass., Dept of Ed. and Dept of Mental Health (RRTC 24QD).

lationship between demographic variables, such as integrity of the family and chronic illness, and aspects of the child's growth, such as personality, creativity, and academic achievement, was to be determined.[1]

Two additional publications need special mention. The report of a conference on teacher-learning processes which featured new methodologies to describe and analyse affective–social interactions among disturbed pupils and the teacher exemplified emerging concern to deal with ecological issues.[2] A collection of original research papers and selected review articles which focused upon child psychiatry and child development revealed increased recognition of mutual interest, and needed *rapprochement* of methodology in psychiatry, pediatrics, psychology and education.[3]

Close of the decade

Learning theory was becoming more influential in both research and service. Public school programmes flourished numerically: states and territories reporting special education for the emotionally disturbed increased more than threefold since 1960. In a comprehensive review of behaviour disorders, Glavin and Quay noted growing reliance on teacher ratings of behaviour, citing an extension of Bower's earlier work[4] which seemingly confirmed his conclusions about the predictive value of teachers' ratings of pupils' behaviour. Progress in epidemiology was impaired by variation in definition of behaviour disorder; estimates of prevalence ranged from 4 to 22 per cent in school populations studied.[5] Among studies of school achievement was a project in which children were characterized as having psychosomatic problems, exhibiting aggressive behaviour, having school difficulties, being school phobic, or displaying neurotic-psychotic behaviour, and these categories related to school performance. All categories scored lower in arithmetic than in reading, children with school difficulties had the lowest mean performance in reading and arithmetic, and the highest academic achievement was found among neurotic-psychotic children.[6] Social and psychological research on parent–child, and especially mother–child, relationships increased in amount. In one such study, four patterns of child–parent involvement in therapy were

1 R. Soar, *Home and School Factors in Pupil Mental Health, 1968–1969*, Gainesville, Fla., Univ. of Fla., College of Ed. (RRTC 24OG4).

2 R. Knoblock & J. Johnson (eds), *Teaching Learning Process in Educating Emotionally Disturbed Children*, Syracuse, N.Y., Syracuse Univ. Press, 1967.

3 S. Chess & A. Thomas (eds), *Annual Progress in Child Psychiatry and Child Development*, New York, N.Y., Robt Brunner Inc., 1968.

4 Bower, op. cit.

5 J. Glavin and H. Quay, 'Behavior Disorders', *Rev. Educ. Res.*, Vol. 39, No. 1, February 1969, p. 83–102.

6 L. Schroeder, 'A Study of the Relationships Between Five Descriptive Categories of Emotional Disturbance and Reading and Arithmetic Achievement', *Except. Children* (Arlington, Va), Vol. 32, October 1965, p. 111–12.

evaluated: no treatment for parent or child, treatment for child alone, group therapy for parents alone, and a combination of individual treatment for the child and group therapy for parents. The reported findings were, respectively, slight improvement, a decline, significant improvement, and in the last arrangement, no change.[1] A similar study reported by Glavin and Quay concluded that treatment approaches which focused on parents and teachers, and excluded the disturbed child, were most effective in improving the child's behaviour when teachers' perceptions of childrens' behaviour were used as the criterion of behaviour disorder.

A study of therapeutic education is of interest. In this work, an intervention curriculum was designed to explore ways of helping delinquent children overcome social and academic deficits. The curriculum and methods were derived from assumptions about the effect of the disorganized family and social *milieu* on the child's learning style from which a profile of the child's cognitive-affective style was drawn. Pupils alternately served as participant or observer and were coached in rating other children's responses and identifying behaviours which helped or hindered learning.[2] Research on the classroom behaviour style of teachers included a study which reported that in a sample of five treatment centres, teacher styles differed; a child-permissive pattern was commonest, followed by a teacher-centred structured style. The permissive style was associated with high non-directiveness and nurturance, and low dominance and orderliness.[3]

The Glavin and Quay review concluded with a useful discussion of past and prospective research. Some selected comments include:

... While research on classroom behavior styles of teachers suggested that teachable techniques can be delineated for facilitating improved class room behavior, the research also suggested that with these techniques the disturbed child could often be managed in the regular, as well as the special class. Furthermore, research on the effects of special class placement has often been conflicting.

... the emphasis for educational intervention perhaps should be placed on eliminating concrete observable behavior of immediate concern and remediating the frequently concomitant academic learning problems rather than on the more ambitious restructuring of personality. Of equal importance to educators, recent learning theory research has shifted from the use of conditioning to influence an individual child's behavior to the application of operant principles to the entire classroom ...

These reviewers also concluded that research showing the importance of parental influences on the child suggested the need for a more encompassing intervention programme. They recognized and emphasized that implemen-

1   R. D'Angelo *et al.*, 'An Evaluation of Various Therapy Approaches', *J. Psychol.* (Provincetown, Mass.), Vol. 67, September 1967, p. 59–64.
2   S. Minuchin *et al.*, 'A Project to Teach Learning Skills to Disturbed Delinquent Children', *Am. J. Orthopsychiat.* (Broadway, N.Y.), Vol. 37, April 1967, p. 558–67.
3   J. Johnson, *Classroom Behavior Styles*, East Lansing, Mich., Mich. St. Univ., 200 p. (Dissertation Abstracts 26:4450, No. 8).

tation of such a programme would require a broader concept of the accountability of special education in the socialization of disturbed children inasmuch as it would necessitate more intimate and intensive involvement with parents.

Decreasing support of research in this area by USOE was reflected in the availability of only two summaries of projects supported in 1969. One aimed at producing a training film for use in the in-service training of teachers of disturbed children. Principles and practices of crisis intervention with adolescents were to be portrayed.[1] The other consisted of a grant to a research organization in support of an intensive evaluation effort. A previously developed programme for training teachers to manage social and emotional problems in the classroom was to be revised, adapted and refined in broader practice, and given a full-scale field try-out and evaluation.[2]

Several special reports and scholarly publications suggest major trends at the close of the decade. The Joint Commission on Mental Health of Children urged attention to several broad research issues. Among these were longitudinal studies of human development that cover the entire life span, multivariate research directed toward the multiple criteria which characterize the mentally healthy child and adolescent, and the need to obtain more basic knowledge of the nature of social structures and their impact on people. Cross cultural studies were urged because, 'Cross cultural studies provide wider ranges of variation in normal practice than can be found in any single society . . . They provide a crucial test for distinguishing between what is programmed in genetic human nature and what is culturally induced'.[3]

The report of a major conference on the acquisition and development of values reflected growing concern to get at the cognitive, affective and motivational roots of moral values. Psychological, social and cultural, and historical factors are considered in a way which gives a 'feel' for a variety of contemporary positions on these issues.[4] The report of a 'panel of visitors' who had scrutinized Project Re-ED from its beginning is of interest. The 'panel' was composed of an eminent member of each of the fields of education, psychiatry, psychology and sociology, who concluded:

. . . Project Re-ED represents a conceptually sound, economically feasible, and demonstrably effective approach to helping emotionally disturbed children, including the moderately disturbed and some seriously disturbed . . . We therefore recommend the adoption of the Re-ED program as a primary resource for the help of emotionally disturbed children of the Nation.[5]

1   F. Wilderson, *Crisis Intervention, Secondary Schools, 1969*, Minneapolis, Minn., Univ. of Minn. (USOE G 0-9-332018-2777.)
2   G. Gropper, *Evaluation of a Program to Train Teachers to Manage Social and Emotional Problems in the Classroom, 1969*, Pittsburgh, Pa, Am. Inst for Research (USOE OEC 0-9-482025-3726).
3   *Crisis in Child Mental Health* . . ., op. cit.
4   'The Acquisition and Development of Values', *Perspectives on Research* (Bethesda, Md), NICHHD, May 1968.
5   Project Re-ED, op. cit.

A collection of readings, *The Nature of Teaching*, is notable. The editor assembled, integrated and interpreted in a most helpful manner a number of original works which have been influential in theory, research and practice in the sixties. Among five sections, two—'Teaching as Social Interaction' and 'Teaching as the Emergence of Human Potential'—bear directly on issues vital to the education of the emotionally disturbed.[1]

The decade in retrospect: summary and impressions

Summary

In the early sixties there were relatively few educational programmes for emotionally disturbed children. Most research was designed to provide the necessary background for establishing and administering programme in the schools. The research was primarily atheoretical, and aimed at determining the incidence of disorder, systematizing definitions in the area of juvenile delinquency and emotional disturbance, and developing ways whereby emotionally disturbed children could be identified and diagnosed in the public school system. By the end of the decade there was a substantial increase in the number of programmes for emotionally disturbed children in the public schools and a corresponding increase in research on methods of educations. Teacher behaviour in the classroom was being more carefully scrutinized and attention was given to the conduct and academic progress of emotionally disturbed pupils. Alternative classroom structures were considered. Special methods of reinforcement, such as rewarding entire groups instead of individuals, were weighed. The role of parents, peers, psychological therapists, courts and schools was studied in isolation and in combinations to determine optimum methods of influencing the behaviour of the child.

Simultaneously with the search for effective teaching styles and classroom structure, researchers began to evaluate the long-range results of established programmes. A growing body of research pointed to the dominant influence of social class on the diagnosis, treatment and disposition of emotionally disturbed children and juvenile delinquents. Ties between emotional disturbance and factors such as family stability, social class and the child's early behavioural characteristics cast serious doubts on the effectiveness of special classes or psychological therapy in combating emotional and social disturbance. The new directions in research gave rise to several theoretical trends.

Impressions

Increasing willingness to rely upon the observation and analysis of the behaviour of disturbed children was a striking trend. Two developments encouraged the trend. First was the growing acceptance of teachers' observations and appraisals of children's behaviour and the systematization of these obser-

1 L. Nelson (ed.), *The Nature of Teaching: a Collection of Readings*, Waltham, Mass., Blaisdell Publishing Co., 1969.

vations by the use of behaviour inventories, behaviour check lists, etc. Second was the 'dramatic return to learning theory, specifically behaviorism, for the treatment of disturbed behavior'.[1] Both the theory, and the technology generated from the theory, focus on behaviour *per se* as the primary datum of concern to theorist, therapist or teacher.

A trend toward more modest expectations in the treatment and the education of the disturbed child became apparent in the latter part of the decade. Thus, Glavin and Quay's suggestion that more emphasis be put upon the elimination of concrete disturbing behaviours and the remediation of academic learning problems, rather than upon restructuring the personality.[2] Hobbs presented the view that the problem of the disturbed child is basically one of the breakdown of an ecological system composed of child, family, neighbourhood, school and community.[3] Asserting that traditional mental health approaches have borrowed too heavily from the medical tradition, where anything less than a cure is regarded as a failure, he wrote:

... *Cure is a meaningless concept in mental health.* Effective living is intrinsically problematic. Our goal should be to help restore small social systems to a point of adequacy where the probability of continued successful function outweighs the probability of failure. The task is to get child, family, neighborhood, school and community just above the threshold in the requirement that each component makes of other components, and then to get out of the system. Mental health agencies cannot take over indefinitely the responsibilities of the normal socializing agencies of our society.

The move toward the experimental explication of the ecological point of view was important. The work of Minuchin and colleagues who constructed profiles of children's cognitive-affective style on the basis of observation of the child and his family *milieu*,[4] and a study of the interaction of temperament and environment by Thomas and his group,[5] who have recently described their work in monograph form,[6] are illustrative. Another instance appears in a report describing efforts by special educators to modify deviant social behaviours in a variety of classroom settings. The authors acknowledge a focus on reinforcing contingencies in the classroom, but also subscribe to a social learning emphasis which takes form in their attempt to develop a 'psychology of the dispenser', reflecting their concern to study the dispenser of reinforcers, the teacher, as a crucial social agent.[7]

1 Balow, op. cit.
2 Glavin and Quay, op. cit.
3 N. Hobbs, 'Reeducation, Reality and Community Responsibility', in: J. Carter (ed.), *Research Contributions from Psychology to Community Mental Health,* chap. 2, p. 7–19, New York, N.Y., Behavior Publications Inc., 1968.
4 Minuchin, op. cit.
5 S. Chess *et al.,* 'Interaction of Temperament and Environment . . .', op. cit.
6 A. Thomas *et al., Temperament and Behavior Disorders in Children,* New York, N.Y., New York, Univ. Press, 1968.
7 A. Benson (ed.), *Modifying Deviant Social Behaviors in Various Classroom Settings,* Eugene, Oreg., Dept of Special Ed., Univ. of Oregon, 1969, 79 p.

One of the most comprehensive and sophisticated attempts to approach behaviour ecologically is found in the work of Kelly. Beginning with the premise that the functions of individuals and organizations are interdependent, he has set about systematically explicating the processes that mediate between the setting in which behaviour occurs and the behaviour of individual group members. A primary focus of the work is upon the coping styles and preferences of teenagers in their high school environment. Regarding this ecological approach to behavioural-social events, he has written:

... The interest in this work is in knowing as much about adaptive societies as adaptive persons. The approach to this integrative task is to study both processes in contrasting environments, and to learn how people emerge in changing societies, without limiting the development of either themselves or the evolution of the society...[1]

It was noted before that although requests for support of research on emotional disturbance increased, USOE grants declined. The best available explanation of this discrepancy is that the proposed research was not basically educational in nature. The role of education in emotional disturbance is a fundamental issue and some research of the decade points toward clarification if not resolution of the issue. The trends toward a focus on the behaviour of children, the acceptance of more modest expectations of therapy and education, and the developing ecological orientation offer the most immediate, albeit tenuous, promise of clarification of the issue. Most of us—theorists, researchers, administrators and practitioners, and the institutions we serve—follow a map of the mind which marks it off into three provinces: the cognitive, the affective, and the conative. Many, perhaps most, legal, administrative and clinical provisions for handicapped children are based on this age-old view of the mind. There is a desperate need for a new and better cognitive map as a guide toward a common language to facilitate communication among those with responsibilities in education, mental health and corrections, and for the development of procedures co-ordinated with that language. Hopefully, such a map would clarify the role of education in the prevention and management of emotional disturbance and behaviour disorders in children.

---

1   J. Kelly, 'Toward an Ecological Conception of Preventive Interventions', in: J. Carter (ed.), *Research Contributions from Psychology to Community Mental Health*, chap. 6, p. 76–100, New York, N.Y., Behavior Publications Inc., 1968.

Research on the
hearing-impaired

Research in this area tends to fall into two categories: work with the deaf and work with the hard of hearing. The pre-lingually deafened child poses the most severe challenge to educational research because of his marked educational retardation. This educational retardation and other evidence that the pre-lingually deaf differ significantly from normal hearing children in their cognitive functioning have been the subject of much speculation and considerable research. A persistent question is whether an individual deprived of oral-aural language experience from birth or shortly thereafter can develop 'normal' cognitive capabilities. If he does develop these capabilities can they be demonstrated by the use of tests and measures standardized on normal hearing and normal speaking subjects? Some of the most promising as well as the most provocative research of the decade aimed at explicating factors underlying these educational and cognitive concerns.

Early developments

DiCarlo reviewed work with the deaf and hard of hearing in a 1959 review.[1] He noted basic research by Wever, Davis, Galambos and Bekesy in the preceding five years and the lack of comparable progress in research on education and rehabilitation. He stressed the need for study of the adjustments required at critical periods in the life of the deaf and urged more longitudinal studies. Failure to standardize definitions of hearing impairment was a major problem which DiCarlo attributed to lack of agreement as to whether to take account of the effect of hearing loss on oral communication. He cited research on differential diagnosis which made use of galvanic skin responses (GSR) and electroencephalography (EEG) as a means of testing auditory sensitivity. Studies of incidence yielded ranges of 0.5 to 0.7 per cent as the estimated proportion of school-age children in need of special education. DiCarlo estimated that less than 25 per cent of those in need received special education services. He noted an increase in pre-school training and attributed this to improved transistorized hearing aids and increased interest on the pert of speech and hearing centres; e.g. the John Tracy Clinic Correspondence Course for Home Instruction. Several studies confirmed according to

1   L. DiCarlo, 'The Deaf and Hard of Hearing', *Rev. Educ. Res.*, Vol. 29, No. 5, December 1959, p. 497–518.

DiCarlo, '. . . previous findings that deaf children are at least four years educationally retarded, even when first-rate instruction is provided'. He referred to an earlier review of research and clinical experience which indicated that if the child's residual hearing was not utilized, auditory perception would atrophy,[1] and a number of studies which suggested that early auditory training complemented by the use of hearing aids resulted in better language learning. Gesell's observation that early hearing loss resulted in retarded comprehension, sound production, social rapport and social behaviour was cited as illustrative of the impact of impaired hearing on personality.[2]

USOE-sponsored research included a six-year study of cognitive development and performance in children with normal and defective hearing which had the aim of assessing performance in children of three age-groups in different areas of cognition, in learning and in non-language tasks, and with respect to information either acquired incidentally or under test conditions. The approach was to gather information that would permit cross-sectional as well as longitudinal comparison as a function of age, sex, and residential versus day-school status among the hearing-impaired.[3]

In a 1963 survey, Lane cited a recent estimated rate of 0.14 per cent of hard of hearing in the United States.[4] He described research on differences in audiometric responses, work on EEG and GSR indices of hearing acuity, and attempts to determine the reliability of testing procedures. Other research included study of the use of hearing aids in combination with auditory training, the relative value of monaural and binaural aids, and the dangers of excessive amplification. Research in the communications area included a monograph which recorded the visual communication system of the American deaf for the first time.[5] Furth reported extensive work on the role of language in concept development and concluded from studies of the deaf that language was not essential.[6] A major study of the influence of institutionalization on psychoeducational development reported that pupils in residential schools were better adjusted personally and socially but lagged in oral communication skills when compared with day-school pupils.[7]

1   L. DiCarlo, 'Auditory Training: Research Trends and Practical Applications', *Volta Rev.* (Washington, D.C.), Vol. 56, October 1954, p. 351–3.
2   A. Gesell, 'Psychological Development of Normal and Deaf Children in Preschool Years', *Volta Rev.* (Washington, D.C.), Vol. 58, March 1956, p. 117–20.
3   M. Templin, *Study of Cognitive Development and Performance in Children with Normal and Defective Hearing, 1958–1964,* Minneapolis, Minn., Univ. of Minn. (USOE CSAE 7775).
4   H. Lane, 'The Deaf and the Hard of Hearing', *Rev. Educ. Res.,* Vol. 33, No. 1, February 1963, p. 48–61.
5   W. Stokoe, 'Sign Language Structures: An Outline of Visual Communications Systems of American Deaf', *Studies in Linguistics,* Buffalo, N.Y., Dept. of Anthro. and Ling., Univ. of Buffalo, 1960, 78 p. (Occasional Papers No. 8).
6   H. Furth, 'Influence of Language on Development of Concept Formation in Deaf Children', *J. abnormal Soc. Psychol.,* Vol. 63, November 1961, p. 386–9.
7   S. Quigley *et al., Institutionalization and Psychoeducational Development of Deaf Children,* 1961 (CEC Research Monogr., Series A., No. 3).

In another 1963 review, Quigley surveyed the hard of hearing, summarizing studies between 1931 and 1960 chosen for their focus on behavioural and social effects of hearing loss.[1] He expressed the conviction that a completely adequate definition of the hard of hearing must take account of three variables: degree of loss as measured in decibels, age of onset of hearing loss, and type of hearing loss. Age of onset was stressed because of its importance to language and speech development, e.g. prelingual versus postlingual loss. Type of loss applied particularly to conduction defects, which can often be compensated by sound amplification, in contrast to sensori-neural impairments which are much less amenable to compensatory devices. In his concluding comments he urged that behavioural definitions of hearing impairment be developed, making use of the techniques of audiology, psychology, sociology and education. He argued that such definitions are especially necessary to research on educational environments and procedures.

In another review in 1963, Mangan, who reviewed research on the deaf, defined the deaf child as 'one who was born with little or no hearing, or who suffered the loss early in infancy before speech and language patterns were acquired'.[2] He summarized studies of intelligence, adjustment and education in the period 1918–60. The studies cited showed a shift of interest away from broad comparisons of intelligence in hearing and deaf subjects toward more specific aspects of intellectual functioning of the deaf. Studies of the social behaviour and competence of the deaf revealed deafness as a potent social handicapper. In his conclusion he noted that, whereas research had indicated where the deaf stood as a group, it had too seldom shed light on the reasons for their educational deficiencies or on programmes and procedures that promise better results.

Two USOE-supported studies illustrate directions of inquiry in this period. A three-year project aimed at the development of a 'non-verbal' language for the profoundly deaf young child got under way in 1960.[3] Evaluation of a programme of educational audiology was the purpose of a six-year grant which began in 1961. The subjects were hard of hearing children from 6 to 42 months of age of whom twelve were placed in a *unisensory* programme and sixteen in a multisensory programme. The unisensory or experimental group got hearing aids, auditory training at home, and took part in special group sessions. At age 3 they entered an enriched nursery school programme which featured similar emphasis upon auditory training.[4]

1   S. Quigley, 'The Hard of Hearing', in: Kirk and Weiner (eds), op. cit., p. 155–82.
2   K. Mangan, 'The Deaf', in: Kirk and Weiner (eds), op. cit., p. 183–225.
3   M. Meier, *The Role of Non-verbal Symbols in the Education of the Deaf, 1960–1962,* Flushing, N.Y., Queens College (USOE CSAE 8412).
4   J. Stewart, *An Evaluation of the Effectiveness of Educational Audiology upon the Language Development of Hearing Handicapped Children, 1961–1966,* Denver, Colo., Univ. of Denver (USOE GSAE 89966).

Middle years

Rosenstein in a 1966 overview of research[1] called attention to two recent compilations of research; a 1963 issue of the *Volta Review* and the *Proceedings of the International Congress on Education of the Deaf*.[2] Prevalence estimates of 0.2 to 0.4 per cent of children in need of special education, and 3 to 6 per cent with milder hearing loss were cited. Etiological studies inquired into the relationship of climate to type of hearing loss, the possible deleterious effects of newer antibiotics on the inner ear, and the incidence of early total deafness due to heredity, e. g. an estimate of 50 per cent due to genetic factors of which 40 per cent was attributed to recessive genes.[3] Research on intelligence as cited by Rosenstein continued to show the deaf inferior to the hearing in verbal comprehension and abstract figural reasoning, and the question of whether the deaf were inferior when the criterion of language was removed remained a lively issue. The value of early training in finger-spelling was seen as an issue in communications research. Speech research focused on study of the intelligibility of deaf speech and on variables involved in the self-monitoring of the loudness of speech by the deaf. Speech-reading research aimed at the relationship of speech-reading to intelligence, specific cognitive abilities, personality, and motivation, but was generally inconclusive. Major developments in research on auditory training included comparison of normal and hard of hearing subjects with respect to auditory discrimination, articulation and lip-reading, analysis of serial rote learning ability in hard of hearing and deaf subjects. Research on educational achievement again confirmed that the severely hearing impaired are educationally retarded. Language-learning research reflected an interest in improving grammatical competence. A number of studies explored programmed instruction as a means of more efficient language learning.

Four USOE studies initiated in 1964 illustrate a focus on problems of learning and of teaching. In a project to develop instructional materials for the very young deaf, emphasis was placed upon syntactical properties of language. The approach was to teach word order in sentences making use of such visual aids as blocks of wood, colour coded according to grammatical units.[4] Another study evaluated programmed visual presentation of verbal materials as a means of teaching reading to hearing impaired children. It was concluded that a comprehensive programme would be prohibitive; e. g. to

1   J. Rosenstein, 'The Deaf and the Hard of Hearing', *Rev.Educ.Res.*, Vol.36, No.1, February 1966, p.176–98.
2   *Proceedings of the International Congress on Education of Deaf and 41st Convention of American Instructors of Deaf, 1964.* Washington, D.C., U.S.Govt Printing Office.
3   D. Sank *et al.*, 'The Role of Heredity in Early Total Deafness', *Volta Rev.* (Washington, D.C.), Vol.65, November 1963, p.461–70.
4   R. Krug, *A Project to Develop and Evaluate the Effectiveness of Instructional Materials for the Deaf: Designed to Emphasize the Syntactical Meaning of Words, 1964–1966,* Boulder, Colo., Univ.of Colo. (USOE G 32-15-0180-1019).

take children from beginning to fourth grade reading level would require 800 programmes of thirty to forty frames each.[1] Analysis of verbal and non-verbal learning aimed at exploring variables that determine the child's preference for a single modality in verbal learning; e.g. visual versus auditory presentation.[2] A hearing clinic undertook a demonstration of home teaching for the parents of young deaf children in which parents and other family members visited the clinic for instruction. The approach was sufficiently superior to the traditional clinic procedure to cause the clinic to adopt the home teaching approach as a permanent procedure.[3]

Studies begun in 1965 included use of motion picture films in teaching speech reading. The effectiveness of self-instruction with films, teacher instruction plus practice with films, and instruction by teacher alone, was compared.[4] The value of visual display of acoustic co-ordinates of speech as an aid in teaching intonation and inflection was studied. It was reported that speech volume and duration were most significant factors in visual display.[5] Another grant enabled the development of an English curriculum for deaf students at the high school level. The approach was to construct teaching materials on the basis of analysis of the learning difficulties of secondary school deaf students, and normal hearing students learning a second language and to apply methods of structural linguistics and mathematics in putting together the curriculum.[6] A plan for the systematic development of a master survey plan to be utilized in conducting a national prevalence survey of speech and hearing problems in school children was funded by USOE.[7] Deployment of USOE resources in 1966 took form in a project to compare the categorization behaviour of deaf and hearing children. Through the use of a forced choice technique, children categorized visual stimuli on dimensions derived from Vigotsky's work.[8] Another effort aimed at enlarging the American sign language. The approach was to create 500 to 1,000 new signs, test them for recognition, acquisition and retention, and develop ways of teaching them. The subjects were to be upper-class students at Gallaudet

1 B. Karlsen, *Teaching Beginning Reading to Hearing Impaired Children, Using a Visual Method and Teaching Machines, 1964–1966*, Minneapolis, Minn., Univ. of Minn. (USOE G 7-33-0400-230).

2 J. Gaeth, *Verbal and Non-verbal Learning in Children Including Those with Hearing Losses, Part II: 1964–1967*, Detroit, Mich., Wayne State Univ. (USOE C 4-10-033).

3 E. Lowell, *Home Teaching for Parents of Young Deaf Children, 1964–1966*, Los Angeles, Calif., John Tracy Clinic (USOE G 32-14-0000-1014).

4 A. Neyhus, *Self-teaching in the Development of Speech Reading in Deaf Children, 1965*, Evanston, Ill., Northwestern Univ. (USOE G 32-23-0790-5002).

5 L. Dolansky, *Teaching Intonations and Inflections to the Deaf, 1965*. Boston, Mass., Northeastern Univ. (USOE C 5-10-356).

6 H. Bornstein *et al.*, *An English Curriculum for Deaf Students at the Secondary Level, 1965–1968*, Wash., D.C., Gallaudet College (USOE C 5-10-006).

7 F. Hull, *National Prevalence Survey of Speech and Hearing Disorders in School Children, 1965–1968*, Fort Collins, Colo., Colorado State Univ. (USOE G 32-15-0050-5010).

8 T. Silverman, *Categorization Behavior and Achievement in Deaf and Hearing Children, 1966*, New York, N.Y., New York Univ. (USOE G 32-42-0930-6030).

College.[1] Development of a home teaching programme for parents of deaf children under age 3 in which parent, child and tutors were to work together in a model residence which simulated a homelike atmosphere was undertaken to develop techniques of teaching speech, speech-reading, and auditory skills which could be intensively applied in the child's home.[2] Another grant underwrote a plan to develop a system for the annual collection of demographic, audiometric and educational information about children in the nation who need special educational services because of hearing impairment.[3]

Craig, who summarized selected studies in the period 1960–68, centred on educational considerations, occupational assessment, psychosocial aspects of deafness and communication modalities.[4] In this treatment of the work he examined exemplified growing awareness in the field of the need to separate and control the effects of variables often confounded in earlier research. A doctoral dissertation which dealt with the major causes of secondary handicaps in deaf children is an example of this trend. Over 1,400 children, 3 to 21 years of age, with hearing loss of sixty-five decibels or more, were studied. The aim was to determine etiology where possible, and to ascertain the relationship of etiology to the variables, multiple handicap, brain damage, audiometric status, emotional adjustment, intelligence, communication skills and educational achievement. The etiological factors found were (by percentage): heredity, 5.4; Rh factor, 3.1; prematurity, 11.9; meningitis, 8.1; maternal rubella, 8.8; unknown, 30.4; other, 32.3. The genetic group had by far the lowest incidence of multiple handicap (6.5 as compared with 71, 68, 38 and 54 per cent respectively for the other designated etiologies), the least evidence of brain damage, the least maladjustment, the highest intelligence, and except for speech and speech-reading, the highest educational achievement.[5]

A procedure for assessing the written language of deaf students was developed from compositions of residential and day students of ages 10 to 19. It made use of such criteria as length of composition, variety and versatility of word choice and usage, grammatical correctness and spelling plus teachers' standard grading procedures.[6] Provisions for the education of mentally retarded deaf students in residential schools for the deaf were summarized.[7]

1   H. Bornstein, *Enlarging the Sign Language for Instructional Purposes, 1966–1969,* Washington, D.C., Gallaudet College (USOE GEOG 2-6-061624-1890).
2   F. McConnell, *A Home Teaching Program for Parents of Very Young Deaf Children, 1966–1968,* Nashville, Tenn., Vanderbilt Univ. (USOE G 32-52-0450-6007).
3   A. Gentile, *Annual Census of Hearing Impaired Children, 1966–1968,* Washington, D.C., Gallaudet College (USOE G 32-18-0070-6009).
4   W. Craig, 'Hearing Impaired', in: Johnson and Blank (eds), op. cit., p. 135–80.
5   M. Vernon, 'Multiply Handicapped Deaf Children: Study of Significance and Causes', (unpublished doctoral dissertation, Claremont Grad. College, Claremont, Calif., 1966).
6   E. Stuckless *et al., Assessment of Written Language of Deaf Students,* Washington, D.C., 1966 (USOE Coop. Research Project No. 2544).
7   R. Anderson *et al., Provisions for Education of Mentally Retarded Deaf Students in Residential Schools for Deaf,* Washington, D.C., Dept HEW, U.S. Office of Ed., 1966.

A sociometric investigation of the self concept of deaf children in residential and day-care settings, revealed that institutionalized children were more self-accepting than day-care students and hearing children who were controls.[1] The relationship between early manual communication and later achievement and adjustment was the object of research which led to the conclusion that early acquisition of a manual communication system was advantageous.[2] A later study arrived at similar conclusions.[3]

Three quite disparate studies initiated in 1967 under USOE auspices are of interest. The relationship of air and bone conduction in the testing of hearing was examined with the aim of determining if threshold responses at high levels of intensity in children with sensorineural pathology were mediated through auditory or vibro-tactile channels, or both. The vibro-tactile pathways were blocked with local anesthesia and hearing retested. Anesthesia blocked all responses from the totally deaf, shifted the air conduction threshold five decibels for deaf children with residual hearing, and had no effect on the threshold of normal hearing children.[4] Research on frequency transposition in hearing aids was the object of a three-year experiment with various combinations of frequency selectivity, frequency-response pro-emphasis, and frequency transposition applied to the incoming speech signal before presentation to the listener.[5] Comparative study of the most and the least creative students in grades four to eight was begun. Students were studied by procedures ordinarily used with normal hearing subjects with provocative results; e.g. the most creative deaf males had considerably higher intelligence test scores than others, whereas work with hearing subjects indicates a positive but low correlation between intelligence and 'creativity', etc.[6]

Studies that got under way in 1968 took several directions. A grant to staff in a school for the deaf went to provide descriptive data on the deaf child's reading vocabulary.[7] Study of the communication patterns in classes for the deaf was the intent of a study in which Flander's technique for assessing

1   H. Craig, 'Sociometric Investigation of the Self Concept of Deaf Children', *Am. Ann. Deaf* (Washington, D.C.), Vol. 110, 1965, p. 456–78.

2   J. Birch *et al.*, 'Relationship Between Early Manual Communication and the Later Achievement of the Deaf', *Am. Ann. Deaf* (Washington, D.C.), Vol. 111, 1966, p. 444–52, 499–504.

3   K. Meadows, 'Early Manual Communication in Relation to the Deaf Child's Intellectual, Social, and Communicative Functioning', *Am. Ann. Deaf* (Washington, D.C.), Vol. 113, 1968, p. 29–41.

4   E. Nober, *Air and Bone Conduction Thresholds of Deaf and Normal Hearing Subjects Before and During the Elimination of Cutaneous-tactile Interference with Anesthesia, 1967*, Syracuse, N.Y., Syracuse Univ. (USOE G 1-7-063073-2198).

5   J. Pickett, *Research on Frequency Transposition for Hearing Aids, 1967–1969*, Washington, D.C., Gallaudet College (USOE G 2-7-070070-1522).

6   M. Gallagher, *A Comparative Study of the Most Creative and Least Creative Student in Grades 4 to 8 at the Boston School for the Deaf, Randolph, Mass., 1967*, Chestnut Hill, Mass., Boston College (USOE G 1-7-008771-0480).

7   T. Silverman, *The Deaf Child's Knowledge of Words, 1968–1969*, New York, N.Y., Lexington School for Deaf (USOE GO 8-00419-1792).

communicative interactions in the classroom was to be the basic research tool.[1] Further study of the imagery used by deaf children in learning paired-association material was the subject of another grant.[2] An important follow-up of Nober's earlier study (cited above) of thresholds in the severely deaf aimed at developing audiologic criteria to differentiate between auditory and vibrotactile thresholds.[3] A two-year grant enabled a project aimed at demonstrating the feasibility of using existing vocational and technical schools, and junior colleges, which serve normal hearing students, to serve deaf graduates of secondary schools.[4]

Additional research under varying auspices warrants mention. A project undertaken with local support had the aim of evaluating the Perdoncini method of auditory training. Criterion measures were auditory reception skills and programming was such that subject responses dictated the degree of difficulty of subsequent learning tasks.[5] The U.S. Children's Bureau undertook support of a five-year study of early diagnosis of hearing. In this work children were to be tested during sleep with auditory-evoked responses and these findings checked against otologic, audiologic and neurological evaluation.[6] A treatise on the biological foundations of language by Lenneberg, which presented data from congenitally deaf children and those deafened accidentally early in life, espoused the thesis that biologically based cognitive factors are predominant in the development of human language.[7]

Close of the decade

Research on the deaf and the hard of hearing as surveyed by Quigley led him to comment that there had been a considerable increase in research on the deaf but relatively little with the hard of hearing who make up the largest number of hearing-impaired and are the most neglected educationally. He characterized most of the research on the deaf as being in the area of either psychology or hardware technology. Except for work on manual communi-

1   W. Craig, *Communication Patterns in Classes for Deaf Students, 1968*, Pittsburgh, Pa, University of Pittsburgh (USOE GO 8-000640-1863).

2   D. Allen, *Modality Aspects of Mediation in Children with Normal and with Impaired Hearing Ability, 1968*, Detroit, Mich., Wayne State Univ. (USOE GO 8-070837-1858).

3   E. Nober, *The Development of Audiologic Criteria to Differentiate between Auditory Thresholds and Vibro-tactile Thresholds of Deaf Children, 1968*, Syracuse, N.Y., Syracuse Univ. (USOE GO 8-080321-4463).

4   W. Craig, *Improved Vocational Training Opportunities for Deaf People, Research Component, 1968–1969*, Pittsburgh, Pa, Univ. of Pittsburgh (USOE GVRA-RD-2723-5-68).

5   R. McCroskey, *Evaluation of the Perdoncini Method of Auditory Training, 1968–1969*, Wichita, Kans., Inst. of Logopedics, Wichita State Univ. (RRTC 24GE3).

6   I. Rapin *et al.*, *Early Diagnosis of Hearing Using Auditory Evoked Responses, 1968–1973*, New York, N.Y., Einstein College of Med., Yeshiva Univ. (RRTC 24GB2).

7   E. Lenneberg, *Biological Foundations of Language*, New York, N.Y., John Wiley & Sons, 1967.

cation there were few studies of education of the deaf.[1] He singled out a conference on the education of the deaf sponsored by the U.S. Department of Health, Education, and Welfare as promising future gains.[2]

Discussing incidence, he referred to a national household survey of binaural loss; highlights were that more 4 million persons had some hearing loss, that over 850,000 needed hearing aids to hear and understand speech, almost 750,000 were classified as able to comprehend only a few spoken words, and about 2.5 million could understand most spoken words. About 22 per cent of the hearing-impaired reported current use of hearing aids.[3] He noted that a rubella epidemic which had spread from the eastern to the western seaboard in 1963–65 was currently a significant factor in the cause of hearing impairment of children entering school and cited a recent summary of studies of the etiology of deafness.[4]

Other work included a 1968 summary of fifty years' work on I.Q. and hearing impairment.[5] A major work in the cognitive area was a review by Furth who offered further evidence in support of his position that language is not necessary to the development of logical thinking.[6] In the mental health area, a monograph describing the findings of a long-range programme of research on emotional disorders in the deaf was notable.[7]

Language and communication research received major attention in Quigley's survey. Major contemporary reviews were cited.[8] Major trends in research on language and communication were seen by him to be:

... (a) the design and construction of devices to transform the acoustic signal of speech into another sensory modality (usually visual but vibratory in some cases), which would provide an additional feedback to replace or supplement the deficient auditory feedback ... (b) transformation of the acoustic signal into a visual signal to serve as a receptive means of communication to replace speechreading or to improve the teaching of it, (c) the development of devices to produce a frequency shift in the acoustic signal to utilize whatever residual hearing a deaf child might have, (d) an increased interest

1   S. Quigley, 'The Deaf and the Hard of Hearing', *Rev. Educ. Res.*, Vol. 39, No. 1, February 1969, p. 103–23.
2   *Education of the Deaf*, Washington, D.C., Dept HEW, U.S. Govt Printing Office, 1968.
3   A. Gentile *et al., Characteristics of persons with impaired hearing*. Washington, D.C., Dept HEW, Govt Printing Office, 1967 (Public Health Service Publ. No. 1000, Series 10, No. 35).
4   M. Vernon, 'Current Etiological Factors in Deafness', *Am. Ann. Deaf* (Washington, D.C.), Vol. 113, March 1968, p. 106–15.
5   M. Vernon, 'Fifty Years of Research on the Intelligence of Deaf and Hard of Hearing Children: a Review of Literature and Discussion of Implications', *J. Rehabil. Deaf*, (Knoxville, Tenn.), Vol. 1, January 1968, p. 1–12.
6   H. Furth, 'A Review and Perspective on Thinking of Deaf People, *Cognitive Studies*, Vol. I, Seattle, Wash., Special Child Publications (in press).
7   J. Rainer *et al., Comprehensive Mental Health Services for Deaf*, New York, N.Y., Dept Med. Genetics, N.Y. Psych. Inst., Columbia Univ., 1966.
8   J. Pickett, 'Sound Patterns of Speech: an Introductory Sketch', *Am. Ann. Deaf* (Washington D.C.), Vol. 113, March 1968, p. 120–6.

in the use of manual communication . . ., and (e) application of recent developments in linguistics and psycholinguistics to the language and communication problems of the deaf child.[1]

Of special interest in the language field was a method of 'cued speech' in which hand positions and configurations are used to facilitate speech-reading by supplementing facial and labial cues which are not readily discriminable to the speech-reader. The method may be used to instruct the child in areas of his own speech in which non-visible cues predominate.[2] A remarkable adaptation of technology to the needs of the deaf occurred in the introduction of an eyeglass hearing aid which provides visual cues of speech features not readily visible to the speech-reader.[3] An approach to early amplification and training said to have aroused much interest was that of the 'HEAR' Foundation.[4] Increased interest in manual communication was attributed at least partially to earlier research by Soviet investigators.[5]

According to Quigley, research on language development was marked by the use of newer linguistic techniques. Two studies utilizing the 'cloze' technique in which every nth word is deleted from a reading selection, and the reader must fill in the missing word, reported that the deaf were inferior to normal hearing subjects on both semantic and syntactic aspects of the task. Other research on spoken and written language indicated that the deaf were inferior to the hard of hearing and the normal hearing in quantity of word output, quality of syntax, the use of adverbs, pronouns and auxiliaries, and in the variety and versatility of word choice and usage.[6]

Little objective research on education could be reported. Work cited by Quigley aimed at the adjustment of hard of hearing students in regular colleges, assessment of the abilities and academic progress of graduates of residential schools for the deaf who were attending regular college, and attempts to provide supporting services to deaf and hard of hearing students in regular colleges and vocational schools. Social and vocational studies were characterized by a greater emphasis upon rehabilitation. Among these was an effort to systematize job choice and training in which job sampling tests representative of a number of basic job families were utilized.[7] Quigley also noted the availability of a 1967 publication which centred on projects concerning the utilization of community services for the deaf.[8]

1   Quigley, op. cit.
2   R. Cornett, 'Cued Speech', *Am. Ann. Deaf* (Washington, D.C.), Vol. 112, January 1967, p. 3–13.
3   H. Upton, 'Wearable Eyeglass Speech Reading Aid', *Am. Ann. Deaf* (Washington, D.C.), Vol. 113, March 1968, p. 222–9.
4   C. Griffiths, *Conquering Childhood Deafness*, New York, N.Y., Exposition Press, 1967.
5   B. Morkovin, 'Experiment in Teaching Deaf Preschool Children in the Soviet Union', *Volta Rev.* (Washington, D.C.), Vol. 62, June 1960, p. 260–8.
6   Quigley, op. cit.
7   A. Pimentel, 'The Tower System as a Vocational Test for the Deaf Client', *J. Rehabil. Deaf* (Knoxville, Tenn.), Vol. 1, April 1967, p. 26–31.
8   *J. Rehabil. Deaf* (Knoxville, Tenn.), October 1967.

USOE-funded studies of this period reflected a tendency toward systematic programmatic attacks upon problems of both basic and applied concern. Thus, a grant was made to assist in the development of a 'thinking laboratory' for deaf children. The laboratory was to provide youngsters in a state school for the deaf with daily training in intellectual activities. A regular course of such activities adapted to each age level according to tenets of Piaget's theory of intellectual development was to be offered.[1] A five-year effort aimed to determine the syntactic patterns in language comprehension and production, to describe the rules by which these syntactic patterns are generated, to construct a 'grammar' which would describe crucial aspects of the rules available to deaf children and youth, and ultimately to develop materials for assessing and teaching certain syntactic structures. Transformational-generative grammar was to be used as a model for studying these syntactical characteristics.[2] A study to assess the play activities and gesture output of children with speech and hearing handicaps proposed to develop techniques of assessing such non-verbal behaviours as a means of achieving better understanding of the development of symbolic behaviour.[3] In another study the aim was to compare low-frequency and traditional frequency amplification against such criteria as rate of vocalization, quality of vocalization, and information provided by analyses of sonographs of speech samples.[4]

The decade in retrospect: some impressions

There were no dramatic breakthroughs in the field. Old issues were better explicated and concepts and techniques from other disciplines assimilated into research. The place of oral/aural language in cognitive development continued to be a vital theoretical issue of concern to a number of disciplines. Lenneberg's thesis of the developmental primacy of cognitive over language characteristic in humans[5] took some support from observations made with deaf children and Furth marshalled evidence to support his position that the prelingually deaf are the cognitive equals of the normal hearing.[6] Practical implications of the theoretical issue are revealed in the continuing controversy about whether to emphasize manual or oral/aural communication training

1   H. Furth, *A Thinking Laboratory Adapted for Deaf Children, 1969.* Washington, D.C., Catholic Univ. of Am. (USOE GO 9-182044-0784).
2   S. Quigley, *Development and Description of Syntactic Structure in the Language of Deaf Children, 1969–1973,* Urbana, Ill., Univ. of Ill. (USOE GO-9-232175-4370).
3   A. Drexler, *Study to Assess the Play Activities and Gesture output of Language Handicapped Preschool Children, 1969–1970,* Cincinnati, Ohio, Cincinnati Speech & Learning Center (USOE GO-9-452109-2467).
4   C. Asp, *The Effectiveness of Low Frequency Amplification and Filtered Speech Testing for Preschool Deaf Children, 1969–1971,* Knoxville, Tenn., Univ. of Tenn. (USOE GO-9-522113-3339).
5   Lenneberg, op. cit.
6   H. Furth, 'A Review and Perspective on Thinking of Deaf People', op. cit.

in the early education of the deaf. The adaptation of the newer concepts of psycholinguistic theory to the study of the syntax of the deaf offered hope of new knowledge of direct value in the education of the deaf and help in resolving theoretical issues surrounding cognition and language.[1] There was a potential lesson for all in the work of Nober.[2] If his contention that vibrotactile input contaminates auditory input in high intensity threshold testing is confirmed, it will provide a striking example of the need to continually assess the validity of fundamental methods.

Among all categories of handicaps funded by the Bureau of Education for the Handicapped, USOE, in the period 1964–69, hearing impairment was the only handicap in respect of which more grants were made for demonstration projects than for research projects. If we assume that demonstration projects are more service-oriented than are research projects, it follows that, in contrast to the other areas of handicap, service-oriented concerns exceed knowledge-oriented interests in the field of the hearing-impaired. If this is true, it presents an unusual paradox when examined in the perspective of the potential contribution to our understanding of human behaviour inherent in the resolution of such issues as the relationship of oral/aural language to cognitive development. Were a culture discovered in which all human communication took place in the complete absence of oral/aural inputs and outputs, it would surely arouse great interest within the scientific community. Massive study programmes would no doubt be proposed to take advantage of an opportunity to gain more understanding of human cognitive development by the study of such unique individuals. Such individuals are interspersed throughout all oral/aural cultures; yet they seemingly provoke relatively little interest among those who seek knowledge of human cognitive development and function.

Research on the
mentally retarded

Services and research in mental retardation enjoyed substantial support in the sixties. This support started in 1957 with legislation providing $1 million for co-operative research on the handicapped and received a great impetus from recommendations of the President's Panel on Mental Retardation in 1963. USOE data reveal that activities related to mental retardation con-

1   S. Quigley, *Development and Description of Syntactic Structure* . . ., op. cit.
2   E. Nober, *The Development of Audiologic Criteria* . . ., op. cit.

sistently got more grants and money than any other handicap. The mentally retarded were the focus of 28 per cent of the grants made between 1964 and 1969, and of 15 per cent of the money allocated. Most grants were research-oriented and were administered by colleges and universities.

If one views the ultimate aim of education as the development of cognitive capacities, it is not surprising that this is a high priority, since of all handicaps it is most clearly characterized by defective cognitive functioning. Unlike emotional disturbance, where there is uncertainty as to the locus of defect among cognitive, emotional and motivational systems, there is little comparable ambiguity in mental retardation.

Early developments

Dunn and Capobianco who reviewed the field in 1959 noted expansion of support from national institutes of health and a growth in federal funds for educational research. Problems of terminology were cited but there was movement toward acceptance of mental retardation as a broad generic term for a wide range of syndromes having the common denominator—subnormal intellectual development. In practice, mental retardation was coming to mean an I.Q. score below 75 or 80. In educational terminology, children in the 50–75 I.Q. range were designated the educable mentally retarded (EMR), those in the range 30–50 were called the trainable mentally retarded (TMR), and those children with I.Q.'s below 30 were referred to as the custodial mentally retarded. Prevalence estimates were complicated by inadequacies of definition and of measurement but the vast majority of retarded children were in the range of 50–75 I.Q. scores. It was necessary to distinguish between educational retardation and mental retardation because many children were not retarded but suffered deficits in educational functioning. These reviewers also noted a prevailing belief among educators that only about one half of the children in the 50–75 I.Q. range actually required special education services. Much research on school programmes for the EMR aimed at assessing the relative value of three basic placement procedures: regular class, special class and special day-school placement. Studies indicated that regular class pupils did better academically, whereas pupils in special classes did better in their personal and social adjustment.[1]

Study of the effect of pre-school training on the school performance of EMR pupils indicated that experimental children from both adequate and inadequate homes showed significantly greater gains in social development than control children from similar homes. However, experimental children from adequate homes were not significantly different from their controls after regular school experience, and the potential value of such training for chil-

[1]   L. Dunn and R. Capobianco, 'Mental Retardation', *Rev. Educ. Res.*, Vol. 29, No. 5, December 1959, p. 451–70.

dren from inadequate homes was emphasized.[1] A rapid increase in schooling
for TMR children made research in that area more urgent. Generally, children with I.Q.s in the range of 30–50, who were not totally dependent, and
had potential for self-help gains, social adjustment in home and community,
and for some economic usefulness were considered eligible for special classes.
A controlled study of the outcome of special class training in which matched
pairs of TMR children at home and in special classes were compared, revealed
little difference over a one-year period. When the children were further classified into high and low I.Q. groups, it was found that the only high I.Q. groups
who attended school made significant gains suggesting the desirability of
raising the I.Q. level for eligibility to trainable classes, and making other
arrangements, such as special day care, for children with I.Q.s below 35
or 40.[2]

Sociological studies of the effect of severely mentally retarded children on
family integration increased. Findings included the observation that severely
retarded boys were much more disruptive to the home than girls, that older
sisters are most apt to suffer restrictions due to the severely retarded child
than are boys, and that severely retarded children were most disruptive to
families in the higher socio-economic bracket.[3] Research on speech and
language development attempted to discern speech syndromes peculiar to
the mentally retarded as a group or to sub-groupings of the retarded but no
'mentally retarded speech syndrome' as such was identified. A review of
research on speech and language development concluded that the greatest
needs were for diagnostic scales, evaluation of therapeutic programmes, and
intensive study of speech and language development in the pre-school period.[4]
Research on learning was increasing rapidly but the baseline from which it
was rising was remarkably low. McPherson was able to find barely two dozen
articles between 1904 and 1958.[5] Studies of learning tended toward either
classroom application or basic learning theory.

Among theoretical views the hypothesis that the mentally retarded suffer
a primary deficit in attention was of interest.[6] Many studies illustrated a
characteristic of the time—the transfer of virtually unchanged methods
and concepts of the laboratory into the realm of research on the mentally
retarded.

1   S. Kirk, *Early Education of Mentally Retarded*, Urbana, Ill., Univ. of Ill. Press, 1958.
2   J. Hottel, *An Evaluation of the Tennessee Day Class Program for Severely Retarded (Trainable)
Children*, Nashville, Tenn., Tenn. State Dept of Education, 1958.
3   B. Farber, 'Effects of Severely Mentally Retarded Children on Family Integration',
Monogr. Soc. Res. Child Dev. (Chicago, Ill.), Vol. 24, 1959, No. 2.
4   S. Harrison, 'A Review of Research in Speech and Language Development of the Mentally Retarded Child', *Am. J. ment. Defic.* (Albany, N.Y.), Vol. 63, September 1958,
p. 236–44.
5   M. McPherson, 'Learning and Mental Deficiency', *Am. J. Ment. Defic.* (Albany, N.Y.),
Vol. 62, March 1958, p. 870-7.
6   D. Zeaman *et al.*, 'Use of Special Training Conditions in Visual Discrimination Learning
with Imbeciles', *Am. J. Ment. Defic.* (Albany, N.Y.), Vol. 63, November 1958, p. 453-9.

Dunn and Copabianca saw the field as being on the threshold of an era of intense activity wherein the greatest opportunity was in the creation of new educational approaches, and cited Strauss and Lehtinen's work as an example of needed creativity.[1]

Three activities in particular influenced the direction of research throughout the decade. A symposium on research design and methodology in 1959 had the purpose of clarifying major administrative and technical considerations involved in fostering more and better research. It remains a unique resource to those who must initiate major research campaigns since it deals with a wide range of issues confronting such enterprises.[2]

The second activity took the form of a new manual on terminology and classification intended to reduce confusion and to facilitate uniform statistical reporting on the part of various agencies.[3] The manual offered a new definition of mental retardation, a revised medical classification, a newly developed scheme for behavioural classification and a 'model' statistical reporting format. The definition stated:[4]

Mental retardation refers to subaverage general intellectual functioning which originates during the developmental period and is associated with impairment in one or more of the following: 1) maturation, 2) learning, and 3) social adjustment.

The proposed behavioural classification stimulated research aimed at the delineation of the dimensions of behaviour requisite to such classification.

The third activity led to a publication which played a role in increased interest in research and was the result of the co-operative efforts of the National Association for Retarded Children, NIMH and NINDS of the National Institute of Health. The monograph, *Mental Subnormality*, provided a comprehensive survey and critique of contemporary biological, psychological and cultural information pertaining to the etiology of mental retardation.[5]

Continued growth in interest in mental retardation was noted by Cain and Levine in a 1963 review.[6] New tests such as the Peabody Picture Vocabulary Test (PPVT),[7] and the Illinois Test of Psycholinguistic Abilities (ITPA)[8]

1 Strauss and Lehtinen, op. cit.
2 AAMD, 'Symposium on Research Design and Methodology in Mental Retardation', *Am. J. Ment. Defic.* (Albany, N.Y.), Vol. 64, September 1959, p. 227–432.
3 R. Heber, 'A Manual on Terminology and Classification in Mental Retardation', *Am. J. Ment. Defic.* (Albany, N.Y.), 1961 (monograph supplement).
4 The definition was revised in the second edition to read, 'Mental retardation refers to subaverage general intellectual functioning which originates during the developmental period and is associated with impairment in adaptive behavior'.
5 R. Masland *et al.*, *Mental Subnormality*, New York, N.Y., Basic Books Inc., 1958.
6 L. Cain and S. Levine, 'The Mentally Retarded', *Rev. Educ. Res.*, Vol. 33, No. 1, February 1963, p. 62–82.
7 L. Dunn, *Manual: Peabody Picture Vocabulary Test*, Minneapolis, Minn., Am. Guidance Service, 1959.
8 S. Kirk *et al.*, 'The Illinois Test of Psycholinguistic Abilities—An Approach to Differential Diagnosis', *Am. J. Ment. Defic.* (Albany, N.Y.) Vol. 66, November 1961, p. 399–412.

were seen as most promising, as was a scale to assess the social competence of TMR children.[1] A major study of screening procedures included teacher referrals, group tests of intelligence, group achievement tests and age-grade placement tests. Childrens' scores on the Stanford-Binet were used as the 'validating criterion' against which the efficacy of each of these procedures was gauged. There was great variation between and among schools and grade levels, and teacher referrals agreed with the Stanford-Binet criterion for an average of only 56 per cent.[2] Another study found 16 of 1,000 children in the 6–15 age range in the general population were EMRs, and 2.7 per 1,000 in the TMR group. In the school population, the comparable rates were 16 and 3.1 per 1,000 and EMRs increased progressively until age 14 at which time they decreased rapidly. The rate for TMRs remained constant through the school years.[3]

Basic research featured studies of paired-associate learning, discrimination learning, concept formation and comparison of normal and retarded children of organic etiology and of familial origin. Studies of motivation included assessment of the 'achievement motive' in normal and retarded schoolchildren. Studies were made of the value of verbal praise as a reinforcing agent with the retarded and there were attempts to demonstrate that motivational factors could explain the 'rigidity' of behaviour seen in institutionalized retardates of familial etiology. For example, it was hypothesized that these children are motivated toward compliance and persistence by their great need for approval by adults and not by an inherent cognitive rigidity.[4] In another approach, the effect of tangible and intangible reinforcers on the concept switching ability of M.A. matched normals and retardates was studied. The retarded were said to be less able to change concepts (more 'rigid') and it was concluded that conditions of motivation effected concept changing, e.g. both normals and retardates did better on the concept switching when tangible reinforcers were used.[5]

In educational research, a study of over 1,200 children in the 50–75 I.Q. range, of whom 500 were in a regular classes and the remainder in a special class, led to the conclusion that the regular class group did better academically after one year, but after two years the groups were advancing at the same rate. However, children in the 50–60 I.Q. range, who were in the special class,

1   L. Cain *et al.*, *A Study of the Effects of Community and Institutional School Classes for TMR Children, 1961*, San Francisco, Calif., San Francisco State College (USOE Coop. Res. Proj. 589).
2   C. Elkema *et al.*, *Study of Screening Procedures for Special Education Services to Mentally Retarded Children.* Jackson, Miss., Mississippi State Dept of Education (USOE Coop. Res. Proj. 139).
3   B. Farber, *The Prevalence of Exceptional Children in Illinois in 1958*, Springfield, Ill., Supt of Public Instruction, 1959.
4   R. Shepps, 'Social Deprivation and Rigidity in Performance of Organic and Familial Retardates', *Am. J. Ment. Defic.* (Albany, N.Y.), Vol. 65, May 1961, p. 761–5.
5   E. Zigler *et al.*, 'Concept Switching in Normal and Feeble Minded Children as a Function of Reinforcement', *Am. J. Ment. Defic.* (Albany, N.Y.) Vol. 66, January 1962, p. 651–7.

advanced more rapidly than their counterparts in the regular class through-out the two years.[1] Evaluation of classes for TMR pupils produced conflicting results. Some reported greater progress on a series of behaviour scales for public school children than for retardates who remained at home, while others found no difference in social competency as a function of attending TMR class. Comparison of the social behaviour of institutionalized EMR and TMR subjects with those in family placement revealed no significant differ-ence, but one study indicated that play behaviour was predicted better by I.Q. than by M.A. and the reviewers suggested the possibility that 'predictive criteria for learning social behaviour might differ from those of concept learning or for discrimination learning'.[2] An evaluation of a comprehensive two-year programme of instruction for EMR pupils reported achievement gains said to be only half as great as would be predicted from the children's M.A. Social development advanced at the same rate as chronological age.[3]

Socially oriented research involved comparison of the post-school adjust-ment of graduates of school programmes for the EMR, comparison of employed and unemployed mental retardates, and study of 'successful' and 'unsuccessful' dischargees from residential institutions. A critical review of research on vocational and community adjustment stressed the need for more refined description and analysis of the behavioural characteristics of the re-tarded, better analyses of family variables and sharper criteria of vocational success.[4] Research on the family increased in amount and variety but was generally inconclusive. Typical of this research was comparison of various types of family counselling, study of the effect of the retarded child's partici-pation in classes for the TMR on parental attitude, and evaluations of family dynamics as a function of placement of the child in a residential facility versus remaining at home.

A 1963 review of programmed instruction for the mentally retarded is of special interest.[5] Focused on research on retardates' language and arithmetic learning, it included studies of programmed instruction of sight vocabulary and research in which programmed instruction and traditional teaching were compared. In programmed instruction research on arithmetic which hypothesized that retardates' ability profiles would correlate differentially with a systematic and non-systematic programme sequence, it was found that

1 T. Thurstone, *An Evaluation of Educating Mentally Handicapped Children in Special Classes and in Regular Classes, 1960*, Chapel Hill, N.C., Univ. of N.C. (USOE Coop. Res. Proj. OE-5AE-6452).

2 R. Capobianco *et al.*, 'Social Behavior of Mentally Retarded Children', *Am. J. Ment. Defic.* (Albany, N.Y.), Vol. 64, January 1960, p. 638–51.

3 L. Smith *et al.*, *Effects of a Comprehensive Opportunity Program on Development of EMR Children, 1960*, Iowa City, Iowa, State Univ. of Iowa (USOE Coop. Res. Proj. 145).

4 O. Kolstoe, 'Employability Prediction for Mentally Retarded Adults', *Am. J. Ment. Defic.* (Albany, N.Y.), Vol. 66, September 1961, p. 287–9.

5 L. Stolurow, 'Programmed Instruction for Mentally Retarded', *Rev. Educ. Res.*, Vol. 33, No. 1, February 1963, p. 126–36.

systematic programming correlated highest with specific relevant abilities. The non-systematic sequence was more highly correlated with general ability scores such as I.Q. The need to determine factors that make programmed instruction more effective for learning, retention, and especially for transfer or generalization was emphasized.

In another 1963 review, Heber surveyed EMR research.[1] His comment and critique are helpful in assessing problems of that time. Reviewing studies of environmental influence, he pointed to serious methodological problems such as the inability to randomly assign children to various environmental settings and the difficulty of demonstrating the continuity of intelligence measures obtained early in life with those obtained later in life as well as general inability to identify and evaluate significant attributes of the early childhood environment. Regarding learning and performance in EMRs, he stressed the danger of generalizing about all retardates on the basis of data for institutionalized subjects.

Research on TMR children was reviewed by Charney.[2] He cited a national questionnaire survey directed to teachers in public and private day schools and in residential facilities. The age range was from 3 to 37, the average I.Q. 47. In day schools, 35 per cent of the students had I.Q.s over 50. Teachers stressed the need for better screening of pupils, better teacher preparation, and more training in dealing with the children's parents.[3] Measurement of the activity level of retardates of organic and familial etiology yielded no differences between the groups as a function of visual stimulation, although all became more active when the illumination level was lowered.[4] Learning studies included an analysis of probability learning in normal, slow-learning, EMR and TMR children matched on M.A. The results revealed the normal children most effective in learning, and least perseverative or rigid. Retardates of higher mental ages exceeded those of lower mental age in learning and in flexibility. No differences were found which could be attributed to the etiological classification of the mentally retarded subjects.[5] Research in rote learning, and in learning in which abstraction of common elements facilitated a learning task, indicated TMRs were able to facilitate learning through such abstractions.[6]

1   R. Heber, 'The Educable Mentally Retarded', in: Johnson and Blank (eds), op.cit., p.54–90.
2   L. Charney, 'The Trainable Mentally Retarded', in: Johnson and Blank (eds), op.cit., p.90–115.
3   F. Connor et al., 'Opinions of Teachers Regarding Work with Trainable Children: Implications for Teacher Education', Am. J. Ment. Defic. (Albany, N.Y.), Vol.64, 1960, p.658–70.
4   W. Gardener et al., 'Studies in Activity Level: Effects of Distal Visual Stimulation in Organics, Familials, Hyperactives, and Hypoactives', Am. J. Ment. Defic. (Albany, N.Y.), Vol.63, 1959, p.1028–33.
5   R. Metzger, 'Probability Learning in Children and Aments', Am. J. Ment. Defic., Vol.64, 1960, p.869–74.
6   Zeaman et al., op. cit.

Three USOE-funded studies indicate the range of research in this period. One grant enabled research on the programming of self-instructional devices. The aim was to test principles derived from earlier research by comparison of several levels of criterion difficulty, different sequences of prompting and confirming, etc. A major conclusion was that the child's aptitudes or abilities possibly determined the optimum sequence for presentation of material.[1] A six-year study aimed at exploring the relationship of age, sex and I.Q. to simple and complex learning, and problem-solving situations. Subjects performed discrimination learning tasks of varying complexity levels, and rates of learning, precision of discrimination, etc. were noted.[2] The third study was an investigation of the relationships of selected pre-school experiences of an academic, psychological and social nature to a variety of cognitive and non-cognitive attributes of EMR children.[3]

Two scientific activities helped in 'tooling up' for research. The first was a conference on sociological research which dealt with issues such as the relationship between applied and theoretical research, the study of groups involved in the management of the retarded, e.g. family, institutions, etc., the development of social behaviour, and the role of social factors in the process of becoming mentally retarded.[4] Second, was a seminar on strategies for behavioural research which dealt extensively with intelligence and its deviations, personality concomitants of mental retardation, learning, motivation, and educational treatment and strategies for educational research.[5] The President's Panel on Mental Retardation recommended the establishment of a National Institute of Learning comparable to the National Institute of Health and urged that the research budget of USOE be substantially augmented.[6] The Task Force on Education and Rehabilitation of the President's panel issued a special report which made somewhat more specific recommendations about research.[7] A comprehensive study of past and current efforts to determine the prognosis of the mentally retarded appeared in monograph form. It was aimed at '. . . trying to advance knowledge by presenting the current state of information and suggesting additional research efforts'.[8]

1   L. Stolurow, *Principles for Programming Learning Devices for Mentally Retarded Children, 1960–1962*, Urbana, Ill., Univ. of Ill. (USOE CSAE 8370).

2   K. Jensen, *Factors Influencing Learning and Problem Solving Behavior in Mental Retardation, 1962–1967*, Madison, Wisc., Univ. of Wisc. (USOE C 2-10-345).

3   B. Blatt, *Field Demonstration of Effect on Non-automated Responsive Environments on Intellectual and Social Competence of EMR Children, 1962–1965*, Boston, Mass., Boston Univ. (USOE C 2-10-056).

4   B. Farber (ed.), *Directions of Future Sociological Research in Mental Retardation*, New York, N.Y., Natl Assoc. Retarded Children, 1961.

5   R. Wilcox (ed.), *Strategies for Behavioral Research in Mental Retardation*, Madison, Wisc., Univ. of Wisc., 1961 (USOE Coop. Res. Proj. No. G-1).

6   *A Proposed Program for National Action to Combat Mental Retardation*, op. cit.

7   President's Panel on Mental Retardation, *Report of Task Force on Education and Rehabilitation*, Washington, D.C., Supt of Documents, Govt Printing Office, August 1962.

8   C. Windle, 'Prognosis of Mental Subnormals', *Am. J. Ment. Defic.* (Albany, N.Y.), Vol. 66, No. 5, March 1962 (monograph supplement).

Middle years

Blackman and Heintz who surveyed mental retardation in 1966 set forth three disparate views of etiology: neural inadequacy, cultural deprivation and personal aberration.[1] The third conceptualized mental retardation as a problem of behavioural deficit.[2] They concluded with the recommendation:

> Clearly the next step in educational research with the mentally retarded would involve the development and evaluation of a taxonomy of the school-relevant disabilities of retarded learners. Theoretically, therefore, knowledge of the psycho-educational abilities and disabilities of mentally retarded individuals coupled with an analytical understanding of the psychoeducational demands of specific schools tasks, stated in comparable terms, should lead to maximally efficient matching of learners and materials in terms of whether the former possess the necessary prerequisites for the latter. If not, depending upon relative feasibility, either the learner can be remodeled to meet the specifications of the task, or vice versa . . .[1]

Studies of the structure of intelligence suggested a similarity in the factor analytic structure of the retardate and the normal except that the retardate structure appeared simpler.[3] A review of fifty studies indicated that the WISC was perhaps the most widely used of various intelligence tests.[4] A review of efficacy studies as of 1962 led to the conclusion that retardates in special classes achieve less academically than control retardates in regular classrooms. Slight gains in personal-social adjustment by those in a special class were acknowledged and attributed to a mental hygiene approach by special class teachers.[5] In a major study, EMR students from different geographic locales were randomly assisted to either special classes or kept in regular classes as controls. Comparison of the two groups after four years revealed no differences in academic achievement although both groups made significant gains in I.Q. in the first year of the study.[6]

Learning and memory got much attention. A number of experiments on short-term memory were generated by Ellis' concept that the retarded are characterized by a defective stimulus trace which does not sustain short-term memory long enough to permit the changes which underlie long-term

1 L. Blackman and P. Heinz, 'The Mentally Retarded', *Rev. Educ. Res.*, Vol. 36, No. 1, February 1966, p. 5–36.
2 S. Bijou, 'Theory and Research in Mental Retardation', Psychol. *Rec.* (Granville, Ohio), Vol. 13, January 1963, p. 95–110.
3 C. Meyers *et al.*, 'Primary Abilities at Mental Age Six', *Monogr. Soc. Res. Child Dev.* (Chicago. Ill.), Vol. 27, 1962 (1, Serial No. 82).
4 A. Baumeister, 'Use of WISC with Mental Retardates', *Am. J. Ment. Defic.* (Albany, N.Y.), Vol. 67, November 1962, p. 424–36.
5 G. Johnson, 'Special Education for Mentally Handicapped—a Paradox, *Except. Children* (Arlington, Va), Vol. 29, October 1962, p. 62–9.
6 H. Goldstein *et al.*, *The Efficacy of Special Class Training on Development of Mentally Retarded Children*, Urbana, Ill., Inst. Res. on Exceptl Child., Univ. of Ill. (USOE Coop. Res. Proj. 619).

memory.[1] Attempts to test Ellis' trace hypothesis included measuring the time-span of EEG changes associated with visual attention, comparison of delayed response characteristics of normal and retarded, and the derivation of 'trace factors' from intelligence test items which measure or depend upon short-term memory, e.g. digit span, coding, etc. Research on learning sets continued to arouse interest among experimentalists. There was general agreement that the EMR could acquire learning sets under experimental conditions, but the findings with regard to TMR subjects were mixed and it was pointed out that variations in experimental conditions and in criteria of acquisition of a learning set could account for some of the differences.[2] A number of studies of operant conditioning appeared. In general, the operant approach was used with both the EMR and the TMR to modify a wide range of behavioural abnormalities, to shape desired classroom behaviours, to improve over-all self-help skills by means of 'operant *milieux*' and to improve retardates' work habits. Conceptual differences between normal and retarded were reportedly evidenced by different patterns of clustering of words on recall tasks with greater clustering and retention shown by the normals. The characteristics of verbal clustering of severely retarded individuals were said to resemble those of older patients and those who had been hospitalized a long time. Furth reported that the retarded, like the prelingually deaf, could perform as well or better than normal subjects on conceptual tasks in which language was not considered relevant.[3]

USOE-supported studies in the 1964–66 interval were largely programmatic, multidimensional attacks on the basic educational or vocational problems of mental retardation. One demonstration-research project aimed at evaluating an experimental curriculum and instructional methods for elementary-level EMR children.[4] Another study had the aim of assessing the impact of pre-school programmes which emphasized perceptual and language training for children at marginal socio-economic levels who also suffered learning difficulties.[5] A three-year study of learning patterns in retardates examined the role of such variables as kind of reinforcement, delay of reward, shifts in reinforcement, etc., in institutionalized EMR, TMR and more severely retarded children.[6] A similar study aimed at a mathematical description of

1   N. Ellis (ed.), *Handbook on Mental Deficiency: Psychological Theory and Research*, p. 134–58, New York, N.Y., McGraw-Hill Book Co., 1963.
2   B. House *et al.*, 'Learning Set from Minimum Stimuli in Retardates', *J. Comp. Physiol. Psychol.* (Washinton, D.C.), Vol. 56, August 1963, p. 735–9.
3   N. Milgram *et al.*, 'The Influence of Language on Concept Attainment in Educable Retarded Children', *Am. J. Ment. Defic.* (Albany, N.Y.), Vol. 67, March, 1963, p. 733–9.
4   H. Goldstein, *Demonstration Research Project in Curriculum and Methods of Instruction for Elementary Level for Educable Mentally Retarded, 1964–1967*, New York, N.Y., Yeshiva Univ. USOE G 32-42-1700-1010).
5   C. Deutsch, *Patterns of Perceptual Language Intellective Performance in Children with Cognitive Defects, 1964–1967*, New York, N.Y., New York Univ. (USOE G 32-42-0920-1009).
6   D. Candland *et al.*, *Studying Learning Patterns of Mental Retardates, 1965–1967*, Lewisburg, Pa, Bucknell Univ. (USOE C 5-10-289).

perceptual processes by which normal and retarded subjects synthesize perceptual cues for classification purposes. Subjects performed discriminations in which probability was a major cue to correct response.[1] A four-year study aimed at elucidating relationships between the training, experience and personal characteristics of teachers and the progress of TMR pupils. Teachers from sixty classes and 600 children from the classes were to be followed with the Cain-Levine Social Competence Scale, *et al.*[2]

A study initiated in 1966 had the objective of finding ways to enhance curiosity as a motive in adolescent retardate learning.[3] Cognitive training was the aim of a project in which children in special classes were to undergo training in cognitive flexibility and response productivity utilizing techniques previously developed by the experimenter.[4] A state education department set about analysing class size and the role of teacher aides as factors in the progress of the EMR. Class size, teacher's aides, and grade level were to be systematically varied over a two-year period.[5] A five-year grant went in support of an effort to develop a social learning curriculum for EMR pupils. The approach was to be to develop a centre for research and instruction in social learning to which teachers would come for training.[6]

Research funded by other agencies included an NIMH-supported project on the EMR in which value of paced auditory-visual presentations in improving reading was assessed. Machine-presented auditory material, and auditory-visual materials were compared with teacher-presented auditory-visual items, and with traditional classroom procedures.[7] Automated training for vocational tasks was the object of study of a project supported by the Vocational Rehabilitation Agency. Automated training began in the classroom and continued in the work setting. It was reported that automated training was generally more efficient than conventional and programmed lecture methods, but that a combination of automated and conventional teaching was best, and that machine instruction alone was the poorest of all methods.[8]

1   C. Elam, *Integration of Stimulus Cues by Normal and Mentally Retarded Children, 1965–1967*, Fort Worth, Tex., Texas Christian Univ. (USOE C 5-10-129).

2   M. Semmel, *Relationship Between Training, Experience and Selected Personality Characteristics of Teachers and Progress of TMR Children, 1965–1968*, Lansing, Mich., State Dept of Public Instruction (USOE C 5-10-022).

3   M. Miller, *Curiosity Behavior in Educable Mentally Retarded Adolescents—Characteristics, Modifiability, and Consequences of Training, 1966–1967*, New York, N.Y., Yeshiva Univ. (USOE G 1-6-061378-0584).

4   H. Corter, *Cognitive Training with Retarded Children, 1966–1969*, Chapel Hill, N.C., Univ. of N. Carolina (USOE G 2-6-062009-1566).

5   K. Blessing, *Class Size and Teacher Aides as Factors in the Achievement of the Educable Mentally Retarded, 1966–1968*, Madison, Wis., Wisc. State Dept of Public Instruction (USOE G 3-6-062620-1879).

6   H. Goldstein, *A Center to Develop a Social Learning Curriculum for the Mentally Retarded*, New York, N.Y., Yeshiva Univ. (USOE G 32-42-1700-6018).

7   J. Robinson *et al.*, *Bimodal Education Inputs to Educable Mentally Retarded Children: Final Report, 1966*, Silver Springs, Md, Am. Institute for Research (ECEA 908).

8   H. Platt *et al.*, *Automation in Vocational Training of Mentally Retarded. Final report, 1966*, Devon, Pa, Devereux Foundation (ECEA 754).

Several publications of this period are germane. A review of research on the education of the mentally retarded by Kirk provides a useful integrated description and evaluation of educational research through the early part of the decade with conclusions which remain valid at the close of the decade, e.g. no definitive decisions were possible regarding the efficacy of special classes for the EMR.[1] An informal survey of findings regarding psycholinguistic functioning in retardates included an overview of the Illinois Test of Psycholinguistic Abilities, research utilizing the test, and implications for the education of retarded children who may suffer deficits in automatic, habitual or rote aspects of language usage.[2] In 1966, the first of a series of international reviews of research appeared under Ellis' editorship. These are of particular value to those concerned with research into the conditions of educability, e.g. learning, memory, neural substrate, etc., and as primary sources of information about the theoretical positions of leaders in the field.[3]

In a comprehensive review of studies relevant to education, Spicker and Bartel noted the impact of the Head Start Program on efforts to provide compensatory pre-school experience for poor children.[4] In one project, three types of compensatory education for children of borderline intelligence were compared over a two-year period.[5] In a second study, EMR pupils took part in a two-year cognitively oriented programme of pre-school experience in which experimenters visited homes to enlist mothers' help and to instruct them in supplementary activities. Experimental children gained significantly in I.Q. after two years but after three years there were no significant gains.[6] A third study featured a structured pre-school curriculum designed to remedy cognitive, affective and motoric defects. A group in a traditional nursery school and a home contrast group served for comparison. Dramatic I.Q. gains occurred after a year of the experimental curriculum, but the differences among groups were no longer significant at the end of the first year of school.[7] Spicker and Bartel were critical of weaknesses in design, noting, for example, that the curricula of special classes are usually constructed with the aim of improving performance on specific achievement tests. The Goldstein, Moss

1 S. Kirk, 'Research in Education', in: G. Stevens and R. Heber (eds), *Mental Retardation*, p. 57–99, Chicago, Ill., Univ. of Chicago Press, 1964.
2 B. Bateman *et al.*, 'Psycholinguistic Aspects of Mental Retardation', *Ment. retardation J.*, April 1965.
3 N. Ellis (ed.), *International Review of Research in Mental Retardation*, Vol. 1, New York, N.Y., Academic Press, 1966.
4 H. Spicker and N. Bartel, 'The Mentally Retarded', in: Johnson and Blank (eds), op. cit., p. 38–109.
5 B. Blatt *et al.*, 'Educating Intelligence: Determinants of School Behavior of Disadvantaged Children', *Except. Children* (Arlington, Va), Vol. 33, 1967, p. 601–8.
6 D. Weikart, 'Preliminary Results from a Longitudinal Study of Disadvantaged Preschool Children', *Selected Convention Papers, 45th Annual C.E.C. Convention*, 161–70, Washington, D.C., CEC, 1967.
7 W. Hodges *et al.*, *Effectiveness of a Diagnostic Curriculum for Preschool Psycho-socially Deprived, Retarded Children, 1967*, Bloomington, Ind., Indiana Univ. (USOE Project No. 50350).

and Jordan study[1] was cited as one of the few that had attempted to hold design short-comings to a minimum.

The effect of special classes on the retardate's self-esteem continued to be a subject of research. Retardates who divided school time between special class and regular class participation (integrated group) were compared with retardates in special class full-time (segregated group). When self-esteem was measured on an index of self-derogation developed earlier by Meyerowitz,[2] the segregated group expressed greater self-derogation than the integrated.[3] Other research focused on reading and language. Comparison of adequate and inadequate readers indicated that poor readers were weak in sound blending, vowel and consonant production, substituted words more often and were less able to use context cues. Good readers did better than poor readers on the auditory-vocal sequential test (digit repetition test) of the ITPA.[4] In a study of major proportions, six approaches to learning to read were compared, utilizing 650 EMR students in eighty-five classes in two cities. All subjects were assigned extensive supplementary reading and teachers used the Peabody Language Development Kit to minimize instructional differences. After two years, no differences were apparent among the six approaches when seven standard reading tests were given subjects.[5] In several studies of language development, the ITPA had a central role. Some research is aimed at the simultaneous improvement of multiple aspects of school behaviour. Behaviour modification was used to develop a motivational system for strengthening achievement and desired behaviours among apathetic or rebellious EMR children. Cognitive tasks and reinforcement schedules were individualized and the children, though together in a classroom, worked alone with direction and support from a teacher.[6]

Another multiple target project attacked reading, language and intellectual development (I.Q.) in culturally disadvantaged children whose mean I.Q. was 85. Over 200 first-grade children were divided among four groups for a year of training which featured either Initial Teaching Alphabet (ITA), the Peabody Language Development Kit and ITA, the Peabody kit and basic reader, or the basic reader only.[7] In an innovative inquiry into learning,

1 Goldstein *et al.*, op. cit.

2 J. Meyerowitz, 'Self-derogation in Young Retardates and Special Class Placement, *Child Dev.* (Chicago, Ill.), Vol. 33, 1962, p. 443–51.

3 E. Welch, 'Effects of Segregated and Partially Integrated School Programs on Self Concept and Academic Achievements of Educable Mental Retardates' (unpublished doctoral dissertation, Univ. of Denver, 1965).

4 G. Sheperd, 'Selected Factors in Reading Ability of Educable Mentally Retarded Boys', *Am. J. Ment. Defic.* (Albany, N.Y.), Vol. 71, 1967, p. 563–70.

5 R. Woodcock *et al.*, *Efficacy of Several Approaches for Teaching Reading to EMR, 1967*, Nashville, Tenn., George Peabody College (USOE Project No. 5-0392).

6 S. Bijou *et al.*, 'Programmed Instructions as an Approach to Teaching of Reading, Writing, and Arithmetic to Retarded Children', *Psychol. Rec.* (Granville, Ohio), Vol. 16, 1966, p. 505–22.

7 L. Dunn *et al.*, 'The Effectiveness of Peabody Language Development Kits and Initial Teaching Alphabet with Disadvantaged Children in Primary Grades', *Inst. on Mental*

gifted, normal and retarded children were compared on equally novel tasks which by design of the experimental procedure ultimately became equally understandable to all subjects. In this procedure there were five progressive levels of instruction regarding the task to be learned. At the first instructional level, the rank order of success was gifted, normal and EMR. At the fifth level, however, the retardates had improved very much and some exceeded the mean performance of the gifted group.[1] The relationship of card sorting and verbal ability was analysed in TMR, EMR and normal children matched on M.A. When subjects were asked to 'select those cards which go together' there were no differences in performance among the three groups. When, however, subjects were asked, 'what way do these cards go together', the order of success became normal, EMR and TMR child.[2]

Studies designed to understand hypothesized motivational attributes of the retarded are of interest. Research on the effect of tangible and intangible rewards on concept switching in middle- and lower-class children of normal intelligence and retardates of similar mental age revealed that the lower-class and the retarded did best under tangible reward; the middle-class did best with intangible reward. All did equally well when operating under the incentive they preferred.[3] Persistence was the dependent variable in research on the effect of the incentives, praise, reproof, and competition, on task performance involving pairs of EMR subjects. Pairs of children were formed in various combinations according to whether they did well or poorly initially on a simple marble dropping task. The pairs then performed the task together with variable patterns of the incentive conditions, e.g. one praised, the other reproved, one reproved, the other urged to compete, etc. The measure of persistence was the number of trials the pair chose to make on the task. Least persistence occurred in groups where one partner was reproved and the other praised. Greatest persistence occurred when one was praised and the other urged to compete. Initial performance level affected the outcome in a complex manner, e.g. if both were of the same initial performance level, the incentive conditions were not as influential as when they differed, etc.[4]

Perceptual distortion was the dependent variable in a study of failure-induced stress in EMR and C.A. matched normal children. Each was assigned to either a failure or a non-stress condition. The task was to match stimuli on a paper given the child with stimuli flashed on a screen by tachistoscope. Among the flashed stimuli some were true copies, others were distorted.

Retardation and Intellectual Development Science Monograph, Nashville, Tenn., George Peabody College, 1966 (Serial No. 2).

1　A. Jensen, 'Learning Ability in Retarded, Average and Gifted Children', *Merill-Palmer Quart.* (Detroit, Mich.), Vol. 9, p. 123–40.

2　N. Milgram, 'Verbalization and Conceptual Classification in Trainable Mentally Retarded Children', *Am. J. Ment. Defic.* (Albany, N.Y.), Vol. 70, 1966, p. 763–5.

3　E. Zigler *et al.,* 'Concept Switching in Middle Class, Lower Class and Retarded Children', *J. abnormal soc. Psychol.,* Vol. 65, 1962, p. 267–73.

4　D. McManis, 'Marble Sorting Persistence in Mixed Verbal Incentive and Performance Level Pairings', *Am. J. Ment. Defic.* (Albany, N.Y.), Vol. 71, 1967, p. 811–17.

Subjects performed the task under normal conditions. Then half were told that they had done poorly and it was necessary to repeat the task. Others were told that the apparatus had broken and were asked to repeat the task for the experimenter's purposes. On the second run, the mentally retarded in the failure stress group substituted significantly more of the distorted symbols for the true stimuli than did normal subjects who were not affected by the failure-stress treatment. Retarded and normal children did not differ on the task under non-stress conditions.[1] A doctoral study dealt with the effect of teachers' expectancies upon the performance of borderline children. Teachers were each assigned a child to tutor in a specific task. Unknown to teachers, the children had been randomly divided into a 'low'- or a 'high'-ability group, e.g. high or low had no relation to their true ability. Teachers receiving a 'low' child got a 'professional' profile which characterized the child as having a poor academic prognosis due to severe cultural disadvantage. Protocols on 'high' ability children predicted a good prognosis in spite of cultural disadvantage. Teachers tutored individual children in a simple sign-reading task, following which they estimated the child's intelligence. Significant differences were found between the learning task scores of 'high' and 'low' groups and teachers' estimates of intelligence paralleled these learning scores. Children's true I.Q.s bore no relationship to either the learning scores or to estimates of their intelligence.[2] A study of post-school adjustment was distinctive. Discharges from a residential institution for the mentally retarded were followed up by personal interviews with the patient, friends and relatives in an effort to characterize their life in the community. A major finding was that this group went to great effort to deny their retardation and to escape the stigma of institutionalization.[3]

USOE projects directed at a wide range of problems were initiated in 1967. These included research aimed at testing the feasibility of using compressed speech to facilitate learning in educationally disadvantaged students. Major variables included the mode and speed of presentation of learning materials.[4] One project aimed at determining the quality and amount of verbal skill that could be taught severely retarded children by means of an intensive programmed language curriculum. Procedures for assessing sensory impairment and specific learning deficits were featured.[5] A 1968 study, aimed

1   T. Wachs et al., 'Perceptual Distortions by Mentally Retarded and Normal Children in Response to Failure Information', *Am. J. Ment. Defic.* (Albany, N.Y.), Vol. 70, 1966, p. 803–6.

2   W. Beez, 'Influence of Biased Psychological Reports on Teacher Behavior', Indiana Univ., 1968 (unpublished doctoral dissertation).

3   R. Edgerton, *The Cloak of Competence: Stigma in the Lives of the Retarded,* Berkeley, Calif., Univ. of Calif. Press, 1967.

4   H. Lewis, *An Experimental Study using Compressed Speech with Educationally Retarded Students, 1967,* Boulder, Colo., Univ. of Colorado (USOE G 2-7-078195-4490).

5   W. Bricker, *The Use of Programmed Language Training as a Means for Differential Diagnosis and Educational Remediation among Severely Retarded Children, 1967–1969,* Nashville, Tenn., George Peabody College for Teachers (USOE G 2-7-070218-1639).

at predicting academic achievement in EMR children, compared the predictive power of combinations of individual tests, i.e. ITPA, group tests, special learning tasks, and selected sub-tests of standard achievement tests. Some combinations permitted correlations above 0.75 after seven months of schooling. Individually administered tests were most efficient with younger children.[1] Development of an integrated curriculum focused on self-help skills and the language of pre-school children with Down's Syndrome was the aim of a project which made extensive use of behaviour modification and task analyses. Subjects were residents of a children's centre and 24-hour programming was done with emphasis upon the use of events of daily living and on recreational activities as a vehicle for both training and motivation.[2] Another project had the purpose of determining parameters of auditory perception and language acquisition so as to generate models for language stimulation and therapy in young retardates. The plan was to gather data by electrophysiological and behavioural techniques as children performed on a variety of standardized tasks.[3]

The last third of the decade was marked by the appearance of theoretical formulations which centred on retardate learning. Zeaman and House proposed that the level of intelligence is associated with differences in attention rather than differences in learning and that if one can engineer the retardate's attention so that it is immediately focused on relevant task dimensions, learning is faster and variance due to intelligence minimized.[4] Bijou posited that retarded development is the result of limited opportunity to acquire and maintain essential behavioural building blocks and that the greater the restriction the greater the retardation. These assumptions led to a combined clinical-research approach to the child in which material to be learned is broken down through task analysis and reorganized so that the child can respond effectively to the components, the child is motivated to respond to these components, supporting behaviours such as attention to task are strengthened, and interfering behaviours are weakened.[5] Scott reviewed several theoretical positions, the findings, and the persistent methodological difficulties that plague work in short-term memory. His discussion of the methodological problems surrounding the use of the simple digit span as a crucial experimental task in the study of short-term memory is a sobering

1   J. Bonfield, *Predictors of Achievement for Educable Mentally Retarded Children, 1968,* University Park, Pa, Pa State Univ. (USOE GO-8-082082-3593).

2   J. Chalfant, *A School Program for Young Mongoloid Children: a Curriculum Development Project, 1968,* Urbana, Ill, Univ. of Ill. (USOE GO-8-001025-1777).

3   J. Graham, *Auditory Perceptual Ability Related to Language Acquisition in Mentally Retarded Children, 1968–1970,* Atlanta, Ga, Emory Univ. (USOE GO-8-00124-1797).

4   D. Zeaman *et al.,* 'The Relation of IQ and Learning', in: R. Gagne, (ed.), *Learning and Individual Differences,* Columbus, Ohio, Charles Merrill Books, 1967. p.192–212.

5   S. Bijou, 'Studies in the Experimental Development of Left-right Concepts in Retarded Children using Fading Techniques', in: N. Ellis (ed.), *International Review of Research in Mental Retardation,* Vol.3, p.66–95, New York, N.Y., Academic Press, 1968.

reminder of the complexity which underlies 'simple' human behaviours.[1] The relationship of specific learning disabilities to the development of mental retardation was the focus of a treatise by Kirk who undertook to demonstrate that some children diagnosed as mentally retarded could better be classified as suffering specific learning disabilities. By use of the ITPA and related diagnostic measures it can be shown that retardation in certain psycho-linguistic abilities (perceptual, conceptual, and memorial) is not necessarily general.[2] Farber gave an incisive analysis of mental retardation from a social and cultural vantage point. On the basis of the empirical findings of educators, psychologists, sociologists and anthropologists, he posits that in modern industrial societies 'institutional efficiency' is a predominant goal and as a consequence in such societies there exist superfluous populations of which the mentally retarded make up one segment.[3]

Close of the decade

In a 1969 review, Prehm and Crosson noted the impact on classification of a changing concept of the nature of mental retardation, citing work by Skeels, Clausen and Bijou.[4] Skeels' demonstration that gains in competence attributable to enriched developmental stimulation persisted almost thirty years, strongly supports a major role for 'nurture' in the development of intelligence.[5] Clausen's advocacy of the analysis of ability structures, if proven fruitful, could force radical changes in classification.[6] Bijou's contention that mental retardation should be regarded as a form of behaviour and not as a symptom obviously leads to radical classification possibilities as well as new approaches to the mentally retarded.[7] The Prehm and Crosson review cited major studies confirming the validity and reliability of the WISC and the Stanford-Binet in moderate, mild and borderline retardation, and research into the relationships between these two tests and the PPVT which produced conflicting findings as to the equivalency of the three tests. They described studies which reportedly succeeded in developing shorts forms of the WISC which retained

1 K. Scott et al., 'Research and Theory in Short Term Memory', in: N. Ellis (ed.), International Review of Research in Mental Retardation, Vol. 3, p. 135–62, New York, N.Y., Academic Press, 1968.
2 S. Kirk, 'Amelioration of Mental Disabilities through Psychodiagnostic and Remedial Procedures', in: G. Jervis, (ed.), Mental Retardation, chap. 13, Springfield, Ill., Charles Thomas Publishers, 1967.
3 B. Farber, Mental Retardation: its Social Context and Social Consequences, Boston, Mass., Houghton Mifflin Co., 1968.
4 H. Prehm and J. Crosson, 'The Mentally Retarded', Rev. Educ. Res., Vol. 39, No. 1, February 1969, p. 5–24.
5 H. Skeels, 'Adult Status of Children with Contrasting Early Life Experiences', Monogr. Soc. Res. Child Dev. (Chicago, Ill.) Vol. 31, No. 3, 1966 (Serial No. 105).
6 J. Clausen, Ability Structure and Subgroups in Mental Retardation, New York, N.Y., Spartan Books, 1966.
7 S. Bijou, 'The Mentally Retarded Child', Psychology Today, Vol. 2, June 1968, p. 46–51.

acceptable validity and reliability. Reviewing sociometric and personality inventories they referred to a revision of the Syracuse Scales of Social Relations for use with mentally retarded children down to the third grade.

A series of studies by Zigler *et al.* derived from factor analysis of pre-admission social histories, evaluated a scale designed to rate the degree of social deprivation of children.[1] Behaviour modification studies displayed a trend toward a broader range of behavioural targets and greater complexity of application. For example, one study in which a cottage for trainable level retarded was totally programmed using a token economy was designed so as to expedite integration at ist advanced stages into the normal reinforcement systems of the extra-institutional community.[2] Research on learning, memory, language and communication, personality and social adjustment flourished. A study of learning set acquisition, in which M.A., I.Q. and motivation were varied systematically, revealed primarily that the higher the I.Q. and the higher the M.A., the faster learning sets were acquired. There was a suggestion that social reinforcement acted as a distracting stimulus inasmuch as the learning set performance of retardates deteriorated when social reinforcement was used.[3]

Two studies focused on creative thinking in the mentally retarded. In one, special class retardates, regular class retardates, and non-retarded subjects matched on M.A., exhibited comparable performance on a battery of productive thinking tests.[4] In the second investigation, regular class EMR and age-matched normal subjects were compared through twenty-two Guilford-type tests of creative thought. Although the retardates displayed some creativity, they fell below the normals on thirteen of the tests. However, when analysis of covariance was used to control C.A., I.Q. level of academic achievement and M.A., the EMR and the normal pupils differed only in word fluency.[5] In a study of socialization, severely retarded individuals selected on the basis of low initial rates of social interaction were trained to present each other with candy. Their rates of social interaction were said to increase as a function of the number of training days.[6] Another project compared three types of reinforcement programmes involving institution-alized retardates. A token economy, social reinforcement and primary food

1   E. Zigler, 'A Measure of Preinstitutional Social Deprivation for Institutionalized Retardates', *Am. J. Ment. Defic.*, (Albany, N.Y.), Vol. 70, May 1966, p. 873–85.

2   J. Lent, 'Mimosa Cottage Experiment in Hope', *Psychology today*, Vol. 2, June 1968, p. 51–8.

3   S. Harter, 'Mental Age, IQ and Motivational Factors in the Discrimination Learning Set Performance of Normal and Retarded Children', *J. exp. Child Psychol.*, (New York, N.Y.), Vol. 5, June 1967, p. 123–41.

4   J. Cawley *et al.*, 'Productive Thinking in Retarded and Non-retarded Children', *Brit. J. Educ. Psychol.* (London), Vol. 37, November 1967, p. 356–60.

5   R. Smith, 'Creative Thinking Abilities of Educable Mentally Handicapped Children in Regular Grades', *Am. J. Ment. Defic.* (Albany, N.Y.), Vol. 71, January 1967, p. 571–5.

6   A. Wiesen *et al.*, 'The Retarded Child as a Reinforcing Agent', *J. Exp. Child Psychol.* (New York, N.Y.), Vol. 5, March 1967, p. 109–13.

rewards, were found to differ in that food and tokens were generally more effective. Food was best for the younger subjects, while tokens were more powerful with older retardates.[1] Studies of short-term memory included work by Ellis which suggested that the memory deficit was due to an encoding deficit.[2]

Prehm and Crosson concluded their 1969 survey with the observation that the level of sophistication of research questions had increased. Researchers were posing more manageable questions, concern for the intrinsic validity of research procedures and tools was more in evidence, and the practice, so common in the past, of comparing retardates and normals in lieu of substantive hypotheses was dwindling.[3]

Work initiated under USOE auspices reflected an increasing emphasis upon the systematic analysis of cognitive, motivational, and social aspects of mental retardation. A growing tendency to make use of more formal theoretical formulations as a guide to research interventions was apparent. For example, one project studied the impact of success experiences upon the classroom performance of retardates. Working within Rotter's social learning theory, and noting past emphasis upon the effect of failure on retardate expectancies and performances, the plan was to examine success in the naturalistic context of the classroom.[4] A study of information processing as a function of task complexity and motivation had the objective of further testing Zigler's developmental theory of retardation which predicts that retardates of familial etiology and normal children of the same M.A. do not differ in cognitive performance.[5] Research on social behaviour took form in a project in which the aim was to adapt a role-taking task, developed for use with normal individuals, to mentally retarded of varying M.A. and C.A.[6] A major research and training programme had the purpose of determining the sequence of development of the lexicon and the syntax of retarded children. An ultimate aim was to use such developmental data in attempts to construct more effective language training programmes.[7] Two projects with a more immediate focus on instruction are of interest. In one, the aim

1   V. Baldwin, 'Development of Social Skills in Retardates as a Function of Three Types of Reinforcement Programs', *Dissertation Abstract*, Vol. 27, No. 9, 1967, 2865A, Eugene, Ore., Univ. of Oregon (doctoral dissertation abstract).

2   N. Ellis *et al.*, 'Short Term Memory in the Mental Retardate', *Am. J. Ment. Defic.* (Albany, N.Y.), Vol. 72, May 1968, p. 931-6.

3   Prehm *et al.*, op. cit.

4   H. Spicker, *The Effect of Interpolating Success Experiences into Classes for the Retarded, 1969*, Bloomington, Ind., Indiana Univ. Foundation (USOE G 5-9-242086-0029).

5   G. Gruen, *Information Processing in Retarded and Normal Children as a Function of Task Complexity and Motivation, 1969–1971*, Lafayette, Ind., Purdue Univ. (USOE OEG-0-9-242119-4078).

6   M. Feffer, *Role Taking Behavior in the Mentally Retarded, 1969*, New York, N.Y., Yeshiva Univ. (USOE GO-9-422029-0713).

7   S. Seitz, *A Research and Training Program in Selected Aspects of Lexical and Syntactic Development in the Mentally Retarded, 1969–1973*, Houston, Tex., Texas Research Inst. of Mental Sciences (USOE GO-9-532163-4698).

was to make use of gross body movement in teaching retarded children such skills as pattern recognition, serial memorization and spelling. The plan was to have children hop, walk lines, jump, and in other ways carry out 'academic' tasks by use of total body movement, e.g. in pattern recognition the child is told, 'find and stand on the triangle', or, in a serial memory task, the child is told, 'go through the same movements John just went through', etc.[1] In a second, the proposal was to develop a total academic curriculum to emphasize general learning skills, specific subject-matters, and social skills.[2]

An exchange of views by Milgram, Zigler, and Ellis regarding the basic nature of mental retardation explicated some fundamental theoretical issues.[3,4,5] Choice of a developmental, a difference, or a defect view of retardation was a central theoretical issue. Zigler's study characterized these views as follows. The developmental view assumes that variation in cognitive development is determined largely by polygenic variations and that the familially retarded represent the lower end of the genetic distribution. It is assumed that even if 'environment' could be made identical for all, variations in genetic distribution would still produce major differences in I.Q.

According to Zigler, difference and defect theories assume that the rate and level of development of cognitive functioning of the mentally retarded is modified by some factor(s) over and above those assumed to operate in the developmental view. Hence, difference and defect theories predict different cognitive performances by persons at the same M.A. The difference theories assume that those factors (above and beyond development) which affect I.Q. vary continuously with variations in I.Q. whereas the defect theorists assume that they operate to affect I.Q. only in the mentally retarded range of intelligence. Within this schemata, Zigler identified his own position as developmental, that of Spitz[6] and Kounin[7] as difference theories, and those of Luria,[8] Milgram[9] and Ellis as defect theories. Ellis observed that when 'develop-

1   B. Cratty, *The Effect of a Program of Gross Body Movement upon Selected Abilities of Retarded Children, 1969–1971*, Los Angeles, Calif., Univ. of Calif. (USOE GO-9-142710-4449).

2   S. Ross and D. Ross, *An Intensive Training Curriculum for the Education of Young Educable Mentally Retarded Children, 1969–1972*, Palo Alto, Calif., Palo Alto Medical Research Foundation (USOE GO-9-142106-2444).

3   N. Milgram, 'The Rational and Irrational in Zigler's Motivational Approach to Mental Retardation', *Am. J. Ment. Defic.* (Albany, N.Y.), Vol. 73, January 1969, p. 527–32.

4   E. Zigler, 'Developmental Versus Difference Theories of Mental Retardation and the Problem of Motivation , *Am. J. Ment. Defic.* (Albany, N.Y.), Vol. 73, January 1969, p. 536–56.

5   N. Ellis, 'A Behavioral Research Strategy in Mental Retardation: Defense and Critique', *Am. J. Ment. Defic.* (Albany, N.Y.), Vol. 73, January 1969, p. 557–66.

6   H. Spitz, 'Field Theory in Mental Deficiency', in: N. Ellis (ed.), *Handbook on Mental Deficiency* . . ., op. cit., p. 11–40.

7   J. Kounin, 'Experimental Studies of Rigidity: II', *Character Person.* (London), Vol. 9, 1941. p. 273–82.

8   A. Luria, *The Role of Speech in Regulation of Normal and Abnormal Behavior*, New York, N.Y., Liveright Publication Corp., 1961.

9   N. Milgram, 'The Rationale and Irrational . . . , op. cit.

mentalists' allude to developmental factors as 'explaining' the difference between the normal and the retarded child, they achieve no more explanatory leverage than when one attributes the cognitive difference between a normal three-year-old and a normal twelve-year-old to 'developmental differences.[1] Much controversy was polarized by the publication of a review by Jensen of efforts at compensatory education in which he charged these with failure to yield lasting effects on children's I.Q.s and academic achievement.[2] He contended that failure occurred because genetic factors are much more important than environmental ones in producing I.Q. differences, that the major impact of environment is in prenatal life, and that environment operates primarily as a 'threshold variable' in relation to I.Q. In the same review Jensen proposed that educational efforts be directed toward teaching specific skills and influencing motivation and values rather than toward increasing the I.Q.

Jensen's analysis and conclusions evoked critical reaction from both geneticists and environmentalists. Most critics asserted that Jensen's premise that compensatory education had failed was invalid because these programmes had not been adequately tested. Kagan[3] and Hunt[4] noted recent findings regarding the import of social class differences in mother–child tutorial relationships in language acquisition, and environmental stimulation in early perceptual development, as indicating the need for caution in assigning weight to environmental factors. Hirsch, a behavioural geneticist, criticized the apportionment of genetic and environmental variance with respect to a complex polygenetic trait such as intelligence on the grounds that it is presently conceptually and methodologically impossible to make a general statement about such proportions in reference to either the individual or to differences observed among members of a population.[5] Bereiter observed that with further social progress, heritability of intelligence would undoubtedly increase because of the elimination of such present-day sources of environmental variance as gross differences in the quality of health, education and welfare services.[6]

Jensen distinguished between 'mammoth programmes' which he asserted had not got at the specific, fine-grained cultural and cognitive needs of experientially-socially deprived children, and programmes which permitted intensive educational intervention. In one such intensive intervention pro-

1 N. Ellis, 'A Behavioral Research Strategy . . . , op. cit.
2 A. Jensen, 'How Much Can We Boost IQ and Scholastic Achievement , Harvard Educ. Rev. (Cambridge, Mass.), Vol. 39, winter 1969, p. 1–123.
3 J. Kagan 'Inadequate Evidence and Illogical Conclusions , Harvard Educ. Rev. (Cambridge, Mass.), Vol. 39, spring 1969, p. 274–7.
4 J. Hunt, 'Has Contemporary Education Failed? Has It Been Attempted?', Harvard Educ. Rev. (Cambridge, Mass.), Vol. 39, spring 1969, p. 278–300.
5 J. Hirsch, 'Behavioral-genetic Analysis and its Biosocial Consequences' (paper read at Symposium on Heredity, Environment, and Intelligence, Univ. of Ill., December 1969).
6 C. Bereiter, 'The Future of Individual Difference', Harvard Ed. Rev., Vol. 39, spring 1969, p. 310–18.

gramme, Karnes tested five methods of pre-school compensatory education to determine the most effective type of programme, the length of time required to produce stable cognitive changes, the optimum age for intervention, and the role of paraprofessionals in the classroom and mothers in the home.[1] Subjects were 4-year-old disadvantaged children representative of a wide range of ability levels. The programmes included two variants of traditional nursery school, a Montessori programme, and two highly structured approaches. The last two were an ameliorative programme directed toward specific learning disabilities,[2] and a direct verbal programme which concentrates on skills thought basic to academic achievement. Karnes' conclusions are of interest in relation to Jensen's thesis and as an independent evaluation of the current status of intensive intervention efforts:

> No intervention program was entirely successful in providing the impetus necessary to sustain at the end of the first grade the gains in intellectual functioning and language development made during the preschool years ... however, a major accomplishment of this study remains: serious learning deficits of the disadvantaged children in the Ameliorative and Direct Verbal groups were eliminated during the preschool years. In the Direct Verbal program, where an extensive intervention was sustained over a two year period, continued growth occurred. The deterioration in language and intellectual functioning which occurred at the termination of intensive programming demonstrates the need for continued intervention characterized by low pupil–teacher ratios which make possible the interaction needed for language development and which provides the opportunity to design and implement learning experiences to achieve specific goals.

As part of the above study, Farber, Lewis and Harvey investigated social and psychological factors in the intellectual functioning of culturally disadvantaged children.[3] Their research dealt largely with the description and analysis of family and kinship, neighbourhood and community variables that bear on children's readiness and competence to enter into formal education, the transition from home to school in the perspective of the interaction of private and public cultures and life style of members of a white, lower-class, semi-rural culture. The major argument and conclusion of these investigators was that curriculum development which neglects social context is likely to be unsuccessful. In a final overview of their findings they wrote:

> ... our findings compel us to warn against placing faith (and of course, funds) in a narrow technical approach. *Technical emphasis in educational reform* (particularly that which is intended for the dispossessed) may preclude any possibility of educators making a positive contribution to the obliteration of the social and economic in-

1   M. Karnes, *Research and Development Program on Preschool Disadvantaged Children.* Vol. I: *May, 1969,* Urbana, Ill., Univ. of Ill. (USOE Project No. 5-1181, OE-6-10-235).

2   K. Scott, 'Intelligence and Learning', in: C. Haywood (ed.), *Psychometric Intelligence,* New York, N.Y., Appleton-Century, 1970.

3   B. Farber *et al., Research and Development Program on Preschool Disadvantaged Children,* Vol. III, Urbana, Ill., Univ. of Ill. (USOE Project No. 5-1181, OE-6-10-235).

justices which victimize millions of Americans. In the end such programs may well unwittingly contribute to the collapse of the existing social order.

Technical emphasis in education, as it is in welfare services, is a symptom of a condition which may be termed, *progressive status-quoism* . . . We have chosen this label because the condition it characterizes is social contradiction. Progressive status-quoism occurs when there is a symbolic (or apparent) attack on a social problem. Such an attack seldom acknowledges or deals adequately with the structural roots of the problem . . .

The decade in retrospect: summary and impressions

Summary

In general the etiology of mental retardation was not shown to require separate strategies of education. As the decade progressed it became more widely accepted that teaching techniques should be based upon behavioural characteristics rather than etiological factors. Increasingly research focused on the behavioural origins of mental retardation and educational programmes sought strategies of prevention which had their origin in the child's behavioural environment. Much research aimed at assessing the relative merits of special classes, day schools, and integration of the mentally retarded into regular classrooms. Studies throughout the decade indicated that special class placement yielded no advantage in academic achievement or heightened I.Q. when compared with regular class placement for EMR children. In fact, research suggested more that special class placement tended to lower the children's self-esteem. Special classes proved most successful for TMR children, especially those with I.Q.s in the top half of the TMR range. An early study by Kirk[1] which emphasized the long-range effects of early intellectual stimulation on later intelligence rating confirmed the desirability of pre-school educational programmes especially for the mentally retarded who came from culturally and socially disadvantaged settings.

By mid-decade, a substantial portion of the research effort had turned to the psychological foundations of special education and more precise theoretical formulations of the nature of retardate cognitive functioning became available. Learning and language deficiencies received a great deal of attention. A variety of theoretical formulations had been articulated. Kirk proposed that some children called mentally retarded could be more accurately diagnosed as having specific learning disabilities in areas such as perception and memory because they were normal or near normal in other cognitive functions. Zigler attributed mental retardation to a naturally occurring polygenic variation in the population. Bijou argued that mental retardation is caused by defective learning which arises from one or more of three conditions: physiological abnormality, stimulus deprivation, and acquired behavioural

---

1   Kirk, 'Research in Education', op. cit.

mechanisms that militate against further learning and adjustment. Zeaman postulated that defective learning originates in defective attention. Ellis developed a theory which made use of the inference that a deficiency in short-term memory prevents the transference of information into long-term memory.

A separate area of research aimed at discovering the motivational characteristics of the retarded. This direction of inquiry led to the proposal that mental retardation is in part due to an abnormal sensitivity to social cues which operates to prevent or seriously reduce experiences necessary to the normal development of intelligence and adaptive behaviour. Studies in the motivational area concentrated on different strategies of reinforcement, on the effects of stress and anxiety in learning situations, and on the role of cultural and family influences. A great number of empirical studies utilized the principles and techniques of operant conditioning to modify the behaviour of the retardate.

There was a growing plea for the development of a taxonomy of the school-relevant disabilities of the retarded learner. Increasing numbers of USOE-funded research projects aimed at developing curricula which took account of current understandings of the unique verbal, perceptual and motivational capabilities and liabilities of the mentally retarded. The precise role of the educational system in the prevention or the remediation of behavioural deficits due to differences in social, cultural and economic factors in the larger society was the subject of much soul-searching at the close of the decade.

Impressions

Future historians of science may find this period in mental retardation of unusual interest. Seldom has so much money and manpower been allocated to a previously neglected human handicap in such a brief period of time. The move into mental retardation was unique because of the scope and complexity of the problem and the limited store of relevant scientific knowledge on hand when the enterprise got under way. Another unique condition was (and remains) the isolation of the scientific community from the problem of mental retardation and the concomitant gulf between the scientific and the service communities. Small wonder that in the beginning scientists often quite literally transposed theory and technique from the laboratory to the study of the retarded. The miracle is that in the short space of ten years promising methods, principles and theories based upon scientific study of the retarded have begun to appear.

The single most important influence in research and service was the adaptation of the principles and techniques of the functional analysis of behaviour to this area of handicap. The most immediate impact of this has been more in training than in education. The beneficiaries have been the custodial and trainable level retardates rather than the educable individuals. Nevertheless, the demonstration that the behaviour of the most severely retarded individuals can be shaped so as to be more adaptive and the individual brought to a point of greater control of his own behaviour has given new hope to many. The demonstrated value of attending to the behaviour of the handicapped child has had a salutary effect on work at all levels of mental retardation.

One of the most disturbing conclusions to be drawn from this review of research is that the education provided for less severely retarded children is not adequate to develop their academic proficiency at a rate equal to their limited rate of mental development. The technology of behaviour which is a product of the behaviour modification and operant conditioning approaches will be of value in improving the education of the retarded, but it will most likely be of major utility in laying a foundation for educability. Such a foundation would provide underpinnings for the more complex special guidance and assistance needed by the educationally handicapped.

Virtually all educational programmes and procedures rest upon various convictions about the relations between learning and intelligence. Yet our basic understanding of these relations is at best tenuous. An examination of these issues by Scott highlights the complexities and pitfalls.[1] An immediate problem is to define learning and intelligence to the satisfaction of the diverse schools and theoretical positions represented. Scott was able to cite only one study which deals directly with the vital question of the separate contributions of M.A., C.A. and I.Q. to a specific type of learning ability.[2] The stores of basic psychological information needed to generate strategies for the education of the mentally retarded are still very limited. The same is true of other disciplines.

Research on the
speech-impaired

Most research in this field was directed toward defects of articulation, fluency and stuttering, and problems of voice quality. However, as the decade progressed the scope of theory and investigation was broadened to include inquiry into language and communication disorders and there was an upsurge of interest in the development of speech, language and communication behaviours. The proportion of USOE support allocated to research on speech impairment increased from 1964 to 1969. This growth was said to be associ-

1   K. Scott, 'Intelligence and Learning', in: C. Haywood (ed.), *Psychometric Intelligence*, New York, N.Y., Appleton-Century, 1970.
2   J. Paraskevopoulos, 'Symmetry: Its Effect on Recall, Preference and Discrimination of Visual Patterns in Relation to Age and Intelligence', (unpublished doctoral dissertation, Univ. of Ill., 1967).

ated with an increased desire to work with children's speech problems in educational settings rather than in the more traditional clinical settings.[1]

Early developments

In a 1959 review Murphy cited estimates that from 12 to 15 per cent of elementary schoolchildren had serious functional deficits in articulation and an additional 1 per cent suffered stuttering and voice disorders.[2] Boys exceeded girls, particularly in stuttering.[3] A major study of nearly 500 children indicated that all speech sounds are normally mastered by the age of 8, that children in higher socio-economic brackets are usually superior on language tests, and that the standard speech and language measures are highly intercorrelated.[4] Stuttering was a major research target and Murphy cited as major theoretical positions Johnson's diagnosogenic hypothesis,[5] several variations of themes derived from learning theory, and a number of theories based upon neuro-physiological hypotheses. A review of a number of studies of the incidence of speech disorders in the mentally retarded produced estimates ranging from 5 to 75 per cent depending upon definition, population examined, and methodology.[6] The proceedings of a symposium on congenital aphasia were cited as the most comprehensive and current on childhood aphasia; participants in the symposium unanimously expressed doubt as to the validity of the concept of aphasia.[7] Reference was made to Myklebust's efforts to differentially relate hearing impairment, mental retardation, emotional disturbance and brain injury to the etiology of children's language disorders.[8]

Projecting trends in research, Murphy foresaw increased collaboration between academic and service workers around common research concerns, improved instrumentation and more precise representations of speech processes, more attention to clarification of the neurological and behavioural bases of linguistic structures, and increased recognition of the value of the case study and the longitudinal approach.

1 Mueller, op. cit.
2 A. Murphy, 'The Speech Handicapped', *Rev. Educ. Res.*, Vol. 29, No. 5, December 1959, p. 553–65.
3 R. Milisen, 'The Incidence of Speech Disorder', in: L. Travis (ed.), *Handbook of Speech Pathology*, p. 246–66, New York, N.Y., Appleton-Century-Crofts, 1957.
4 M. Templin, *Certain Language Skills in Children: Their Development and Interrelationships*, Minneapolis, Minn., Univ. of Minn. Press, 1957.
5 W. Johnson and R. Leutenegger (eds), *Stuttering in Children and Adults: Thirty Years of Research at University of Iowa*, Minneapolis, Minn., Univ. of Minn. Press, 1955.
6 J. Matthews, 'Speech Problems of Mentally Retarded', in: L. Travis (ed.), *Handbook of Speech Pathology*, p. 531–51, New York, N.Y., Appleton-Century-Crofts, 1957.
7 S. Brown (ed.), *The Concept of Congenital Aphasia from the Standpoint of Dynamic Differential Diagnosis*, Washington, D.C., American Speech & Hearing Assoc., 1958.
8 H. Myklebust, *Auditory Disorders in Children: a Manual for Differential Diagnosis*, New York, N.Y., Grune & Stratton, 1955.

Two monographs published in 1957 influenced theory and research in the sixties although their theoretical positions were at polar extremes. Chomsky's *Syntactic Structures*, described his transformational model for linguistic structures. He proposed a strategy in which one begins with the study of a core of simple sentences and derives all other sentences from these by a process of transformation. Syntax or grammar was conceived as comprised of an integrated sequence of rules. One sequence governs the making of phrases, another guides the conversion of morphemes into chains of phonemes, and the third is a set of rules to be used in connecting the phrases making rules with the morphophonemic rules. From these evolved the concepts of deep structure, which has to do with semantic interpretation, and surface structure, which deals with the interpretation of phonetic information. In this paradigm the co-ordination of deep and surface structure is the function of syntax. Chomsky designated as generative grammar that grammar which has the function of explicating the relationships between deep and surface structures.[1] In the monograph, *Verbal Behavior*, Skinner applied principles of functional analysis of behaviour to speech and language, characterizing verbal behaviour as behaviour which is reinforced through the mediation of other humans. As such it is to be analysed in terms of contingencies arising in the environment. Consistent with his 'atheoretical position' Skinner stressed the necessity of avoiding the postulation of non-observable events as 'explanations' of verbal behaviours and pointed to the historical succession of utilization of the concepts of images, ideas, meanings, and most recently, information, to explain verbal behaviour, as having deterred the functional analysis of such behaviour.[2]

Ainsworth began a 1963 review with a survey of work on testing and research techniques, citing several projects focused on the problem of scaling both normal and abnormal articulation.[3] Attention was called to the newly created Arizona Articulation Proficiency Scale.[4] Significant research effort was aimed at the determination of minimal language samples required to yield acceptable reliability and validity in assessing various attributes of speech.[5] Studies in language development probed several parameters of language behaviour including the acquisition of vocabulary, growth of ability to produce phonemes, and patterns of development of speech fluency. Extensive review of research indicated that the first word appeared at about one year of age but that this bore no significant relationship to later articulatory disorders. However, appearance of the first word past 18 months was said to

1   N. Chomsky, *Syntactic Structures*, The Hague, Mouton & Co., 1957.
2   B. Skinner, *Verbal Behavior*, New York, N.Y., Appleton-Century-Crofts, 1957.
3   S. Ainsworth, 'The Speech Handicapped', *Rev. Educ. Res.*, Vol. 33, No. 1, February 1963, p. 20–37.
4   J. Barket *et al.*, 'A Numerical Measure of Articulation: Further Developments', *J. Speech Hear. Disorders* (Washington, D.C.), Vol. 27, February 1962, p. 23–7.
5   F. Darley *et al.*, 'Reliability of Language Measures and Sizes of Language Sample', *J. Speech Hear. Res.* (Washington, D.C.), Vol. 3, June 1960, p. 166–73.

increase the probability of later difficulty.[1] Performance on the digit-symbol sub-test of the WISC was used to compare children with mild and those with severe articulatory defects. Those with mild defects were said to do better.[2] A correlation was reported between phonetic word-synthesis ability and the number of articulatory errors and children with articulatory defects were said to do poorly on a test of pitch discrimination.[3] Normal children and children with a variety of articulatory defects were compared through use of a battery of tests of motor function, hearing, intelligence, and estimates of socio-economic level. Children displaying omission type of errors ranked lower in motor skills, digit span, intelligence, and socio-economic status.[4]

Ainsworth directed attention to two monographs on stuttering. The first dealt with the relationship of child-rearing variables and stuttering in North American Indians;[5] the second with speech disfluency among both normal speakers and stutterers.[6] Considerable experimental effort also went toward analysing the phenomena of adaptation, evidenced when stuttering decreases on successive reading of the same material, the spontaneous return of stuttering after a respite from reading, and the tendency to make a consistent stuttering response to specific words or other stimulus conditions. In one project of this type it was found that the probability of stuttering was high for words which were associated with words known to have high stuttering potential for the individual.[7] Other approaches included analysis of the ability of naïve listeners to differentiate stuttering speech from non-stuttering speech and efforts to identify unique parent–child interactions. Methodological barriers to the reliable description of stuttering speech were the subject of a comparative analysis of four methods of measuring the phenomenon of adaptation.[8] Among studies of childhood aphasia were a project in which auditory discrimination in aphasic and control children was compared, and a study of visual spatial memory in aphasic children. Evidence of a specific deficit in auditory learning, independent of C.A., M.A. and hearing loss, was

1   F. Darley et al., 'Age of First Word: Review of Research', J. Speech Hear. Disorders (Washington, D.C.), Vol. 26, August 1961, p. 272–90.

2   E. Trapp et al., 'Functional Articulatory Defect and Performance on a Nonverbal Task', J. Speech Hear. Disorders (Washington, D.C.) Vol. 25, May 1960, p. 176–80.

3   C. Menge, 'Relationships Between Selected Auditory Perceptual Factors and Articulation Ability', J. Speech Hear. Res. (Washington, D.C.) Vol. 3, March 1960, p. 67–74.

4   T. Prins, 'Motor and Auditory Abilities in Different Groups of Children with Articulatory Deviations', J. Speech Hear. Res. (Washington, D.C.), Vol. 5, June 1962, p. 161–8.

5   J. Stewart, 'The Problem of Stuttering in Certain North American Indian Societies', J. Speech Hear. Disorders (Washington, D.C.), 1960, (Monogr. Suppl. No. 6).

6   W. Johnson et al., 'Studies of Speech Disfluency and Rate of Stutterers and Nonstutterers', J. Speech Hear. Disorders (Washington, D.C.), 1961 (Monogr. Suppl. No. 7).

7   R. Peters et al., 'Generalization of Stuttering Behavior Through Associative Learning', J. Speech Hear Res. (Washington, D.C.), Vol. 3, March 1960, p. 9–14.

8   M. Tate et al., 'Measurement of Adaptation in Stuttering', J. Speech Hear. Res. (Washington, D.C.), December 1961, p. 321–39.

reported in the first study,[1] as was a deficiency in visual spatial memory in the second.[2]

In an examination of broad issues, Ainsworth discussed several contemporary influences. The appearance of several major studies of the profession was seen as indicative of growth and differentiation in the field. One presented the findings of a national study of research needs.[3] The status and trends in public school speech and hearing programmes in the nation were the subject of another.[4] The initiation in 1960 of a quarterly series of abstracts concerning deafness, speech and hearing, was seen as an event of prime importance to investigators.[5] The development of the ITPA was noted and it was predicted that it would be valuable in work with cerebral palsy, congenital aphasia, and other instances of retarded speech development.[6] Ainsworth concluded his review with an analysis of trends in the field. A more systematic move toward co-operation in research, both within the profession and among disciplines, an active interest in developing more definitive tests and measures of speech disability, and further growth in the basic speech sciences, were seen as significant.[7]

In another 1963 review, Schiefelbusch, who surveyed research on speech and language impairment, distinguished between the two. Speech impairment was said to refer to deviations in the process of speech *per se* whereas language impairment denoted difficulty in projecting or comprehending ideas through the medium of speech. A study which hypothesized a relationship between articulatory competence and reading readiness was of interest. More than 600 first-grade children were tested on the Gates Reading Readiness Test and their speech was evaluated. A relationship was reported in which the Gates scores declined as articulatory errors increased; the correlation between reading readiness and articulatory errors was -0.20.[8] A clinical research project on stuttering exemplified early efforts to submit therapeutic procedures to objective appraisal. The aim was to compare the efficacy of three techniques of negative practice with one another and with control procedures by observation of their effect on the phenomenon of adaptation in stutterers' reading. The treatment methods were imitation of stutter-

1   L. Wilson *et al.*, 'Auditory Discrimination Learning by Aphasic and Nonaphasic Children', *J. Speech Hear. Res.*, (Washington, D.C.), Vol. 3, June 1960, p. 130–7.
2   D. Doehring, 'Visual Memory in Aphasic Children', *J. Speech Hear. Res.* (Washington, D.C.), Vol. 3, June 1960, p. 138–49.
3   M. Steer *et al.*, 'Research Needs in Speech Pathology and Audiology', *J. Speech Hear. Disorders* (Washington, D.C.), 1959 (Monogr. Suppl. No. 5).
4   M. Steer *et al.*, 'Public School Speech and Hearing Services', *J. Speech Hear. Disorders* (Washington, D.C.), 1961 (Monogr. Suppl. No. 8).
5   *Adsh Abstracts Quarterly.* Washington, D.C., Deafness, Speech & Hearing Publications, October 1960.
6   J. McCarthy *et al.*, *Examiner's Manual, ITPA Experimental Edition*, Urbana, Ill., Univ. of Ill. Press, 1961.
7   Ainsworth, op. cit.
8   C. Weaver *et al.*, 'Articulatory Competency and Reading Readiness', *J. Speech Hear. Res.* (Washington, D.C.) Vol. 3, 1960, p. 174–80.

ing pattern, voluntary repetition of syllables (bounce), and voluntary prolongation (slide). Analysis of performance throughout the study indicated that imitation retarded adaptation whereas the other two procedures improved it. However, by the criterion of performance on a final test trial, no difference was seen between the three procedures.[1]

Concluding his review, Schiefelbusch stressed the need for more objective studies of therapy and the potential utility of operant conditioning methods.[2]

Two USOE studies are of interest in this period. One aimed at the empirical refinement and validation of a test for the prediction of articulatory maturation. Children with functionally defective articulation were tested and the test items analysed for their capacity to discriminate children who spontaneously recovered from articulatory errors from those who did not recover.[3] The second attempted to describe the development of articulation of consonant phonemes and the relationships between articulation and non-articulation variables. Over 400 pre-kindergarten children were followed through the fourth grade and records made of their performance on articulation tests and tests of reading, spelling, auditory and visual ability, intelligence, etc. Children who were initially poor in articulation remained so throughout the study period. Attempts to relate performance on non-articulation measures to specific phoneme defects were unsuccessful.[4]

Middle years

In 1966, Canter and Trost examined a wide range of studies of the speech handicapped.[5] With regard to delayed speech and language development, Canter and Trost noted the growth of interest among linguists in the development of speech and language, citing an entire issue of the *Harvard Educational Review* devoted to research on language learning[6] and publication of a collection of studies on language acquisition.[7] The potential heuristic value of generative or transformational models of grammar was demonstrated in a

1   J. Sheehan, 'Stuttering as Conflict: Comparison of Therapy Techniques Involving Approach and Avoidance', *J. Speech Hear. Disorders* (Washington, D.C.), Vol. 22, 1957, p. 714–23.
2   R. Schiefelbusch, 'Children with Speech and Language Impairments', in: Kirk and Wiener (eds), op. cit., p. 259–91.
3   C. Van Riper, *A Predictive Screening Test for Children with Articulatory Speech Defects, 1962–1966*, Kalamazoo, Mich., Western Mich. Univ. (USOE C 2-10-089).
4   M. Templin, *Longitudinal Study Through the Fourth Grade of Language Skills of Children with Varying Speech Sound Articulation in Kindergarten, 1963–1967*, Minneapolis, Minn., Univ. of Minn. (USOE C 3-10-129).
5   C. Canter and J. Trost, 'The Speech Handicapped', *Rev. Educ. Res.*, Vol. 36, No. 1, February 1966, p. 56–74.
6   J. Emig *et al.*, 'Language and Learning', *Harvard Educ. Rev.* (Cambridge, Mass.), Vol. 34, Spring 1964, p. 131–68.
7   U. Bellugi *et al.* (eds), 'The Acquisition of Language', *Monogr. Soc. Res. Child Dev.* (Chicago, Ill.), Vol. 29, 1964 (Serial No. 1).

study of the nature of 'infantile' speech in pre-school children. Language samples of infantile speech and that of normally speaking children were analysed to determine differences in the use of syntactic structures. The analysis indicated that the older children using infantile speech were not simply using a grammar such as that used by younger normal children. It was concluded that the children with infantile speech were using a different coding process for the production and perception of language and that it was a misnomer to label their speech 'infantile'.[1] An attempt to devise an objective measure of stuttering was described. The measure, or 'disfluency index', which consisted of the ratio between number of syllables spoken and the rate of speaking was said to correlate highly with listener judgements of stuttering severity and to be consistent for individual stutterers.[2]

In other work the hypothesis that the phenomenon of adaptation in successive reading of the same material is associated with anxiety reduction received support when palmar sweat was used as an index of anxiety. In a study cited as important by the reviewers, it was demonstrated that when several measures of adaptation were repeated over a period of time, they were unreliable.[3] The diagnosogenic or evaluational theory, which attributes the etiology of stuttering to adults' evaluation of normally disfluent speech as abnormal, prompted numerous studies, but a comprehensive review of research relevant to the theory led to serious questioning of its value.[4] In an ingenious study growing out of the evaluation theory, listeners evaluated simulated disfluent speech, e.g. single repetitions of syllables versus double repetitions. Listeners judged double repetitions of disfluent speech as 'stuttering' twice as often as single repetitions.[5]

An increase in interest in speech and language disorders in the mentally retarded was reflected in several ways. A monograph of the *Journal of Speech and Hearing Disorders* was devoted to the retarded and introduced a new language test, the Parsons Language Sample.[6] A systematic study of a large sample of children in an institution for the mentally retarded indicated that those whose retardation stemmed from demonstrable prenatal causes were much more prone to language difficulty than those who suffered postnatal injury or infection.[7] The ITPA profiles of TMR children were said to reveal

1   P. Menyuk, 'Comparison of Children with Functionally Deviant and Normal Speech', *J. Speech Hear. Res.* (Washington, D.C.), Vol. 7, June 1964, p. 109–21.
2   F. Minifie *et al.*, 'A Disfluency Index', *J. Speech Hear. Disorders* (Washington, D.C.), Vol. 29, May 1964, p. 189–92.
3   W. Cullinan, 'Stability of Adaptation in Oral Performance of Stutterers', *J. Speech Hear. Res.* (Washington, D.C.), Vol. 6, March 1963, p. 70–83.
4   M. Wingate, 'Evaluation and Stuttering II and III', *J. Speech Hear. Disorders* (Washington, D.C.), Vol. 27, August and November 1962, p. 244–57, 368–77.
5   E. Sander, 'Frequency of Syllable Repetition and Stutterer Judgments, *J. Speech Hear. Disorders* (Washington, D.C.), Vol. 28, February 1963, p. 19–30.
6   R. Schiefelbusch *et al.*, 'Language Studies of Mentally Retarded Children', *J. Speech Hear. Disorders* (Washington, D.C.), 1963 (Monogr. Suppl. No. 10).
7   I. Blanchard, 'Speech Pattern and Etiology in Mental Retardation', *Am. J. Ment. Defic.* (Albany, N.Y.), Vol. 68, March 1964, p. 612–17.

poor encoding ability and better performance on visual-motor tasks than on auditory-vocal.[1] Research on cerebral palsy took many directions. One project had the aim of correlating selected characteristics of speech movements and non-speech movements such as opening and closing the lips with the teeth together. The results suggested a negligible relationship between speech and non-speech movements.[2]

Interest in automated training, programmed instruction, and various mechanized approaches to speech modification was evident in the USOE-funded research initiated in this period. A project initiated in 1964 is representative of this interest. Children with functional articulatory difficulties were given auditory discrimination training by means of programmed instruction delivered by teaching machine. Auditory discrimination programmes were prepared for the ten most frequently misarticulated English consonants.[3] A longitudinal study set about to correlate school achievement and speech defects severe enough to require therapy. The study revealed no difference in school achievement between children with defects of this severity and those with normal speech; nor did speech therapy change the relationship. A low but significant relationship between perceptual abilities and both articulation and school achievement was reported.[4] An automated speech correction programme designed to test the use of programmed instruction in the remediation of functional articulatory errors was evaluated in a 1965 study. The design permitted comparison of students' correction or non-correction of his errors, and therapists' correction or non-correction of errors at critical points in training. The programme was said to be effective in improving auditory discrimination and articulation but the correction variables produced no differences in outcome.[5]

A project which centred on the reduction of severity of stuttering made use of an electronic sound-making device (worn like a hearing aid) in order to break the circle of non-fluency by interrupting auditory feedback during speech therapy sessions. After six months of bi-weekly therapy it was reported that experimental subjects surpassed controls in reduction of stuttering severity.[6] A five-year programmatic attack on stuttering had the broad objectives of gaining more information about variables associated with the severity of

1   M. Mueller *et al.*, 'Psycholinguistic Abilities of Institutionalized and Non-institutionalized Trainable Mental Retardates', *Am. J. Ment. Defic.* (Albany, N.Y.), Vol. 68, May 1964, p. 775–83.

2   T. Hixon *et al.*, 'Restricted Mobility of Speech Articulators in Cerebral Palsy', *J. Speech Hear. Disorders* (Washington, D.C.), Vol. 29, August 1964, p. 293–306.

3   A. Holland, *Training Speech Sound Discrimination in Children who Misarticulate: a Demonstration of the Use of Teaching Machine Techniques in Speech Correction, 1964–1965*, Boston, Mass., Emerson College (USOE G 32-31-0280-1031).

4   J. Wepman *et al.*, *School Achievement as Related to Developmental Speech Inaccuracy, 1964–1967*, Chicago, Ill., Univ. of Chicago (USOE C 4-10-006).

5   E. Garret, *Correction of Functional Misarticulation Under an Automated Self-correct System, 1965*, University Park, N. Mexico, New Mexico State Univ. (USOE C 5-10-179).

6   J. Wepman *et al.*, *Treatment of Stammering Through the Use of a New Electronic Device, 1965*, Chicago, Ill., Univ. of Chicago (USOE C 5-10-396).

stuttering, conducting experimental studies of therapy for children, and the development of improved programmes and procedures of therapy for stutterers in public schools.[1] A study of stuttering begun in 1966 aimed at analysing visible and audible attributes of stuttering speech through the use of sound motion picture records of stutterers. Correlations among those visible and audible features which differentiated among stutterers were factor analysed and ten factors such as over-all stuttering severity, type of audible dysfluency, etc., identified.[2] In research on cleft palate speech, the effect of listening instruction on mothers' ability to comprehend content and assess nasality and intelligibility from recorded cleft palate speech was investigated.[3] Another cleft palate study aimed to demonstrate the effectiveness of a preschool remedial speech programme for children as young as 18 months in age and to gather data regarding the early articulation of cleft palate children, to assess the anxieties and pressures felt by the parents, and to study the further speech training needs of the children on school entry.[4]

A psycholinguistically oriented conference on language development illustrated the impact of heightened concern with human development *per se* and the growing influence of the psycholinguistic approach. The role of social, psychological and biological factors in language development were examined at length. The hazards of interpreting the speech and language of the child from the perspective of adult speech was stressed as was the danger of using standards derived from one social class, e. g. the middle class, in assessing the intrinsic communicative merits of the language of another social class.[5]

A 1968 review by Smith and Lovitt considered research on speech, language and communication disorders in the period 1957–67.[6] Their concern with research which extends beyond speech and language reflected a movement in the field to view speech impairment in a broader perspective. They cited evidence of a 50 per cent increase in remedial services in the preceding ten years and an authoritative estimate that about half of speech-handicapped children had access to remedial programmes.[7] In research on the relationships between auditory discrimination ability and articulation,

1   D. Williams, *Therapy Research Program for the School-aged Child who Stutters, 1965–1969,* Iowa City, State Univ. of Iowa (USOE G 32-25-0420-5014).
2   D. Prins, *A Study of the Behavioral Components of Stuttered Speech, 1966–1968,* Ann Arbor, Mich., Univ. of Mich. (USOE G 3-6-062382-1882).
3   G. Shames, *Effects of Listening Instruction and Severity of Cleft Palate Speech on Listeners,* Pittsburgh, Pa, Univ. of Pittsburgh (USOE G 1-3-062115-1590).
4   R. Harrison, *A Demonstration Project of Speech Traning for the Preschool Cleft Palate Child, 1966–1967,* Miami, Fla, Univ. of Miami School of Medicine (USOE GEOG-2-6-061101-1553).
5   F. Smith and G. Miller (eds), *The Genesis of Language: A Psycholinguistic Approach,* Boston Mass., MIT Press, 1966.
6   J. Smith and T. Lovitt, 'Speech and Communication Disorders', in: Johnson and Blank (eds), op. cit., p. 226–61.
7   R. Mackie, 'Spotlighting Advances in Special Education', *Except Children Rev.,* Vol. 32, 1965, p. 77–81.

children with defects in the 'r' sound, were tested for their ability to discriminate the defect in their own speech versus their ability to discriminate between auditory stimuli presented by another speaker. The children were more successful in detecting errors in their own speech than in making auditory discriminations based on a standard test of articulation.[1] Smith and Lovitt interpreted these findings as pointing the way to systematic exploration of new dimensions of diagnosis and therapy in which direct vocal training and self-monitoring would receive greater emphasis. The relative efficacy of group and individual speech therapy was investigated in a study of children with articulatory defects. Primary-grade children were randomly assigned to individual therapy or to groups of four to five children for therapy which extended over eight months. All therapists divided their time between the two treatment approaches. Comparison of scores on a standard test of articulation administered before and after therapy revealed no differences in therapeutic gains between the two approaches.[2] A doctoral dissertation illustrated the application of the operant conditioning approach to articulatory behaviour. Mentally retarded males with articulatory errors of a substitution type, and who had the ability to articulate at least one of their defective phonemes when it began a word or appeared in isolation, were the subjects. Each was given training with words which began with a phoneme which was habitually misarticulated but which the subject had shown some ability to articulate properly in isolation. First, correct articulation in isolation was positively reinforced. When a given level of competence was reached, a series of training steps were set in motion with the aim of shifting the correct articulatory response to the control of stimuli (pictures, graphemes, and verbal chains) which had not previously evoked correct articulation.[3]

Other operant studies focused on fluency. The effect of verbal punishment on disfluency in normal speakers was the object of research in which the statement 'wrong' was made immediately after a repetition or interjection of words or sounds by subjects who were reading. Such verbal punishment contingent with disfluencies reduced their frequency significantly whereas the random use of verbal punishment produced no changes in fluency.[4] In a later study these investigators worked with stutterers. They applied verbal punishment ('not good') immediately in each instance of stuttering and a verbal reward ('good') after each 30-second interval of fluency. This procedure reduced stuttering in the two male subjects. A strap attached to the subject's wrist was shown to develop similar control features as a result of

1   L. Aungst, 'Auditory Discrimination Ability and Consistency of Articulation of "r"', *J. Speech Hear. Disorders* (Washington, D.C.), Vol. 29, 1964, p. 76-85.
2   R. Sommers *et al.,* 'The Effectiveness of Group and Individual therapy', *J. Speech Hear. Res.* (Washington, D.C.), Vol. 9, 1966, p. 219-26.
3   J. McLean, 'Shifting Stimulus Control of Articulation Responses by Operant Techniques' (unpublished doctoral dissertation, Univ. of Kansas, 1965).
4   G. Siegel *et al.,* 'Verbal Punishment of Disfluencies in Normal Speakers, *J. Speech Hear. Disorders* (Washington, D.C.), Vol. 8, 1965, p. 245-51.

having been paired with the verbal stimuli.[1] A study of operant control of continuous speech in young children was especially ingenious. The children were confronted with a papier mâché clown whose nose was a red light bulb. The reinforcing event was the lighting of the bulb. They were asked to talk to the clown to 'keep him happy'. It was possible to control the rate and duration of speech, and the rate of utilization of speech components such as personal pronouns, through the use of the clown's light-bulb nose as a reinforcer.[2]

Among language studies was a study of home background variables and speech development in normal pre-adolescents. Data were systematically collected from parents, teachers and speech specialists and subjected to extensive correlational analyses. The results suggested that neither permissive child-rearing practices nor parental demands were related to speaking ability. However, higher scores in speaking ability occurred where speech-training techniques were used in the home. A substantial difference was found between the speech ratings of teachers and those of speech specialists.[3] Research aimed at isolating variables and procedures involved in developing verbal behaviour in children with retarded speech illustrated the clinical utilization of the operant approach. Four children, aged 3 to 7, whose speech was limited to partially adequate imitation of sounds, words and phrases, were first helped to improve their repertoire of imitative verbalizations, and new ones were added. When this repertoire reached a desired point, the units were chained together to form longer response units. In the final phase of training, stimulus control was shifted from imitative stimuli to pictures, objects, questions, etc. The procedure was said to be effective in establishing limited repertoires of normal verbal behaviour in the four subjects.[4] Continued effort to discover and refine predictors of speech competence and to relate these to academic achievement characterized much of the USOE research initiated in 1967. A study in 1967 aimed at further validation of a predictive screening test of articulation which was developed in an earlier study.[5] Another study began as a follow-up to earlier effort to establish relationships between articulatory defects, perceptual abilities and academic achievement. Children previously followed through grade three were to be studied through grade six with intensified analysis of auditory and visual discrimination and memory, and other

1 R. Martin *et al.*, 'Effects of Simultaneously Punishing Stuttering and Rewarding Fluency', *J. Speech Hear. Res.* (Washington, D.C.), Vol. 9, 1966, p. 466–75.

2 S. Salzinger *et al.*, 'Operant Conditioning of Continuous Speech in Young Children', *Child Dev.* (Chicago, Ill), Vol. 33, 1962, 683–95.

3 M. Marge, 'The Influence of Selected Home Background Variables on the Development of Oral Communication Skills in Children', *J. Speech Hear. Res.* (Washington, D.C.), Vol. 8, 1965, p. 291–309.

4 T. Risley, 'The Establishment of Verbal Behavior in Deviant Children' (unpublished doctoral dissertation, Univ. of Washington, 1966).

5 C. Van Riper *et al.*, *Cross Validation of a Predictive Screening Test for Children with Articulatory Speech Defects, 1967–1968*, Kalamazoo, Mich., Western Mich. Univ (USOE G 3-7-068717-0198).

perceptual and conceptual characteristics of the subjects.[1] Another project had the aim of comparing selected visual dimensions in children with language problems and those with normal language. Tests of visual closure, figure-ground relationships and perceptual speed were to be made and related to the children's language behaviour in the hope of improving the teaching of children with language disorders.[2] The development of clinical skills in speech pathology was the aim of study which made use of videotape confrontation. The approach was to compare the efficacy of traditional training, videotape confrontation in which trainees and trainer review trainees' clinical performance on videotape, and a method of double confrontation. In this last the trainee and trainer are confronted with a videotape of themselves as they behaved in the initial video confrontation.[3] A demonstration of a programme of stuttering therapy based on principles of family therapy and operant conditioning was the objective of a two-year project. The plan was to train parents in the utilization of re-enforcing events and behaviours designed to emit or evoke, strengthen and maintain fluent speech in the child, and ultimately to give the parent primary responsibility for treatment.[4]

Among other activities, a conference on research on speech and language problems of the mentally retarded needs mention. Research on these problems was approached from psycholinguistic, psychological and developmental points of view and attention given to the correlation of prelingual processes with subsequent lingual behaviour, the evaluation of both receptive and expressive language and the language training of the retarded.[5] In a 1967 treatise on the biological foundations of language, Lenneberg set forth a theory significant to psychoeducational theory and practice. The theory is based on conclusions drawn from a wide range of data about language development. These included the relative lack of a need to teach language, the relative ineffectiveness of programmed instruction in speeding-up language acquisition, the universal regularity of the age of onset of language, and the seeming similarity of strategies of language acquisition in different cultures, and data from studies of generative grammar. In brief, the theory assumes that language is a species-specific characteristic which is a derivative of biologically determined cognitive capacities peculiar to the human. Cognitive function is taken to be a more basic and primary process than is language and language is viewed as an extrapolation of the cognitive processes of

1 J. Wepman, *School Achievement as Related to Speech and Perceptual Handicaps, 1967–1969*, Chicago, Ill., Univ. of Chicago (USOE G 2-7-070461-4543).
2 N. Wood, *Visual Psychophysics of School-aged Children with Language Learning Problems, 1967–1969*, Los Angeles, Calif., Univ. of Southern Calif. (USOE G 4-7-062088-0386).
3 D. Boone, *The Development of Clinical Skills in Speech Pathology by Audiotape and Videotape Self-confrontation, 1968–1969*, Denver, Colo., Univ. of Denver (USOE GO-8-071318-2418).
4 G. Shames *et al.*, *Experimental Therapy for School-age Children and their Parents, 1968–1969*, Pittsburgh, Pa, Univ. of Pittsburgh (USOE GO-8-080080-3525).
5 R. Schiefelbusch *et al.* (eds), *Language and Mental Retardation*, New York, N.Y., Holt, Rinehart & Winston, Inc., 1967.

categorization and abstraction. Lenneberg's thesis is that language development is a resultant of the interplay of biologically determined language readiness (maturation) and environmentally induced experience with language. Because the primitive stages of language were judged too different from adult forms to be due to passive modelling by the developing human, it is theorized that the human synthesizes the building blocks from which he forms his language. The raw material for this synthesis is the input provided by the language environment. Lenneberg draws an analogy between this postulated language synthesis and the biochemical process which occurs when organisms break down and reassemble metabolites to meet their individual physiological needs.[1] In an appendix to the Lenneberg monograph, Chomsky gives a summary of his view of the formal nature of language. Most germane is his conclusion that the developing human acquires a generative grammar appropriate to his natural language on the basis of very limited experience. This conclusion and others leads to the postulate that children are biologically endowed with an internal structure which equips them with the equivalent of a 'universal grammar' or a master template from which they construct their own language out of the 'raw materials' supplied by their language environment.

In the section above, 'Research on the Crippled or Otherwise Health-impaired', reference was made to Chalfant's survey and synthesis of research on central processing dysfunction. Although the focus of this work is learning disabilities, it has much relevance to speech impairment. Of special value are discussions of research on kinesthetic factors in articulation, the assessment of auditory or receptive language, and the task analyses of the steps involved in tutoring children who suffer from defective receptive and expressive language. These task analyses also generate a number of suggestions for further educational research.[2]

Close of the decade

In a 1969 survey of the speech handicapped, Starr observed that there were no adequate theories or models to account for the acquisition or maintenance of articulation.[3] Review of relevant research indicated that a positive relationship between speech-sound discrimination and articulation is most likely to occur in children under 9 who have severe articulation disorders.[4] Starr called attention to the publication of a collection of studies involving the use of

---

1   Lenneberg, op. cit.
2   J. Chalfant *et al., Central Processing Dysfunctions in Children ...*, op. cit.
3   C. Starr, 'The Speech Handicapped', *Rev. Educ. Res.*, Vol. 39, No. 1, February 1969, p. 38–51.
4   P. Weiner, 'Auditory Discrimination and Articulation', *J. Speech Hear. Disorders* (Washington, D.C.), Vol. 32, February 1967, p. 19–28.

operant conditioning with articulation problems.[1] The application of operant conditioning to stuttering and the linguistic analysis of the stutterer's output were concerns of research. Research on linguistic variables included a study of relationships between grammatical function of words and stuttering in young children in which it was concluded that a true grammatical factor does not exist during the initial phases of stuttering.[2] The major thrust of clinical research on delayed speech and language was seen as the identification of perceptual factors which might account for delay and the use of operant conditioning procedures to develop speech in the mute children. Among studies of perception was an analysis of the sequencing abilities of aphasic children using sequencing sub-tests of the ITPA, a tapping test and the Knox Cube Test with results which were interpreted as placing temporal sequencing at the core of aphasic disabilities.[3] Another research into disturbances in perceptions of auditory sequencing in children with minimal cerebral dysfunction arrived at the conclusion that defective auditory sequencing and reduced attention are basic to these children's language problems.[4] In the area of diagnosis and therapy, operant techniques were used to test speech-sound discrimination in normal and aphasic children and it was reported that the two were equal in ability to discriminate isolated sounds but that aphasics were inferior when the sounds were embedded in words.[5]

The summaries of only three USOE studies were available for examination for this report. Two are presented here. A project in the area of stuttering focused on the use of delayed auditory feedback of the stutterer's speech and the utilization of several operant paradigms in an effort to improve fluency.[6] An extensive project initiated in 1969 aimed at the further refinement and evaluation of a programme of perceptual, social and language learning in a day school for pupils who suffer speech disorders. The programme centred on a method called mediated language acquisition which is based upon a combination of programmed learning and operant conditioning. Sub-goals were to develop improved instrumentation and mechanical control over task components and more efficient programmes for language acquisition.[7]

1   H. Sloane *et al.*, *Operant Procedures in Remedial Speech and Language Training*, Boston, Mass., Houghton Mifflin Co., 1968.
2   O. Bloodstein *et al.*, 'Grammatical Function in Relation to Stuttering in Young Children', *J. Speech Hear. Res.* (Washington, D.C.), Vol. 10, December 1967, p. 786–9.
3   J. Stark, 'A Comparison of the Performance of Aphasic Children on Three Sequencing Tests', *J. Commun. Disorders*, Vol. 1, May 1967, p. 31–4.
4   J. Aten *et al.*, 'Disturbances in the Perception of Auditory Sequence in Children with Minimal Cerebral Dysfunction', *J. Speech Hear. Res.* (Washington, D.C.), Vol. 11, June 1968, p. 236–45.
5   L. McReynolds, 'Operant Conditioning for Investigating Speech Sound Discrimination in Aphasic Children', *J. Speech Hear. Res.* (Washington, D.C.), Vol. 9, December 1966, p. 519–28.
6   R. Webster, *Effects of Stutterer's Self Monitoring on Retention of Fluency Generated by Delayed Auditory Feedback, 1969*. Hollins, Va, Hollins College (USOE G-2-7-078290-3550).
7   B. Gray, *Mediated Language Acquisition for Dysphasic Children, 1969–1972*, Monterey Calif, Montery Inst. for Speech & Hearing (USOE G-0-9-142144-3554).

The decade in retrospect: some impressions

The bulk of research focused on specific impairments of speech. The introduction of the principles and techniques of operant conditioning influenced the form and direction of this research. Concern with language development and vigorous growth in several areas of linguistics had considerable impact. Lenneberg and Chomsky's thesis that experience alone is not sufficient to explain a child's knowledge of language spotlighted the genetic component of the nature–nurture equation. But such emphasis upon biological factors did not diminish the imperative to acquire more information about the role of experience in language acquisition, a need well illustrated by Kagan's work. Attempting to discover factors underlying differences in the verbal behaviours of lower-, middle- and upper-class members, he subjected mother–infant verbal interactions to intensive analysis. A major finding was that mothers of the upper socio-economic classes directed distinctive vocalizations to their infants more often than did mothers in the lower classes. No significant differences attributable to social class were apparent when the variable was the amount of child-directed vocalization.[1] These and related findings accruing in the field of sociolinguistics are a reminder of the shallowness of our knowledge of essential relationships of the developing human and his language environment.

It is difficult to escape the impression that neither practice nor research in the field of speech impairment is as well integrated into educational programming as is true in other areas of handicap. Among many studies reviewed, very few (such as that of Wood,[2] for example) clearly set forth the objective of seeking principles and procedures of prevention or remediation which might be incorporated into routine grammar school curricula. Most school-related research seemed limited largely to the improvement of the identification of children with speech and language problems, with relatively little emphasis upon devising or testing strategies of prevention or remediation which would operate as an integral part of the educational programme and make use of the instructional skills of the teacher. Ainsworth provides an excellent overview of the function of the individual classroom teacher in this area of handicap but there appears to be little hard research on the matter.[3] If the estimates of the incidence of speech disorders among school-age children are valid, the sheer magnitude of the need is such as to necessitate optimum utilization of the schools and teachers in combating speech impairment.

1   J. Kagan, 'On Cultural Deprivation', in: D. Glass (ed.), *Environmental Influences*, p. 211–50, New York, N.Y., Rockefeller Univ. Press, Russell Sage Foundation, 1968.
2   Wood, op. cit.
3   S. Ainsworth, 'The Education of Children with Speech Handicaps', in: W. Cruickshand and O. Johnson (eds), *Education of Exceptional Children and Youth*, 2nd ed., p. 389–431, Englewood Cliffs, N.J., Prentice-Hall Inc., 1967.

Research on the
visually impaired

Throughout the decade there was increasing emphasis upon educationally functional criteria in distinguishing between blindness and partial sightedness and a lessened reliance upon medical and legal criteria. Associated with this trend was increased acceptance of the philosophy of maximum utilization of residual vision in the partially sighted individual. The virtual eradication of retrolental fibroplasia resulted in a significant decrease in incidence of early blindness. Research with the blind was influenced by technological advances which allowed a direct attack on the problem of improving the information access of the blind through such approaches as speech compression and the conversion of visual into tactile information. By the end of the decade there were significant new efforts toward improved understanding and adaptation to the unique cognitive and developmental characteristics of the young blind child.

Early developments

Ashcroft, who surveyed progress in research on the blind and partially seeing as of 1959, spoke of three trends in the six years preceding his review.[1] These were the rise and decline in the incidence of blindness due to retrolental fibroplasia (RLF), an increase in provisions for the visually impaired in regular classrooms, and the utilization of optical aids and the adaptation of technological advances from other fields. Among general research contributions, Ashcroft noted the role of the National Society for the Prevention of Blindness in the solution of the problem of retrolental fibroplasia, which at its peak was the cause of 80 per cent of pre-school blindness.[2] The definition of visual impairment was evolving away from a dependence upon visual acuity. Criteria for the partially sighted were moving toward the use of such indices as the utilization of vision as the chief channel of learning, benefit from the use of special facilities, and the recommendations of eye and educational specialists in individual cases. The standard for the blind was coming to be the presence of a degree of loss requiring major reliance on braille, audio aids and special equipment. The best estimates of prevalence of school-age

---

1 S. Ashcroft, 'The Blind and Partially Seeing', *Rev. Educ. Res.*, Vol. 29, No. 5, December 1959, p. 519–28.
2 A. Reese, 'An Epitaph for Retrolental Fibroplasia', *Sight Sav. Rev.* (New York, N.Y.), Vol. 25, Winter 1955, p. 204–6.

partially seeing was given as 1 child in 500, and 1 in 3,000 children was believed blind. The reduction in RLF and other diseases and accidents had resulted in prenatal factors of genetic or unknown origin becoming the major causes of blindness in children.[1] The effects of early blindness on the later development of perceptual and intellectual competence was the object of a major study in which early and late blinded subjects were compared. The study suggested that time of onset of blindness did not effect touch sensitivity nor did it impair ability to deal with spatial concepts. Impairment in intellectual development was noted but the possibility of associated brain damage could not be ruled out.[2] Much research on the pre-school blind child focused on RLF and its relation to mental development. An extensive longitudinal project with nearly 300 pre-school blind children found no evidence of an association of generalized brain damage and RLF and concluded that opportunities for learning were the most important determinants of the child's functioning.[3] Two major developments were noted in technical research. An IBM-704 computer was programmed so as to convert printed text directly into braille.[4] Secondly, the continuing development and refinement of optical aids for those with severe visual impairment was cited.[5]

Inquiry into the educational aspects of visual impairment took several directions, including efforts to determine the competencies required of teachers. The Stanford Achievement Tests were adapted to large type for the partially seeing and into braille for the blind. Special study of the arithmetic skills of the blind indicated that on the average they scored below the norms for sighted children.[6] The most current study of residential school students indicated that about 15 per cent were mentally retarded as well as blind.[7]

A 1963 review by Lowenfeld put stress on problems of identification and classification, reading and writing, social psychology of the blind and the multiply handicapped blind.[8] Evidence that the incidence of blind children had decreased 25 per cent in the preceding three years was cited and this was contrasted with a decrease of 70 per cent in the three years before that. These sharp drops in incidence were attributed to the prevention of RLF.

1   C. Kerby, 'Causes of Blindness in Children of School Age', Sight Sav. Rev. (New York, N.Y.), Vol. 28, spring 1958, p. 10–21.
2   S. Axelrod, Effects of Early Blindness, New York, N.Y., Am. Foundation for the Blind, June 1959 (Research Series, No. 7).
3   M. Norris et al., Blindness in Children, Chacago, Ill., Univ. of Chicago Press, 1957.
4   IBM Corporation, IBM Computer is Programmed to Transcribe Braille. White Plains, N.Y., The Data Processing Division, January 1959.
5   B. Gettes, 'Optical Aids for Low Vision', Sight Sav. Rev. (New York, N.Y.) Vol. 28, summer 1958, p. 81–3.
6   C. Nolan et al., 'The Stanford Achievement Arithmetic Computation Tests: a Study of Experimental Adaption for Braille Administration', Int. J. Educ. Blind. (Louisville, Ky), Vol. 8, May 1958, p. 89–92.
7   P. Paraskeva, 'A Survey of the Facilities for the Mentally Retarded Blind in the United States', Int. J. Educ. Blind. (Louisville, Ky), Vol. 8, March 1959, p. 89–92.
8   B. Lowenfeld, 'The Visually Handicapped', Rev. Educ. Res., Vol. 33, No. 1, February 1963, p. 38–47.

Lowenfeld emphasized the educational consequences of a widespread shift from concern with sight preservation to sight utilization. Prior to this shift the legal definition of blindness by visual acuity (20/200 in the better eye after maximum correction or a visual field which subtends an angle of 20 degrees or less) had been satisfactory as a guide to educational placement. With these new attitudes came the need to develop behaviourally and educationally functional criteria for educational placement and planning, e.g. creation of an education research department within the American Printing House for the Blind.[1]

Research in the areas of reading and writing focused on the role of tactile and auditory input in the learning of the visually impaired as well as upon methods of teaching skills based upon these inputs. An early investigation of the feasibility of increasing auditory input by presenting more information per unit of time involved comparison of the comprehension and retention by blind children of verbal material recorded at slow and fast rates.[2] A learning aptitude test for the blind which made use of haptic items appeared in preliminary form.[3] Parental attitude toward the visually disabled adolescents was said to be the best predictor of the individual's adjustment.[4]

A second survey of work with the visually impaired by Nolan reflected both the behavioural-educational orientation underlying the 1963 CEC review and the growing emphasis upon functional criteria of visual impairment.[5] With regard to the total research enterprise, Nolan emphasized the paucity of integrated research and attributed this state of affairs to the lack of systematic, sustained, institutionalized support for investigation in the area of visual impairment. He cautioned against the tendency to base educational programmes on analogies between the visual processes and those of the tactual, kinesthetic and auditory modalities and cited Axelrod's discussion of the educational errors that arise from fallacious analogies.[6] His review of research on educational development and evaluation led him to conclude that, except for the area of arithmetic computation, the blind equalled the normally sighted of their grade level. Emphasis was placed upon the apparent absence of research in which various methods in instructing the blind was the object of inquiry. In his appraisal of progress in research with the partially

1 C. Nolan, 'An Overview of the Educational Research Program at the American Printing House for the Blind', *Report of 45th Biennial Convention of American Association of Instructors of the Blind*, p. 25–6, St. Louis, Mo., The Association, 1960.

2 M. Enc et al., 'A Comparison of the Effects of Two Recording Speeds on Learning and Retention', *New Outlook Blind* (New York, N.Y.), Vol. 54, February 1960, p. 39–48.

3 T. Newland, 'The Blind Learning Aptitude Test', *Report of Proceedings of Conference on Research Needs in Braille*, p. 40–51, New York, N.Y., Am. Foundation for the Blind, 1961.

4 E. Cowen et al., *Adjustment to Visual Disability in Adolescence*, New York, N.Y., Am. Foundation for the Blind, 1961.

5 C. Nolan, 'The Visually Impaired', in: Kirk and Weiner (eds), op. cit., p. 115–54.

6 S. Axelrod, *Effects of Early Blindness. Performance of Blind and Sighted Children on Tactile and Auditory Tasks*, New York, N.Y., Am. Foundation for the Blind, 1959.

seeing, Nolan referred to Pintner's comment in 1941 to the effect that there was almost total ignorance of the psychology of the partially seeing child.[1] The comment was said to be equally applicable in 1963.

Only one USOE-funded study initiated in this period was available for the present review. This was a two-year project aimed at determining the feasibility of adapting programmed learning materials and techniques to blind students in grades six to ten. Four stimulus-response modes were tested and a braille stimulus–braille response mode was found better than audio–audio, audio–braille and braille–audio stimulus–response paradigms. The best braille stimulus–braille response format was found to be a simple booklet. Commercially developed science programmes were modified for use with the blind and a number of symbols developed in braille to represent the most frequently used science terms. Junior high students reportedly did best on the programmed material and high school subjects were said to have reacted negatively.[2]

Middle years

The visually handicapped were reviewed in 1966 by Ashcroft and Harley who noted that technological advances exceeded behavioural research gains in the period of their survey.[3] Among major works were the *Proceedings of the International Congress on Technology and Blindness,*[4] and *Human Factors in Technology,*[5] both of which dealt with technology in the service of the handicapped. Attention was called to the initiation of the *Research Bulletin,*[6] by the American Foundation for the Blind, and to the *Bibliography of Research on the Blind* by the American Printing House for the Blind.[7] Also cited was the annual, *Blindness,* sponsored by the American Association of Workers for the Blind, which was to provide annual summaries of research supported by major federal agencies.[8] A major development in identification and definition was the initiation of the Model Reporting Area for Blindness Statistics by the National Institute Neurological Diseases and Blindness (NINDB) in co-

1 R. Pintner *et al., The Psychology of the Physically Handicapped,* New York, N.Y., Crofts & Co., 1941.
2 G. Mallinson, *Programmed Learning Materials for the Blind, 1963,* Kalamazoo, Mich., Western Michigan Univ. (USOE G 7-32-0580-191).
3 S. Ashcroft and R. Harley, 'The Visually Handicapped', *Rev. Educ. Res.,* Vol. 36, No. 1, February 1966, p. 75-92.
4 American Foundation for the Blind, *Proceedings of the International Congress on Technology and Blindness,* p. 1-4, New York, N.Y., The Foundation, 1963.
5 E. Bennett *et al., Human Factors in Technology,* New York, N.Y., McGraw-Hill, 1963.
6 American Foundation for the Blind, *Res. Bull.,* No. 1, January 1962, New York, N.Y., The Foundation.
7 C. Nolan *et al., Bibliography of Research on the Blind, 1953–1963,* Louisville, Ky, Am. Printing House for the Blind, 1964.
8 American Association of Workers for the Blind, *Blindness,* Washington, D.C., The Association, 1964.

operation with other concerned agencies.[1] A highlight of technological research was the development of a centre for research on sensory aids and one
for tactile research at the Massachusetts Institute of Technology (MIT) and
Stanford University, respectively.

Attitudinal research noted dealt largely with assessment of the attitudes
of the visually normal. Included were studies which indicated that among
sighted children those who had prior contact with blind children were more
positive in their attitude than those without such experience, and research
suggesting that among adults information about the blind was more effective
in improving attitudes than contact with the blind. A factorial study of the
attitudes of the sighted toward the blind provided an empirical analysis of
these attitudes.[2] Work with tests and other measures included development
of a haptic intelligence scale for adults, and a tactual form of the Raven's
Progressive Matrices for use with blind school-age children.[3] Efforts to assess
personality characteristics of the blind included use of tests developed for use
with sighted children, e. g. the Children's Locus of Control Scale, and an attempt to develop an inventory of emotional factors for use with adolescents. A
comparison of the behaviour of normal sighted and blind pre-schoolers
indicated that the blind demanded more attention.[4] Research on higher
intellectual functions took diverse directions. The hypothesis that congenitally blind adults are inferior in abstract functions to the sighted and those
blinded later in life was partially confirmed.[5] A block-sorting test was utilized
in an attempt to determine the type of sensory input blind children use in
concept formation and the means whereby they arrive at concepts based on
multisensory information.[6] Research also aimed at assessing the degree to
which blind children made excessive use of visual terminology (verbalism).

Speech compression was explored in several projects. Generally it was
reported that comprehension equal to that possible with braille or normal
speech rates was achieved under moderately rapid rates of speech presentation. One study compared two methods of speech compression, the pitch-
altering method and the speech-sampling approach, and found the latter
more effective.[7] Programmed instruction in braille became available.[8] Evi-

1   H. Goldstein *et al.*, 'The Model Reporting Area for Blindness Statistics, *Sight Sav. Rev.*
     (New York, N.Y.), Vol. 32, summer 1962, p. 84–91.
2   M. Whiteman *et al.*, 'A Factorial Study of Sighted People's Attitudes to Blindness', *J. Soc.
     Psychol.* (Princetown, Mass.), Vol. 64, December 1964, p. 339–53.
3   D. Rich, *The Validity of Adaptation of Raven's Progressive Matrices's Test for Use with Blind Chil-
     dren* (Doctoral Dissertation Abstract, 24:1711, No. 4, Texas Technological College, 1963).
4   S. Imamura, *Mother and Blind Child*, New York, N.Y., Am. Foundation for the Blind,
     March 1965 (Research Series, 14).
5   E. Rubin, *Abstract Functioning in the Blind*, New York, N.Y., Am. Foundation for the Blind,
     February 1964 (Research Series, 11).
6   E. Foulke, 'A Multy-sensory Test of Conceptual Ability', *New Outlook Blind* (New York,
     N.Y.), Vol. 58, March 1964, p. 75–7.
7   J. McLain, 'A Comparison of Two Methods of Producing Rapid Speech'. *Int. J. Educ.
     Blind* (Louisville, Ky), Vol. 12, December 1962, p. 40–3.
8   S. Ashcroft *et al.*, *Programmed Instruction in Braille*, Pittsburgh, Pa, Stanwix House, 1963.

dence that children who were braille readers could be trained to make use of residual visions was collected and confirmed in several studies.[1] Research on psycholinguistic processes in partially seeing children indicated that their visual and motor abilities were inferior to their auditory and vocal abilities. The possibility was raised that many children in programmes for the partially sighted suffered primarily from reading problems or learning disorders.[2] Experimental mathematical programmes were tested and reported effective in speeding up the achievement of visually impaired children.[3] Studies of the blind's mobility included inquiry into the relationships among combinations of mobility, intelligence, use of auditory cues, and personal adjustment. Concern for an objective means of assessing mobility led to the development of an obstacle course for the blind.[4] A study of developmental data on emotionally disturbed blind children noted the similarity of these children to visually normal schizophrenic and autistic children and stressed the role of defective information processing in the production of the behavioural abnormalities.[5] Other work also focused on abnormalities of information processing as factors in such mannerisms as vigorous prolonged rocking and handclapping.[6]

In their final overview of the field, Ashcroft and Harley spoke of the need for studies which examined assumptions underlying traditional teaching methods, research aimed at modifying relevant behaviours through direct manipulation of the behaviours and active involvement of the child, and process studies which aim at improving knowledge of perception, learning and concept development as a basis for improved training.[7]

Studies supported by the USOE between 1964 and 1966 illustrate activities divided between attempts to improve conditions underlying educability and those aimed at improving methods of instruction. An operation started in 1964 aimed at the evaluation of four methods of adapting rapid or compressed speech to blind schoolchildren.[8] Partially sighted children were the subject of a study of an experimental teaching approach in which they were given daily specialized instruction in visual discrimination. Compared with

1   C. Nolan, 'Blind Children: Degree of Vision, Mode or Reading', in: *Inspection and Introspection of Special Education*, p. 86–94, Washington, D.C., CEC, 1964.

2   B. Bateman, 'Mild Visual Defect and Learning Problems in Partially Seeing Children', *Sight Sav. Rev.* (New York, N.Y.), Vol. 33, spring 1963, p. 30–3.

3   C. Nolan, 'Research in Teaching Mathematics to Blind Children', *Int. J. Educ. Blind.* (Louisville, Ky), Vol. 13, May 1964, p. 97–100.

4   J. Mickunas *et al.*, 'Use of an Obstacle Course in Evaluating Mobility of Blind', *Res. Bull.*, August 1963, No. 3, p. 35–54, New York, N.Y., Am. Foundation for the Blind.

5   G. Haspiel, 'Communication Breakdown in Blind Emotionally Disturbed Children', *New Outlook Blind* (New York, N.Y.), Vol. 59, March 1965, p. 98–9.

6   A. Stone, 'Consciousness: Altered Levels in Blind Retarded Children', *Psychosom. Med.* (New York, N.Y.), Vol. 26, 1964, p. 14–19.

7   Ashcroft and Harley, The Visually Handicapped', op. cit.

8   S. Ashcroft *et al.*, *Study II: Effects of Experimental Teaching on the Visual Behavior of Children as Though They Had No Vision, 1964*, Nashville, Tenn., George Peabody College (USOE G 32-52-0120-1034).

matched controls those children given special instruction did significantly better on visual discrimination tests.[1] A project initiated in 1965 described the status of braille-reading instruction in the United States and the personal characteristics of a sample of students. At grade four, blind children were 1.2 years older than seeing students but by grade eight the age difference was said to be much smaller.[2] The translation of print into braille by use of computers was the objective of a three-year grant.[3] An extensive project to develop an expanded reading code for the blind got under way in 1966. The strategy was to determine the human capabilities for information processing in the tactual modality and to use as a guide in creating a larger braille code.[4]

In a 1968 review, Tisdall categorized research along the functional lines of braille reading and large type reading and commented on the increase in research in the six-year period of his survey, noting particularly an increase in work with braille readers.[5] Studies of particular interest included a doctoral dissertation which hypothesized that only the very young blind make complete use of the tactual modality, and as they progress in school, verbal skills supplant tactual exploration and experience. The paired associates learning of blind and normal children equated with regard to I.Q., C.A., sex and grade was analysed and the findings interpreted as supporting the hypothesis, e.g. the oldest blind children, sixth graders, were poorest of all groups and ages in responding to haptic cues from randomly shaped objects.[6] Another study aimed at the development of a test of braille-reading readiness based upon ability to discriminate tactual stimuli. The test was reported to yield validities around 0.55 in predicting braille-reading success in first graders.[7] Divergent thinking in blind children was the object of a project in which standard verbal tests of productive thinking were given to blind and normal seeing children of normal I.Q. The blind and normally sighted children did not differ significantly in the results.[8] A doctoral study of mother–child relationships in which normal and blind pre-schoolers were contrasted revealed differences in child behaviour, maternal behaviour and different patterns of mother–child interaction.[9] In a major study of the partially seeing,

1   N. Barraga, *Increased Visual Behavior in Low Vision Children*, New York, N.Y., Am. Foundation for the Blind, 1964 (Research Series, 13).
2   B. Lowenfeld et al., *Methods of Teaching Braille Reading, 1965–1967*, San Francisco, Calif., San Francisco State College (USOE C 5-10-009).
3   R. Haynes, *Computer Translation: Grade 2 Braille from Print, 1966–1968*, Louisville, Ky, American Printing House for the Blind (USOE G 2-6-061190-1578).
4   E. Foulke, *Development of an Expanded Reading Code for the Blind, 1966–1971*, Louisville, Ky, Univ. of Louisville (USOE C 6-10-035).
5   W. Tisdall, 'The Visually Impaired', in: Johnson and Blank (eds), op. cit., p. 110–34.
6   J. Kenmore, 'Associative Learning by Blind Versus Sighted Children with Words and Objects Differing in Meaningfulness and Identifiability Without Vision' (unpublished doctoral dissertation, Univ. of Minn., 1965).
7   C. Nolan et al., 'Development and Validation of Roughness Discrimination Test', *Int. J. Educ. Blind.* (Louisville, Ky), Vol. 15, 1965, p. 1–6.
8   W. Tisdall et al., *Divergent Thinking in Blind Children*, 1967, (USOE OE 32-27-0350-6003).
9   I. Sadaki, 'Mother and Blind Child: the Influence of Child Rearing Practices on the

the relationship between size type and school achievement was examined. Subjects were fifth- and sixth-grade students in several states, each of whom was first administered five equivalent forms of a standard reading test. Each form was in a different type size. The test form on which the pupil got his highest score was assumed to be printed in the type size optimum for him. Each child was then given a battery of achievement tests printed in the preferred type size. A most important finding was that, on the average, the visually handicapped, although of normal intelligence, were retarded one grade in school.[1]

The USOE studies to be summarized primarily illustrate efforts to improve the blind individual's access to information. Some rely on technology, others take a psychoeducational approach. In one, blind high-school students were given practice in speed listening and their pre- and post-training comprehension was measured. After practice in listening to rates as high as 300 per minute (the standard rate is 175), the comprehension of the experimental group increased 10 per cent.[2] A second had the aim of determining the relative efficiency of learning through braille reading and learning through listening. Variables to be explored were the age of blind subjects and various curricular areas.[3] Two studies were based upon the use of advanced hardware. One proposed to develop an instrument which would allow the blind to read print directly. The system would scan the print optically and convert this information into an enlarged tactile facsimile which the blind person would read by touch. The tactile representation would be achieved by vibratory pins in a sensing plate.[4] A second project had the objective of the storage of information on magnetic tape in such a way as to recreate braille characters so that the blind person could read directly from the moving tape.[5]

Close of the decade

Nolan and Ashcroft reviewed the visually handicapped in a 1969 NEA-CEC research review.[6] They noted that the major sources of research and research

Behavior of Preschool Blind Children' (unpublished doctoral dissertation, Harvard Univ., 1962).

1   J. Birch *et al.*, *School Achievement and Effect of Type Size on Reading in Visually Handicapped Children, 1966*, Pittsburgh, Pa, Univ. of Pittsburgh (USOE Project No. 1766).

2   E. Rubin *et al.*, *Speed Listening Skill by the Blind as a Function of Training, 1968*, Chestertown, Md, Washington College (USOE G 3-8-080024-0021).

3   C. Nolan, *Aural Study Systems for the Visually Handicapped, 1968–1972*, Louisville, Ky, American Printing House for the Blind (USOE GO-8-008046-2670).

4   J. Linvill *et al.*, *Proposal for Research and Development of Tactile Facsimile Reading aid for the Blind, 1968–1970*, Stanford, Calif., Stanford Univ. (USOE GO-8-071112-2995).

5   A. Grunwald, *A System for Compact Storage of Information on Magnetic Tape Readable by Touch as Braille Characters by Means of a Portable Reading Machine, 1968–1970*, Argonne, Ill., Argonne National Laboratory (USOE GO-8-080144-4280).

6   C. Nolan and S. Ashcroft, 'The Visually Handicapped', *Rev. Educ. Res.*, Vol. 39, No. 1, February 1969, p. 52–70.

information continued to be the American Printing House for the Blind, the American Foundation for the Blind, and MIT. They cited the contributions of USOE and described a 1966 USOE study as providing valuable information on educational practice and prevalence among school-age children.[1] The reviewers pointed to some challenging, if disquieting, questions about special education for the visually handicapped. Bateman had raised the question of whether special education (beyond the provision of large-type books, etc.) is necessary or beneficial for the partially seeing child,[2] and Birch's study of partially seeing children raised serious questions regarding the efficacy of special programmes.[3]

Among psychological studies, a detailed comparison of 100 blind and 100 sighted children on the WISC led the investigator to conclude that the blind 'tend to approach abstract conceptualization problems from a concrete and functional level and consequently lag behind the sighted children'.[4] An individual diagnostic test of braille perceptual skills was designed to identify perceptual errors.[5] A 1967 work focused on the structure of abilities as related to degree of vision, age of onset of visual loss, length of blindness, etc. Subjects were of varying degrees of blindness and included normally sighted persons.[6] In research concerning the effect of visual handicap on the development of spatial concepts, children blind from birth were compared with sighted children. Blind performance on spatial items were poorer than the sighted at all grade levels, leading the investigator to conclude that vision plays an important role in ability to deal with questions involving space.[7] Listening research centred on means of increasing learning efficiency through substituting listening for braille and large-type reading, the use of compressed speech to speed up listening, and the development of techniques to teach listening. In a study comparing the efficiency of learning by listening with the efficiency of learning by braille or large type it was reported that at the elementary school level the efficiency was equal. At the high school level, listening excelled for literature and social science but not for biological and physical science. However, when time spent listening or reading was taken into account, listening exceeded reading in efficiency by 150 to 350 per cent.[8] A national conference

1 J. Jones *et al.*, *Educational Programs for Visually Handicapped Children*, Washington, D.C., N.S. Dept HEW, Office of Education, Govt Printing Office, 1966 (Bulletin No. 6).
2 B. Bateman, 'Visually Handicapped Children', in: N. I. Haring and R. Schiefelbusch (eds), *Methods in Special Education*, p. 209–56, New York, N.Y., McGraw-Hill, 1967.
3 J. Birch *et al.*, *School Achievement and Effect of Type Size on Reading . . .*, op. cit.
4 M. Tillman, 'The Performance of Blind and Sighted Children on the WISC for Children', *Int. J. Educ. Blind* (Louisville, Ky), Vol. 16, March 1967, p. 106–12.
5 L. Hanley, 'The Construction of an Individual, Diagnostic Test of Braille Perceptual Skills' (Doctoral Dissertation Abstract 28:496A-97A No. 2, Boston Univ., 1967).
6 J. Juurma, *Ability Structure and Loss of Vision*, New York, N.Y., Am. Foundation for the Blind, 1967 (Research Series, 18).
7 L. Hartlage, 'The Role of Vision in the Development of Spatial Ability (doctoral dissertation, Univ. of Louisville, 1967).
8 J. Morris, 'Relative Efficiency of Reading and Listening for Braille and Large Type

on time-compressed speech was cited as a major stimulant to research and an excellent source of current research data.[1]

On the basis of a six-year study of perceptual factors in braille reading, it was suggested that unlike its counterpart in print reading, the process of braille word recognition is the result of the accumulation of pieces of information over a temporal interval. It was concluded also that the perceptual unit is not the whole word shape but the braille character and a probabilistic model of braille reading was proposed. The analysis suggested that training in character recognition should improve reading performance.[2] A study confirming this hypothesis was described.[3] Other studies included correlation of the ease of recognition of braille characters and their frequency of occurrence in print. A study of the importance of cues from the preceding test in braille reading compared the rate of reading and retention of braille material presented in traditional form, a medium-length telegraphic style, and a short telegraphic version. The telegraphed forms took less time to read, but the reading rate of the short telegraphic form was 40 per cent slower than the traditional form, which was interpreted as confirming the importance of cues from the preceding text.[4] Research on mobility aimed at the identification of orientation and mobility skills of young blind children for the purpose of developing a scale of mobility.[5] An investigation of the effects of various types of stimulation on the stereotype often seen in blind children indicated that combinations of objects such as toys, sounds such as recorded music, and sound generating devices (horns and bells) reduced stereotype, whereas sound alone was not effective.[6] Nolan and Ashcroft concluded their review pessimistically. Recalling Ashcroft and Harley's declaration in the 1966 NEA-CEC review[7] that 'a new era in research is needed to match the new era in education' they concluded that, 'the new era of research remains a hope for the future'.

The USOE studies presented next are oriented toward improved understanding and utilization of unique cognitive and developmental character-

Readers', *Am. Association of Instructors of Blind, 48th Biennial Report*, p. 65–70, Washington D.C., The Association, 1966.

1   E. Foulke (ed.), *Proceedings of Louisville Conference on Time Compressed Speed*, Louisville, Ky, Univ. of Louisville, 1967.

2   C. Nolan, 'Perceptual Factors in Braille Word Recognition', in: *Am. Association of Instructors of Blind, 48th Biennal Report*, p. 10–14, Washington, D.C., The Association, 1966.

3   F. Henderson, 'The Rate of Braille Character Recognition as a Function of the Reading Process', in: *Am. Association of Instructors of Blind, 48th Biennial Report*, p. 7–10, Washington, D.C., The Association, 1966.

4   C. Martin *et al.*, *Comprehension of Full Length and Telegraphic Material among Blind Children*, East Lansing, Mich., Michigan St. Univ., 1967 (Ed. Research Series, 42).

5   F. Lord, *Preliminary Standardization of Scale of Orientation and Mobility Skills of Young Blind Children, 1967*, Washington, D.C., Govt Printing Office (USOE Project No. 62464, Grant No. OEG 4-7-062464-0369).

6   D. Guess *et al.*, 'Experimental Attempts to Reduce Stereotyping among Blind Retardates', *Am. J. Ment. Defic.* (Albany, N.Y.), Vol. 71, May 1967, p. 984–6.

7   Ashcroft and Harley, 'The Visually Handicapped', op. cit.

istics of the blind. The design and evaluation of a braille-learning programme was the aim of a project on specific difficulties students encounter in learning braille.[1] In another project it was proposed that principles of development of blind children be incorporated into an educational programme for blind infants and pre-school children. These principles were derived from a long-range research programme directed by the principal investigator.[2] The aims of the study were to develop a home guidance programme, a training programme for professional persons, teaching films for professionals and parents and teaching materials such as toys, games, etc.[3]

The decade in retrospect: some impressions

One of the striking developments of the decade was the move toward an educationally functional definition of visual impairment. An excellent example is seen in Kirk's textbook on the education of the exceptional child, in which the blind are designated as those who are educated through channels other than vision while the partially sighted are those who are able to utilize vision in acquiring educational skills.[4] One basis for this new attitude is found in Barraga's research in which experimental teaching led to increased functional vision although visual acuity was unchanged.[5] Within this definitional framework a major special educational objective is the improvement of the child's access to information. The use of large type and visual aids has benefited the partially sighted as has perceptual training. The drive to increase the flow of information to the blind relied heavily on hardware made possible by technological advances. Compressed speech and its psychological counterpart, speed-listening, underwent vigorous exploitation. More complex transformations of information such as the visual to tactile, or the direct conversion of print to braille, were explored.

Awareness of the need for more basic data about the behavioural development of blind infants and children was sharpened in the decade. The promise of such knowledge is evident in Fraiberg's studies of ego development in blind infants. Her work gives an insight into the difficulties that confront the blind child as he sets about forming object concepts—the concept of 'something out there' and of things that 'exist' independent of his perception of them. The blind infant must construct his concept of objects from information which lacks the immediate multidimensionality provided by the

1   C. Budrose, *Proposal to Design, Fabricate and Evaluate a Braille Learning Aid, 1969–1971*, Cambridge, Mass., Bio-Dynamics Inc. (USOE CO-9-312028-2322).
2   S. Fraiberg *et al.*, 'The Role of Sound in Search Behavior of a Blind Infant', *The Psychoanalytic Study of the Child*, Vol. 21, 1966, p. 327–57, New York, N.Y., Int. Univ. Press Inc.
3   S. Fraiberg, *An Educational Program on Behalf of Blind Infants and Young Children, 1969–1972*, Ann Arbor, Mich., Univ. of Mich. (USOE OEG-0-9-322108-2469).
4   S. Kirk, 'Behavior Deviations in Children', *Educating Exceptional Children*, op. cit., p. 330–64.
5   Barraga, op. cit.

contemporaneous processing of visual, haptic, and auditory information. Fraiberg's finding indicates that one consequence in early development is that the co-ordination of prehension and information provided by distance receptors (the ear in the case of the blind) takes the blind child much longer than the sighted child.[1] The fallibility of our present developmental knowledge is well illustrated by the discovery in this decade that newborn infants can 'see' much better than had been assumed.[2]

Research involving multiple
handicapping conditions

Growth in support of studies involving multiple handicap was a significant trend in the support of research by USOE. Support increased from less than $200,000 in 1964 to more than $3.5 million in 1969. This growth was attributed to a strong trend toward the organization of research and related activities around problems encountered in educational settings instead of around classification systems generated by the physiological, medical or psychological disciplines as in the past.[3] This research takes several forms. The most familiar aims at studying individuals who suffer two or more primary handicapping conditions. Another form is cross-disability research which focuses upon two or more handicapping conditions occurring singly in affected individuals. It often aims at comparative study of specific variables across several discrete handicapping conditions. It is likely to be theoretically oriented and is apt to be focused on disabilities rather than individuals. The third form is the study of administrative matters common to all handicapping conditions. This is pan-disability research. The orientation is administrative. The focus is upon the system whereby services are developed and delivered to handicapped individuals.

The research reviews sponsored by the National Education Association and the Council on Exceptional Children do not utilize the multiple handicap category. Instead these conditions are treated as subsidiary topics in the review of each of the seven primary categories, e.g. the deaf–mentally retarded may be considered under mental retardation, deafness, or both. Since much of this work has been surveyed in previous sections the present review will rely largely on an analysis of studies supported by USOE which does recognize the multiple handicap category.

1   S. Fraiberg *et al.*, 'The Role of Sound in Search Behavior of a Blind Infant', op.cit.
2   H. Haynes *et al.*, 'Visual Accomodation in Humans Infants', *Science*, Vol. 148, p. 528–30.
3   M. Mueller, 'Trends in Support of Educational Research for Handicapped', op.cit.

The individual with multiple handicaps

The demand for services for these individuals increased throughout the sixties because the number of persons with multiple handicaps increased due to an extended life span made possible by medical advances. Research with the multiply handicapped individual remains in an early stage of development. Most studies are in the nature of estimates of incidence and prevalence or narrative descriptions of the administrative-clinical experiences of the few agencies which specialize in service to the multiply handicapped. Studies supported by USOE help to illustrate the nature of this work. A project begun in 1964 aimed at the development of a residential education programme for emotionally disturbed pseudo-retarded blind children. The major goals were to overcome the effects of deprivation of experiences underlying concept formation, sensory input, and the development of physical and social competence.[1] A survey of provisions for mentally retarded deaf students in residential schools for the deaf led to the conclusion that relatively large numbers of mental retardates were enrolled in residential schools for the deaf and that without extensive changes in the existing educational programmes many of the mentally retarded deaf would never achieve social competence.[2]

In a project on mentally retarded emotionally disturbed children, it was reported that the pattern of psycholinguistic disabilities was quite unlike those described in the mentally retarded and the difference was attributed to the presence of the added handicap of emotional disturbance.[3] A pilot programme for the emotionally disturbed deaf child got under way in a state residential school for the deaf, the aim being to devise, refine and evaluate instructional materials and methods tailored to this cluster of handicaps.[4] A 1969 USOE grant went to a project designed to develop a clinically useful evaluation protocol for the structured observation of the behaviour of severely multiply handicapped youngsters. The approach was to identify situations which would elicit critical samples of behaviour. Behaviour in these 'test' situations was to be videotaped and the resultant records presented to clinical experts for evaluation and further refinement of the technique.[5] The final project to be described envisioned a combination pre-school and home teach-

1   M. Rigby *et al.*, *Development of a Residential Education Program for Emotionally Deprived Pseudo-Retarded Blind Children, 1964–1967.* Salem, Oreg., Oregon St. School for the Blind (USOE G-32-47-0000-1007).

2   E. Stuckless *et al.*, *Provisions for the Education of Mentally Retarded Deaf Students in Residential Schools for the Deaf, 1965–1966,* Pittsburgh, Pa, Univ. of Pittsburgh (USOE G-32-48-1110-5008).

3   J. Minskoff, *The Effectiveness of a Specific Program Based on Language Diagnosis in Overcoming Learning Disabilities of Mentally Retarded Emotionally Disturbed Children, 1966–1968,* New York, N.Y., Yeshiva Univ. (USOE G-1-6-068375-1550).

4   R. Brill, *Program with Seriously Disturbed Deaf Children, 1967–1969,* Riverside, Calif., Riverside County Department of Education (USOE OEG-4-7-062422-02-8).

5   W. Curtis *et al.*, *The Development and Evaluation of a Behavioral Examination Protocol for Structuring the Clinical Examination of Children with Severe Multiple Disabilities, 1969–70,* New York, N.Y., Univ. of Syracuse (USOE GO-9-422134-2764).

ing programme for deaf blind children. Teachers would work with children in both home and school and parents would be obligated to take part in the school and home training exercises.[1]

Cross-disability research

Cross-disability research generally has the objective of comparative study of specific variables or treatments across two or more discrete handicaps which occur singly in affected individuals. Most USOE-supported research on multiple handicap is of the cross-disability type reflecting the substantive interests of an increasing number of investigators, and evolving policies of USOE in research support tend toward the preferential support of long-range programmatic research enterprises.[2] Illustrative studies supported by USOE included investigation of strategies of learning in deaf, blind, mentally retarded, and normal children focused on classification schemes and the use of verbalization in the children's approach to associative learning tasks.[3] Another study involved the development of a means of assessing the self-concept of academic ability among hearing impaired, visually handicapped and non-impaired high school students.[4] An operant approach to the learning of the correct usage of prepositions and pronouns characterized a four-year study of schizophrenic and mentally retarded children with emphasis on the child's everyday speech, and objects, situations and events within his language environment.[5]

An important investigation paralleled and extended the collaborative perinatal study cited in an earlier section.[6] The objective was to examine the relationship of conditions of pregnancy, birth and infancy to exceptionality in behaviour and in school performance of almost 2,000 kindergarten, first-grade, and fourth-grade children, followed over a three-year period.[7] A related study anticipated a ten-year follow-up in which predictors of reading disability were to be sought from data collected in the prenatal, natal

1   P. Hatlen, *An Experimental Home Teaching Program for Pre-school Deaf Blind Children, 1969–1971*, Daly City, Calif., Frederick Burk Foundation for Education, San Francisco St. College (USOE OEG-0-9-142147-3740).

2   J. Moss, 'Research and Demonstration', *Except. Children* (Arlington, Va), Vol. 34, No. 7, March 1968, 509–14.

3   C. Martin, *Associative Learning Strategies Employed by Deaf, Blind, Retarded and Normal Children, 1964–1967*, East Lansing, Mich., Michigan State Univ. (USOE G-32-32-0410-1020).

4   E. Erickson *et al., Scales and Procedures for Assessing Socialpsychological Characteristics of Visually Impaired and Hearing Impaired Students, 1966–1967*, Kalamazoo, Mich., Western Michigan Univ. (USOE G 3-6-068720-1594).

5   O. Lovaas, *Establishment of Appropriate Use of Pronouns and Prepositions in Schizophrenic and Retarded, 1966–1969*, Los Angeles, Calif., Univ. of California (USOE G4-6-061188-0814).

6   Heinz, op. cit.

7   B. Balow *et al., Educational and Behavioral Sequelae of Prenatal and Perinatal Conditions, 1966–1971*, Minneapolis, Minn., Univ. of Minnesota (USOE G32-33-0402-6021).

and postnatal period of life.[1] Studies initiated in 1967 further illustrate the broad scope of cross-disability research. One grant underwrote a nationwide survey and planning operation aimed at the exploration of the effects of different types of physical environments upon handicapped children.[2] A programmatic attack on man-machine systems designed for the crippled, the blind and the cerebral-palsied was undertaken by a cybernetics institute.[3]

A Research and Development Center established at Columbia University in 1967 projected a long-range programme of research with mentally retarded, emotionally disturbed, physically handicapped, visually impaired and speech-impaired children.[4] A unique study involving mentally retarded, emotionally disturbed, blind and deaf children got under way in 1969. The aim was to determine the attitudes of these children with regard to selected curricular areas such as language and science, and their attitudes toward teachers, parents, classmates and themselves.[5] The final USOE-supported enterprise represents further implementation of a policy of providing substantial long-range support to research and development centres. The new centre has the mission of producing a detailed educationally functional definition and description of the instruction of handicapped children. The aim is to search for specific characteristics of children which produce desired interaction effects with various instructional-treatment systems.[6]

Administrative research

Research in this field consists mostly of descriptive, and occasionally analytic, accounts of the experiences of individuals or institutions. At their best, most are carefully prepared case studies. Until 1969 the NEA–CEC reviews allotted a chapter to this area of study. These will be reviewed primarily to get the benefit of the reviewers' perceptions of the field and their recommendations for action. Several pertinent USOE studies will be noted. In the 1959 NEA–CEC research review, Baer surveyed studies of organization and supervision in special education.[7] Problems included determining optimum class size,

1   J. Isom, *A Study of Reading Disability in the U.S., the Occurrence, Causes, Characteristics, and Relationship to other Abnormalities, 1966–1971*, Portland, Oreg., Univ. of Oregon (USOE G 32-47-8210-6017).

2   W. Geer, *Physical Environment and Special Education: an Inter-Disciplinary Approach to Research, 1967–1969*, Washington, D.C., CEC (USOE G 2-7-070566-3026).

3   H. Kafafian, *Study of Man-machine Communication Systems for Disabled Persons, 1967–1970*, Washington, D.C., Cybernetics Research Inst. (USOE G 2-7-070533-4237).

4   L. Blackman, *A Comprehensive Research and Demonstration Facility for the Handicapped, 1967–1970*, New York, N.Y., Columbia Univ. (USOE G 2-7-070701-4249).

5   E. Thomas, *School Related Perception in Handicapped Children, 1969*, Charlottesville, Va, Univ. of Virginia (USOE OEG-3-9-562154-0052).

6   B. Balow, *A Center for Research and Development in Evaluation of Handicapped Children, 1969–1973*, Minneapolis, Minn., Univ. of Minnesota (USOE G-0-9-332189-4533).

7   C. Baer, 'Organization and Supervision of Special Education', *Rev. Educ. Res.*, Vol. 29, No. 5, December 1959, p. 566–70.

selection of supervisors, the utilization of lay assistants to teachers, pre-school training for the handicapped, methods of providing post-school guidance to the mentally retarded, and community involvement on behalf of handicapped children. Organization, administration and supervision were the subject of a 1963 review by Voelker and Mullen who noted the scarcity of factual surveys which might form the basis of research hypotheses and cited several efforts to formulate a theory of special education.[1] One attempt stressed the need for a comprehensive taxonomy of special education.[2] Another sought to build upon the social psychology of disability[3] and another stressed the need to base any theory upon knowledge of the interaction of disability and environmental demands upon the handicapped individual.[4] Four lines of investigation seen as urgent were optimum organization of special education programmes, evaluation of instruction, the incidence and prevalence of various exceptionalities, and long-range follow-up studies of handicapped youth and adults.

In 1963 Howe provided useful abstracts of major surveys and exploratory studies in administration, and of prevalence studies which attempted to deal with all types of exceptionality in the state.[5, 6] His major conclusion was, however:

The one most significant generalization on the present status of research would be that substantial behavioral research studies have not been done in the area of administration and supervision of special education.

Willenberg who reviewed organization, administration and supervision in 1966 expressed concern with the paucity of specific research on administration.[7] He noted Mackie's estimate that the number of handicapped children in need of special education averages about 10 per cent of the elementary and high school enrolment[8] and gave evidence of an increase in the number of multiply handicapped individuals. In this treatment of research on the instructional programme and supervision, Willenberg stressed the lack of any significant theory of instruction. Such theory was seen as essential to the conceptualization of the role of automated and programmed learning pro-

1   P. Voelker and F. Mueller, 'Organization, Administration, and Supervision of Special Education', *Rev. Educ. Res.*, Vol. 33, No. 1, February 1963, p. 5–19.
2   T. Jordan, 'Conceptual Issues in Development of a Taxonomy for Special Education', *Except. Children* (Arlington, Va), Vol. 28, September 1961, p. 7–12.
3   S. Levine, 'A Proposed Conceptual Framework for Special Education', *Except. Children* (Arlington, Va), Vol. 28, October 1961, p. 83–90.
4   B. Wright, *Physical Disability—a Psychological Approach*, New York, N.Y., Harper & Bros, 1960.
5   B. Farber, *The Prevalence of Exceptional Children in Illinois in 1958*, op. cit.
6   S. Wishik, 'Handicapped Children in Georgia: a Study of Prevalence, Disability Needs, and Resources', *Am. J. Publ. Hlth.* (New York, N.Y.), Vol. 46, 1956, p. 195–203.
7   E. Willenberg, 'Organization, Administration and Supervision of Special Education', *Rev. Educ. Res.*, Vol. 36, No. 1, February 1966, p. 134–50.
8   R. Mackie, 'Special Education Reaches Nearly 2 Million Children', *School Life*, Vol. 47, December 1964, p. 8–9.

cedures as well as the role of the teacher. Chalfant and Henderson examined research on administration in a 1968 review.[1] Acknowledging the continuing scarcity of such research they offered a number of reasons for this. 'Administrative research' had not been adequately defined: it lacked an identity. There was no relevant theoretical base. Such research is inherently complex due to the many levels of administrative responsibility, e.g. federal, state, local and facility levels. This complexity is compounded by the existence of multiple handicaps and multiple disciplines, etc. Among descriptive reports, a study of co-operative programmes in special education,[2] a report delineating problems in providing special educational services in sparsely populated areas,[3] and a description of team teaching with TMR children[4] are especially noteworthy. A project to determine economic and demographic factors underlying public school provisions for exceptional children, and to develop a diagnostic technique for determining if governmental units could be expected to provide special education services is of interest.[5] Chalfant and Henderson emphasized the necessity for evaluation to be established as a priority item early in programme planning so as to force clarification of goals, selection of methods of study, and specification of indices of progress in advance of programme operation.

Recent increase in interest in administrative research is suggested by the fact that of the six USOE projects described next, four were initiated in 1969. A project in 1966 resulted in an instrument designed to simulate critical features of the work of administrators for use in training and as a basis of behavioural research related to special education administration.[6] Another venture aimed at testing the assumption that establishment of a research-demonstration unit in a state department of special education would result in an increase in research-oriented activities in the public schools of the state.[7] In 1969 a one-year grant provided partial support of a projected centre for the pre-school education of handicapped children.[8] Problems of delivery of service in the inner city where there is an inordinate prevalence among the

1   J. Chalfant and R. Henderson, 'Administration', in: Johnson and Blank (eds), op. cit., p. 304–31.
2   F. Lord, *Cooperative Programs in Special Education*, Washington, D.C., NEA, 1964.
3   J. Jordan (ed.), *Special Education Services in Sparsely Populated Areas: Guidelines for Research*, Boulder, Colo., Western Interstate Commission for Higher Education, 1966.
4   H. Taylor *et al.*, 'Team Teaching with Trainable Mentally Retarded Children', *Except. Children* (Arlington, Va), Vol. 30, 1964, p. 304–9.
5   J. Chalfant, *Factors Related to Special Education Services* (Council for Exceptional Children monog., Series B, 1967, No. B-3).
6   D. Sage, *The Development of Simulation Materials for Research and Training Administration of Special Education, 1966*, Syracuse, N.Y., Syracuse Univ. (USOE G-1-6-062466-1880).
7   F. Ayers, *A Proposed Demonstration Project in Development of a Research and Demonstration Unit in the Minnesota Department of Education, 1966–1969*, St. Paul, Minn., Minn. Dept of Ed. (USOE GEOG-3-6-062348-1749).
8   R. Barsch, *A Planning Grant to Establish a Center for Preschool Education of Handicapped Children, 1969*, New Haven, Conn., Southern Connecticut State College (USOE OEG-0-9-162085-1386).

poor of educationally and multiply handicapped elementary schoolchildren was a research target. The investigators proposed to use the regular classroom as the base for a wholistic, cross-discipline, education-treatment programme involving children, family and community with small classes in which handicapped children were to comprise no more than one-third of the enrolment.[1] A major effort to help states evaluate the impact of federal assistance grants got under way with a USOE grant to a technical organization which specializes in the study of social and technical innovation. The project aimed at developing evaluation systems which state departments of education might use to discern and assess the effects of federal programmes designed to help states establish, improve and expand special education services, staff training, vocational training for the handicapped, and demonstration centres and projects.[2] A quite different approach to evaluation is evident in a grant which supports a proposal to develop and test a pilot set of evaluation materials for teachers and other special education personnel. The final product was envisioned as an in-service training package composed of a written resource guide with a co-ordinated automated slide-tape.[3]

Administrative research and development rose in priority throughout the decade in health and welfare as well as education. This was a response to widespread criticism of existing systems of service delivery in these fields. The charge was that too much resource had gone into the development of the components of service and too little into the study of the processes and problems of the delivery of service. The existing knowledge about the delivery of health, education and welfare services is limited in amount, difficult to retrieve, because it is scattered through the literature of many disciplines, and the technology of delivery exists primarily in the lore of administrators and practitioners. The present writer is engaged in an effort to systematize and extend existing knowledge of the delivery of health, education and welfare services to handicapped children as a foundation for an intensive long-range empirical study of delivery systems.[4] In the paradigm which guides this effort, administration is conceived as having the goal of developing and maintaining optimum relationships between needs and resources. Further, administration is assigned the specific objectives of identifying needs, and developing and delivering service appropriate to these needs. This deliberate linkage of responsibility for development and delivery is based on the funda-

1   R. Harris et al., *Overcoming the Problems of the Handicapped Pupil: a Training-research Model for the Inner City Elementary School, 1969–1970*, Richmond, Calif., Richmond Unified School District (USOE G-0-9-142218-4657).

2   G. Rosenthal, *Evaluation of State Administered Programs for the Handicapped, 1969–1971*, Cambridge, Mass., Organization for Social & Technical Innovation (USOE G-0-9-312173-4450).

3   W. Meierhenry, *A Pilot Project to Develop Inservice Training Materials in the Valuation of Special Education Programs for Handicapped Children, 1969–1970*, Lincoln, Nebr., Univ. of Nebraska (USOE G-0-9-372160-3553).

4   W. Hurder, *The Delivery of Services to Handicapped Children*, Urbana, Ill., Inst. for Research on Except. Child., 1970.

mental assumption that the mission of these service enterprises is met only with the ultimate delivery of services to the intended consumer.

Three additional assumptions are central in the conceptualization and empirical study of the processes of delivery. First is that the critical and culminating events of delivery occur at the interface between service and consumer. Two criteria are needed to measure performance at this interface. The first, access, reflects the necessity of contact or contiguity of consumer and service and is the probability that service is available to the consumer. The second, disposition, refers to attitudes of the producer and the consumer which come into play when access has been achieved and is the probability that the consumer will accept the service. In the paradigm, these two criteria are the critical dependent variables. The second assumption is that, within the administrative frame of reference, the delivery of services has two distinct but interdependent objectives: the clinical-prescriptive and the administrative-programmatic. When the clinical-prescriptive objective prevails, the intent is to make a specific sequence of services available to a specific handicapped individual. When the administrative-programmatic objective is uppermost the intent is to make a general class of services available to a class or category of individuals. The third assumption is that the principle delivery-relevant components of health, education and welfare services are specialized knowledge, personnel and organization. Knowledge, personnel and organization comprise the major independent variables in the study of system of delivery. Within the perspective of this paradigm, the central challenge posed by the delivery of services is the active manipulation of knowledge, personnel and organization in such a way as to meet the criteria of access and disposition.

The decade in retrospect: some impressions

Mueller has suggested that from the growth of research on the multiply handicapped there may come a new mode of conceptualizing educational handicaps which would lead to educational programmes based specifically on educationally relevant behaviour. If this is to take place, however, major changes will be required in the mode of conceptualization and conduct of teacher preparation and teacher certification, and in the organization of the services of agencies which provide education to handicapped children. At present, classes are organized and teachers trained and certified in adherence to standards based upon traditional categories of handicap. These place high priority upon specialization in a single area of handicap. It can be predicted that ultimately the considerations which are bringing about change in the direction of research will make themselves felt in the preparation of personnel and the organization of services. But as of yet the impact has been minor.

The impetus to research in this area which has come from sharpened awareness of the deleterious effect of early social and economic disadvantage and deprivation upon the development of children must be recognized. As a result of the war on poverty many practitioners and researchers were brought into significant contact with the children of the poor for the first time. They observed first-hand a striking prevalence of handicapping conditions. They saw children exposed to an overlay of many factors which militate against normal development—unmet health needs, severe experiential deprivation, cultural values antethetical to the values of the educational system, and an umbrella of negative expectation raised by both their own group and the larger society. Under this overlay they found children subject to all of the usual vicissitudes of development which arise out of genetic considerations, adventitious disease and injury. To many who viewed this reality for the first time the issue of the relative significance of genetic versus environmental factors in the production of the handicaps they saw became an irrelevant question.

Another outcome of the condition of the poor has been increased concern with the delivery of services. It has long been known that the poor were less favoured in the distribution of public services but the grossness of the inequities in delivery only became apparent upon closer examination of their circumstances. Within the decade, the poor in America became more vocal and in some cases militant in demanding improved service. In most such instances the complaints centred on failures and inadequacies in the area of delivery. These complaints have played a part in the giving of higher priority to study and research in the area of the delivery of service. The poor are not alone in this discontent. Consumers at all levels of the socio-economic scale have become increasingly critical of the delivery of health services, and to a lesser extent, educational services. But the extreme situation of the poor served to dramatize the problem.

Organization and support
of the research enterprise

The availability of substantial funds for research on the education of the handicapped child is a recent phenomenon. The following summary of this development draws on a very useful overview prepared by Martin.[1] In 1954 the Cooperative Research Act became law. It permitted grants to universities and colleges, and to the states, for co-operative support of educational

1   E. Martin, 'Breakthrough for the Handicapped: Legislative History', *Except. Children* (Arlington, Va), Vol. 34, March 1968, p. 493–504.

research, surveys and demonstrations, but enabling funds were not appropriated until 1957 when $1 million was voted. In 1963 the eighty-eighth Congress passed legislation which provided grants for research and demonstration projects in the area of education of the handicapped, and the Division of Handicapped Children and Youth in the Office of Education was created to administer programmes authorized by this legislation only to be abolished in 1965. In 1965, the Elementary and Secondary Education Act (ESEA) became law. Many view this legislation as the first in which any significant federal aid had been made available to elementary and secondary education. The impact on the handicapped came as a result of a section of the Act, Title I, which earmarked funds for use by local education agencies in work with children from low income areas and permitted aid to states for use on behalf of handicapped children in the states' school systems. The next advance came in 1966 with the enactment of the Education for Handicapped Children bill which came to be known as Title VI of the ESEA. In addition to increasing funds for research, this bill provided for the creation of the present Bureau of Education for the Handicapped, and the National Advisory Committee on Handicapped Children. Since the enactment of Title VI of the ESEA in 1966, federal legislation has provided for the creation of Regional Resource Centers which have the mission of assisting teachers by providing educational evaluation and consultation for all handicaps. Centres and services for deaf-blind children were established separately. An amendment of Title VI of the ESEA in 1968 made it mandatory that 15 per cent of the funds appropriated through Title III should be used for the education of the handicapped. The ninetieth Congress also passed legislation broadening the authority of the Bureau of Education for the Handicapped to support research. Advances in administrative recognition of the handicapped, as exemplified by the creation of the Bureau of Education for the Handicapped, were probably as important as the appropriation of larger amounts of money. Clear designation of priority as reflected in the placement of the bureau near the top of the administrative hierarchy was vital to sustained action on behalf of the bureau's mission. Originally the director of the bureau was an associate commissioner of education and reported directly to the commissioner of the Office of Education. In late 1969, the status of the bureau was changed so that the director was to be thrice removed from the commissioner of education.[1] The consequences for support of education of the handicapped remain to be seen.

Role of government

Elementary and secondary education services are directed and financed almost completely at the state and local level of government. Federal partici-

[1]   J. Allen, Asst. Secretary for Health, Education, and Welfare and United States Commissioner of Education, *Memorandum*, 22 August 1969.

pation is minimal.[1] The relationships among the three levels of government
are almost reversed in the support of research. The federal government is the
major source, the state next, and local government is last in funding research.
These differences make for difficulty in articulating the research and the service enterprises.

Federal role

USOE is the federal agency with major responsibility for research on the
education of the handicapped. Between 1964 and 1969 USOE distributed
$41 million for this purpose. The recently formed Bureau for the Education
of the Handicapped has major concern for research and for the education
and training of personnel. The bureau's outlook was recently described by
its first director, J. J. Gallagher, who foresaw major concentration on the goal
of discovering mechanisms to translate new knowledge into action at the
instructional level.[2] The anticipated use of the bureau's resources in this campaign has been described in greater detail by staff in charge of various programmes.[3,4,5] Moss' description of the research division is most relevant here.
Administratively, the division is divided among units responsible for research
projects and programmes, research laboratories and demonstration, and
curricula and media research. Formal categories of research support include
grants for research and development centres, programme research, research
projects, the development of research competencies within academic departments, demonstration projects, regional demonstration centres, the development and utilization of new educational media, and grants for curriculum
development and evaluation. Other federal agencies fund research which
complements the work of USOE. Among these the NIMH, NINDS,
NICHHD and the Rehabilitation Services Administration, of the Department of Health, Education and Welfare are prominent. The NIMH in
particular supports many projects which are relevant by criteria set forth at
the beginning of this report. One example is the previously cited study of
'the stress of school'.[6] Other examples include a study of the relationships
between teachers' styles of teaching and pupil personality growth,[7] an infant
education project aimed at the early prevention of cognitive defect in children

1   In the state of Illinois in the last budgetary period, local, state and federal contribu-
    tions to the cost of elementary and secondary education were 61, 25, and 5 per cent,
    respectively.
2   J. J. Gallagher, 'Organization and Special Education', *Except. Children* (Arlington, Va),
    Vol. 34, No. 7, March 1968, 485-92.
3   J. Moss, 'Research and Demonstration', op. cit.
4   L. Lucito, 'Division of Training Programs: its Mission', *Except. Children* (Arlington, Va),
    Vol. 34, No. 7, 1968, p. 531-6.
5   F. Withrow, 'Enlarged Responsibilities for Educational Services to Handicapped Chil-
    dren', *Except. Children* (Arlington, Va.), Vol. 34, No. 7, 1968, p. 551-4.
6   Lambert, op. cit.
7   R. Soar, *Pupil Growth in and out of School, 1967-1970*, Gainesville, Fla, Univ. of Florida
    (MH15626).

from disadvantaged homes,[1] and a study of instructional strategies in infant stimulation.[2] Note has already been made of the collaborative perinatal study undertaken by NINDS/ and most recently extended by USOE.[4] NICHHD and the Rehabilitation Services Administration are particularly active in support of research in the areas of etiology and treatment-rehabilitation, respectively, in mental retardation.[5]

State role

The pivotal position of state government in the development and maintenance of educational services for handicapped children has been described in a special report of the President's Panel on Mental Retardation.[6] These responsibilities are discharged primarily through special education units within state departments of education. In states whose special education units have divisions directly concerned with research, the orientation is likely to be toward applied and operational research or problems of dissemination and utilization of research findings. Thus, state departments of education received from 5 to 6 per cent of the research funds allocated by USOE in the period 1964–69, primarily to support research on the education of mentally retarded children and the emotionally disturbed, and the operation of instructional materials centres. State governments provide funds to local school systems to help to defray the higher costs of special education services, prorating this according to the number and types of handicapped children served by the local school system. Another form of state service to handicapped children is the provision of residential facilities for the mentally retarded, the blind and the deaf in practically all states. Some states provide special residential services for the emotionally disturbed and for the crippled child. In some instances these residential facilities have been the site of important research and, with the trend toward placing only the more severely handicapped in residential care, such research becomes increasingly urgent.

Local role

Elementary and secondary school systems get major direction and a substantial amount of their financial support at the local level of government. With the exception of school systems in larger metropolitan areas, administrative provisions for research are informal. Nevertheless, local schools were second only to colleges and universities in the amount of USOE grants and funds between 1964 and 1969, having received 13 per cent of new grants. However,

1 D. Weikart, *Ypsilanti Carnegie Infant Education Project, 1968–1970*, Ypsilanti, Mich., Ypsilanti Public Schools (MH17462).
2 I. Gordon, *Instructional Strategies in Infant Stimulation, 1968–1971*, Gainesville, Fla, Univ. of Florida (MH 17347).
3 Heinz, op. cit.
4 B. Balow et al., *Educational and Behavioral Sequelae . . .*, op. cit.
5 *Mental Retardation Grants*, Washington D.C., U.S. Dept HEW, 1969.
6 W. Hurder et al., *Report of the Task Force on Coordination*, Washington, D.C., Pres. Panel on Mental Retardation, U.S. Dept HEW, 1963.

the percentage of projects operated by schools fell steadily during this period so that in 1969 they received only 7 per cent of the projects and 5 per cent of research and demonstration funds distributed by USOE.

Role of academic and technical agencies

Academic agencies

Over two-thirds of the $41 million awarded by USOE for research on the education of the handicapped in the period 1964–69 went to colleges and universities. Since the majority of the academic centres to which USOE grants were channelled operate within the framework of state government, another facet of state participation in the total research enterprise is revealed. The patterns of intra-university organization for research are extremely varied and complex. There are no data which permit a completely adequate description but the general nature of such patterns can be noted. The basic building blocks of universities and colleges are the disciplines which together form the sciences and the humanities and make up both the foundation and the frame of the academic edifice. Staff and administrative units associated with them are generally knowledge-oriented with primary goals of acquiring, and disseminating to colleagues and students, new information about concepts and phenomena of the discipline. The next level in the structure of the university is composed of the professional schools. The research interests of these schools and their staffs are usually service oriented as their primary aim is to gain and transmit information of utility to the profession and its practice.

Special mechanisms exist to focus the expertise of both the scientific and the professional members of the academic community on pressing social problems. Universities have created a variety of administrative entities designed to pool and focus the know-how of a number of disciplines and professions in pursuit of greater knowledge and improved services in areas of concern, These entities, variously known as centres, institutes, laboratories, offices. etc., have increased in number and variety since the Second World War. The Institute for Research on Exceptional Children (IREC) was one of the first research units of this type to focus on the education of handicapped children. This institute, conceived by S. A. Kirk, has the mission of advancing knowledge about exceptional children so as to make more effective the work of public and private agencies on behalf of such children.[1] IREC has been the source of much research in virtually all exceptionalities, including the gifted child. The contribution to the preparation of research personnel is suggested by the more than seventy-five students who did their doctoral research within the framework of the institute. Current research emphasizes work with the deaf, the mentally retarded, the emotionally disturbed, learn-

1   S. Kirk, *Ten Years of Research in the Institute for Research on Exceptional Children*, Urbana, Ill., Univ. of Illinois, 1964.

ing disabilities, culturally disadvantaged children, the language development of handicapped children and the delivery of services. Another pattern of organization of academic resources is seen in the Research and Development Center at Columbia University which was noted earlier.[1] A $2 million construction grant and other programme support enabled construction of an eleven-storey building and initiation of research in five areas of handicap. The centre is closely linked with the Special Education Department of Columbia and, through the department, with thirty-five schools and facilities serving the handicapped. The application of research findings into teaching and into practice is a major objective. What is perhaps the paramount goal of the centre has been stated by the director as the development of a science of special education.[2]

IREC and the Columbia centre are specialized administrative entities designed to achieve and keep a focus on selected research activities. Another approach is to make research a basic responsibility of an academic department of special education. This approach is seen at the universities of Oregon and Texas where the departments of special education are engaged in a wide variety of research and related activities. The research emphases of the Oregon department include the mentally retarded and the emotionally disturbed among categories of handicap, the early development of all handicapped children, strategic problems of the definition of exceptionality, problems of learning, and the rehabilitation and work adjustment of handicapped youth. A variety of federally supported centres contribute to the research of the special education department. These include a Regional Resource Center, a Materials Instruction Center, a University Affiliated Center for Mental Retardation, and a Center for the Early Education of Handicapped Children.[3] A similar organizational style is found at the University of Texas where the department of special education is quite active in research on the education of the handicapped. Among its resources are a federally funded Instructional Materials Center and a Rehabilitation Research and Training Center in Mental Retardation. Some major research themes of the department are work with minimally brain-injured children, with the emotionally disturbed and with the mentally retarded child.[4]

Technical organizations
Independent privately directed research organizations are a new development in the behavioural and social science fields, but have a long history in the physical sciences. Core staff have specialized knowledge and expertise

1   L. Blackman, *A Comprehensive Research and Demonstration Facility* . . ., op. cit.
2   L. Blackman, 'Research and Demonstration Center for Education of Handicapped Children', *R & D News*, Vol. 1, No. 1, June 1969, New York, N.Y., Teachers College, Columbia Univ.
3   H. Prehm, personal communication, Eugene, Oregon, Dept of Special Education, Univ. of Oregon.
4   H. Jasper, Personal communication, Austin, Tex., Dept of Special Education, Univ. of Texas.

appropriate to the mission of the organization. This mission is usually sharply delineated and clearly spelled out. The organizations are almost always located near major universities and draw on their specialized resources. Examples of technical organizations utilized by USOE are the Organization for the Study of Technical and Social Innovation,[1] the Cybernetics Institute,[2] and the American Institute for Research.[3] The availability of these highly specialized organizations add tactical flexibility to agencies such as USOE. Their utilization by USOE increased from zero in 1964 to seven grants totalling $1,250,000 in 1969.

Professional organizations

These groups also represent a significant resource to USOE which may turn to such groups for special studies such as the project on architectural needs undertaken by the Council on Exceptional Children.[4] Between 1964 and 1969, USOE made arrangements of this type for research on multiple handicaps, six on speech and hearing, six in the area of hearing impairment and two each on mental retardation and on visual handicap.

Role of private and volunteer groups

The contribution of these groups cannot be adequately described here, but their support has been invaluable to the handicapped. Except in the area of the emotionally and socially disturbed child, groups of parents joined by professionals and other citizens have given vigorous support to services, professional training and research in all handicaps. These and related groups are so numerous that the Council on Exceptional Children recently issued a guide to such agencies and organizations.[5] Parent groups in particular have done yeoman service at all levels of government in keeping the needs of the handicapped children before lawmakers. A word must be said about private foundations. Among these the Joseph P. Kennedy, Jr Foundation has made very substantial contributions to the field of mental retardation. In research the foundation conducts an extensive programme of awards to outstanding investigators, makes substantial grants to defray the cost of construction and operation of research facilities, and underwrites career research fellowships for scientists in many disciplines. These activities have especially helped to overcome the isolation of the scientific community from the problem of mental retardation and to narrow the gulf between the scientific and the service communities.

1 Rosenthal, op. cit.
2 Kafafian, op. cit.
3 Gropper, op. cit.
4 Geer, op. cit.
5 A Guide to Agencies and Organizations Concerned with Exceptional Children, Washington, D.C., April 1969, (ERIC Excerpt).

Special problems of organization and support

As might be expected in an enterprise as complex as this, there are many problems which defy adequate solution. A select few of these problems will be dealt with here.

Co-ordination—the process of bringing all necessary resources to bear in the appropriate sequence in order to accomplish a specific mission—is a ubiquitous problem. Three conditions must be met if co-ordination is to occur. These are communication, co-operation, and the delegation of authority among the participants in a given enterprise. Analysis of various circumstances and mechanisms involving co-ordination will substantiate the primacy of these three factors.

Inter-agency co-ordination is a perpetual problem in government, what with multiple agencies having overlapping, conflicting and sometimes competing responsibilities. This is especially true in children's services. The recent creation of the Office of Child Development in the Office of the Secretary of the Department of Health, Education and Welfare, had co-ordination as a major objective. In the statement by President Nixon at the time of the establishment of the office, it was assigned the responsibility to '. . . provide the means for coordination among programs for children administered by the operating agencies of the Department'.[1] Other inter-agency co-ordinating mechanisms have more restricted missions. Some examples are the Secretary's (of the Department of Health, Education and Welfare) Committee on Mental Retardation and the President's Committee on Mental Retardation.

Intra-agency co-ordination is a problem for which adequate and enduring solutions are rare. A major thrust at intra-agency co-ordination in a circumscribed area is illustrated by the creation by USOE of an entity known as the National Laboratory on Early Education which was initially located on the campus of the University of Illinois.[2] The primary function of this laboratory is to co-ordinate certain aspects of the funding and programming of a number of USOE-supported centres for Early Childhood Education which are located at universities throughout the country, e.g. Peabody College, Cornell University, University of Kansas, University of Oregon, and others. Each such centre is assigned a different area of emphasis within the broad spectrum of early childhood education. The challenge to co-ordination is to avoid unnecessary duplication of effort and to expedite the flow of information among the centres. The relationship of the National Laboratory to USOE and to each of the centres might be likened to the relationship of a prime contractor to a number of sub-contractors. In this an overriding concern of USOE is to achieve co-ordination of a complex set of activities.

Academic-service agency co-ordination is often a critical factor in research

1 *Office of Child Development*, Washington, D.C. 20201, Office of the Secretary, U.S. Dept HEW.
2 J. Miller, *National Laboratory on Early Childhood Education, 1969–1971*, Urbana, Ill., Univ. of Illinois (USOE C3-7-070706-3118).

on handicapped children. Broad guidelines for such relationships are available in the report on co-ordination of the President's Panel on Mental Retardation.[1] A prime consideration is clear recognition of the fundamental differences in the objectives of the two agencies. The basic functions of the university are to produce, preserve and disseminate knowledge. Service agencies exist primarily to serve directly the health, education and other social needs of people. These differences must be taken into account in any consideration of joint university-service agency endeavours.

Dissemination and utilization
of research findings

Overview

The period between the close of the Second World War and the sixties witnessed vast expansion of federal support for research. One result was an explosion of knowledge. Another was the question of how to put this knowledge to the best use. This question became so persistent that concern with the utilization of research findings entered the political domain in the sixties. The federal Congress conducted formal inquiries into the matter. Federal agencies established a variety of new administrative units responsible for facilitating the utilization of research findings in practical areas. Much of the unrest and discontent in health, education and welfare stemmed from dissatisfaction with the rate of development and delivery of services. This pressure to narrow the gap between discovery and application remained strong at the close of the decade.

Professional and scientific action first aimed at problems of dissemination and retrieval of scientific and technical information. With the knowledge explosion it became virtually impossible to scan or to retrieve all relevant knowledge in many fields. One direction of attack on these problems was to examine the interface of the scientist and his information system.[2] By the end of the decade, systematic study of the processes and problems of dissemination and utilization had progressed to the point that it could be referred to as the 'science of knowledge utilization'. This development is traced by the Center for Research on Utilization of Scientific Knowledge (at the University of Michigan) which, with USOE support, attempted to assess the current state

1   W. Hurder *et al.*, *Report of the Task Force on Coordination*, op.cit.
2   B. Parker *et al.*, 'Research for Psychologists at the Interface of the Scientist and His Information System', *Am.Psychol.* (Washington, D.C.), Vol.21, No.11, November 1966, p.1061–71.

of knowledge about dissemination and utilization, and to develop a model for the organization of this knowledge which would yield implications of value to researchers, practitioners and policy makers. Growth in this highly specialized field of knowledge was found to be so rapid that an explosion of knowledge about the utilization of knowledge is imminent! The Michigan staff assembled a bibliography of about 4,000 items from the literature up to about 1966–67[1] and predicted 40,000 titles by the seventies. Their study is strongly recommended to the reader who wishes to pursue dissemination and utilization in greater depth.[2]

Activities of USOE

The President's Panel on Mental Retardation recommended the creation within USOE of instructional materials centres 'for the purpose of providing special educators and other related personnel with ready access to valid instructional materials and information for the education of handicapped children'.[3] We have noted earlier Gallagher's goal of discovering mechanisms to translate new knowledge into action at the instructional level.[4] Much of the burden of this aspiration will fall upon dissemination, and more particularly, utilization of research findings. USOE has assumed a leadership role in this campaign and has deployed its resources over several fronts.

The Instructional Materials Centers (IMC) Program of the Bureau of Education for the Handicapped has been recently described by Olshin.[5] Designed to provide instructional material and information to teachers of the handicapped, these centres also carry on research and development activities aimed at the evaluation of materials and the production of new instructional materials. The centres are placed according to demographic characteristics of the areas served. Of a total of 14, 9 are located in the densely populated eastern third of the nation, 12 are administered by universities, 2 by state departments of education. An unsolved problem is accessibility to school systems and teachers. An exploratory effort to bridge the gap between an IMC and its clients got under way in 1968. The objectives were to explore ways in which local funds and facilities could be used to amplify the effect of federally financed dissemination efforts.[6] A pilot evaluation of two univer-

1   R. Havelock *et al.*, *Bibliography on Knowledge Utilization Dissemination*, Ann Arbor, Mich., Center for Research on Utilization of Scientific Knowledge, Univ. of Michigan, 1969.
2   R. Havelock *et al.*, *Planning for Innovation Through Dissemination and Utilization of Knowledge*, Ann Arbor, Mich., Inst. for Social Research, Univ. of Michigan, July 1969.
3   *A Proposed Program for National Action to Combat Mental Retardation*, op. cit.
4   J. J. Gallagher, 'Organization and Special Education', op. cit.
5   G. Olshin, 'Special Education Instructional Materials Center Program', *Except. Children* (Arlington, Va), Vol. 34, No. 7, March 1968, p. 515–23.
6   J. F. Vinsonhaler, *Improving the Dissemination of Instructional Materials for Handicapped Children and Youth, 1968–1970*, East Lansing, Mich., Michigan State Univ. (USOE G-0-8-071321-2673).

sity-based IMCs sheds some light on their mode of operation. A private technical organization collected data through site visits, mail questionnaires, and interviews with teachers and administrators. Of the sample of clients, 90 per cent knew of the IMC, half were familiar with their services, and a quarter of the teachers had visited an IMC library. Teachers reported materials demonstrations conducted at their professional meetings the most helpful service and also cited in-service training institutes and conferences sponsored by the IMC as being valuable.[1]

The IMC programme does not represent the whole extent of USOE dissemination efforts. Olshin also described the part played by the Captioned Films for the Deaf Program, and four Regional Media Centers for the deaf. An important development aimed at helping to co-ordinate the IMC programme and other dissemination efforts was the creation of a national clearing-house within the Educational Resources Information Center (ERIC) under the joint auspices of USOE and the Council on Exceptional Children.[2] More recently, Congress passed a law authorizing a National Center on Educational Media and Materials for the Handicapped.[3] Still another new concept which focuses more sharply on utilization than dissemination is that of the Regional Resource Center. These centres are to focus upon problems of education and are based upon the assumption that the best hope for handicapped children lies in effective teaching. This is an experimental programme which has only begun to explore approaches to these goals. In setting forth the essential purposes and elements of Regional Resource Centers, Congress saw them as providing 'a bank of advice and technical services upon which educators in the region could draw in order to improve the education of exceptional children'. Further, emphasis was seen as being placed upon the special educational problems of individual children and their families.[4]

Demonstration is a form of dissemination often used by USOE and other agencies. Demonstration as a form of dissemination and teaching was first developed in the United States by the federal agricultural extension service which has used this method with remarkable success in programmes of adult education. Demonstration is sometimes incorporated into the core programme of large-scale undertakings such as the Columbia Research and Development Center[5]. Two activities initiated in 1969 illustrate a project

1 G. Johnson *et al.*, *A Pilot Evaluation of Instructional Material Centers, 1967–1969*, Silver Springs, Md, American Institute for Research in Behavioral Sciences (USOE G-2-7-070438-3027).

2 J. Jordan, *Clearinghouse on Exceptional Children, 1967–1971*, Washington, D.C., CEC (USOE G 2-6-062473-1717).

3 *Programs for the Handicapped*, Washington, D.C. 20201, Secretary's Committee on Mental Retardation, U.S. Dept HEW, September 1969.

4 *Policies and Procedures: Regional Resource Centers for Improvement of the Education of Handicapped Children*, Washington, D.C., Bureau of Education for the Handicapped, U.S. Office of Education, March 1969.

5 L. Blackman, *A Comprehensive Research and Demonstration Facility* ..., op. cit.

approach to demonstration. The first is a mobile recreation and physical education unit designed to travel throughout the state providing the latest information about such work with the mentally retarded.[1] The second project has the aim of demonstrating that vocational technical schools and community colleges for the hearing population can with certain modifications also serve graduates of secondary programmes for the deaf.[2] Statistical analyses supplied by USOE indicate that in the period 1964–69, 34 per cent of the activities funded by USOE were classified as more or less directly concerned with demonstration.

Clearing-houses are a direct way of attacking the problem of dissemination of information. The clearest example of this is the ERIC Clearinghouse on Exceptional Children which is largely funded by USOE and is operated by the Council for Exceptional Children.[3] As originally conceived, this clearinghouse is concerned with collecting, abstracting, testing and evaluating literature and materials, as well as developing materials, interpreting research and disseminating information. It will be helpful to examine the Educational Resources Information Center (ERIC) in more detail. Much of the following is taken from a document, *How to Use ERIC*, prepared for potential clients of the system.[4] USOE sponsors the ERIC system as a means of providing the educational community with information about current research in education. ERIC is a national information network made up of a headquarters facility in Washington, D.C., and nineteen decentralized clearing-houses. Each of these nineteen units focuses on a specific area of education and each is located at a university or other institution in various parts of the United States. The basic function of ERIC is to acquire and process research documents and to make these known through its publications. The principal periodical, *Research in Education*, appears monthly and carries data supplied by all of the clearing-houses; hence, it covers a wide spectrum of educational interests.[5] In early 1969, a special service, *Exceptional Child Education Abstracts*, was initiated through the CEC Information Center which functions as the Clearinghouse on Exceptional Children in the ERIC programme and as part of the IMC programme.[6] A more specialized clearing-house service of recent origin is a state-federal computerized legislative information service. A joint endeavour of USOE and CEC, it will analyse and disseminate data about

1 W. Marshall, *Mobile Recreation and Physical Education Unit, 1969–1970*, Frankfort, Ky, Kentucky Association for Retarded Children Inc. (USOE G-0-9-272707-4263 [032]).
2 C. Erickson, Improved Vocational and Academic Training Opportunities for Deaf People, 1969, Seattle, Wash., Seattle Community College (USOE GRD-3268-S-69).
3 J. Jordan, *Clearinghouse on Exceptional Children, 1967–1971*, op. cit.
4 L. Griffin, *How to Use ERIC*, Urbana, Ill., ERIC Clearinghouse on Early Childhood Education, January 1969.
5 *Research in Education*, Washington, D.C., Office of Education, Bureau of Research, U.S. Dept HEW.
6 *Exceptional Child Education Abstracts*, Washington, D.C. 20036, CEC Information Center, 1201 Sixteenth St, N.W.

legislation for the handicapped. An ultimate aim is to establish an independently financed computer-based clearing-house service for professionals in special education.[1]

Dissemination activities of other agencies

Various federal agencies make special efforts to provide current information about research in their area of responsibility. Some examples are a series of bulletins titled, *Research Relating to Children*,[2] and a derivative periodical, *Research Relating to Emotionally Disturbed Children*,[3] prepared by the Children's Bureau of the Department of Health, Education, and Welfare, and the *Mental Retardation Abstracts* issued by the Division of Mental Retardation of the Rehabilitation Services Administration.[4] Each of these differ somewhat in style, format, and in degree of emphasis upon published papers and research projects. Unlike the ERIC publications which tend to concentrate on educational research, these sources attempt to cover a variety of professional and disciplinary studies relevant to handicapped children.

Dissemination and the delivery of services

Major impetus for improved dissemination of information and materials came from interest in the ultimate utilization of knowledge. This interest has been ascribed to '. . . the growing expectations on the part of industrial executives, government leaders, and the general public that most, if not all, of our storehouse of scientific *knowledge should be useful to man*'.[5] It has already been made abundantly clear that the path from initial discovery or invention is rarely unbroken. With respect to the knowledge *per se*, it is obvious that the inital discovery or invention must have sufficient reliability *and* validity to survive transmission from researcher to researcher, researcher to practitioner, and practitioner to practitioner. And yet the knowledge which underlies special education—knowledge derived from the behavioural-social sciences—is peculiarly difficult to conserve as it passes through this knowledge-to-action cycle. We do not know if this instability is attributable to the intrinsic

1 F. Weintraub, *Development and Evaluation of State-federal Computerized Legislative Information. Clearinghouse for Handicapped Children and Youth, 1969–1972*, Washington, D.C., CEC (USOE G-0-9-182013-3451).
2 *Research Relating to Children*, Washington, D.C., Social and Rehabilitation Service, Children's Bureau, U.S. Dept HEW; Supt. of Documents, U.S. Govt Printing Office.
3 *Research Relating to Emotionally Disturbed Children*, Washington, D.C., Social and Rehabilitation Service, Children's Bureau, U.S. Dept HEW; Supt. of Documents, U.S. Govt Printing Office.
4 *Mental Retardation Abstracts*, Washington, D.C., Division of Mental Retardation, Rehabilitation Services Administration; Supt of Documents, U.S. Govt Printing Office.
5 R. Havelock *et al.*, *Planning for Innovation* . . ., op.cit.

nature of the knowledge, the present status of our ability to formulate such knowledge, or some combination of these and other factors. The important thing is that because both the knowledge base and the practice of special education draw heavily upon the behavioural and social sciences for new knowledge, and for means of evaluating the outcome of practice, it is subject to the hazards of this instability.

Various attributes of the practioner participate in substantial ways in the process of delivery of service to the consumer. The practitioner may accept or reject new information or materials according to highly idiosyncratic dispositional criteria. In addition, teachers (as well as psychiatrists, psychologists and others whose practice draws upon the knowledge stores of the behavioural-social sciences) use the *self* as an instrument of education, training and therapy. Through work such as that begun by Rosenthal[1] and Beez[2] we may some day parcel out these intra-practitioner factors and treat them as we do other behavioural and social data.

Teacher preparation
and research

Two aspects of teacher preparation particularly relevant to research are the part training plays in the development of research manpower and the role of training programmes in moulding teachers' attitudes toward the products and the processes of research. In a discussion of teacher training, Cain has noted that the very rapid growth of special education has required that major attention be given to the initiation and development of new services.[3] For this reason among others, the issues of basic concern in this chapter have received little systematic attention.

One of the most striking areas of growth has been in programmes of teacher preparation. At the beginning of the decade it was estimated that around 4 million children needed special education services. It was thought that about 1 million were getting such service.[4] By 1963 it was estimated that one in three children who were eligible for special education were actually

---

1   R. Rosenthal, *Pygmalion in the Classroom*, New York, N.Y., Holt, Rinehart & Winston Inc., 1968.
2   Beez, op. cit.
3   L. Cain, 'Special Education Moves Ahead: a comment on the Education of Teachers', *Except. Children* (Arlington, Va), Vol. 30, No. 2, January 1964, p. 211–17.
4   R. Mackie *et al.*, *Exceptional Children and Youth*. Washington, D.C., U.S. Dept HEW; Govt Printing Office, 1963.

in such programmes.[1] In 1968, Lucito, the director of training programmes for the Bureau for the Education of the Handicapped, cited an estimate to the effect that 40 per cent of handicapped children were then receiving needed educational services.[2] Lack of trained manpower was an important factor in a continuing shortage of service. Two studies provide information as to the rate of progress toward solution of the problem of teacher shortage. In 1961 Mackie described programmes for teachers and related specialists in the nation. At that time, 224 colleges and universities offered at least a minimum sequence in special education. Within these 224 academic centres, 213 programmes were geared to undergraduates and 164 were for graduate study. There were 18,000 full- and part-time students, of whom 11,000 were undergraduates.[3] In 1969 Saettler[4] gathered comparable data. His study revealed 412 universities and colleges with programmes in special education. There were 774 undergraduate programmes and 794 at the graduate level. There were 85,000 full- and part-time students, of whom about 59,000 were undergraduates. Among the 26,000 graduate students, 23,000 were in master's degree programmes, 2,000 were working toward a doctorate, and the remainder were seeking degrees or certification at levels between the master's and the doctor's degree. In spite of this marked increase in the numbers of students in training, Saettler estimated that at the rate of teacher preparation which existed in 1969 the supply of teachers would fall far short of the demand.

Saettler also provided information on the financing of education which is of value in assessing the relative investment in special education as a whole, and the relative emphasis upon teacher preparation within special education. In 1969, the total national expenditure for education was put at $54,000 million. State and local sources were credited with $50,000 million and the remaining $4,000 million came from federal sources. From the $4,000 million in federal funds, $100 million was allocated to the education of the handicapped (in contrast to $1.5 million in 1960). In 1969, state and local support of special education was said to be $900 million. Thus, at the close of the decade, the total expenditure for education of handicapped children was thought to be $1,000 million. The $100 million of federal funds for the handicapped were distributed as follows: teacher preparation $30 million; research $14 million; direct allocation to state and local school systems for developmental programmes $23 million. The remaining funds went into related administrative and supportive activities such as regional resource centres and model programmes of early childhood education. Saettler's analysis indicated that the impact of federal funding was great. There was a fivefold

1   R. Mackie et al., *College and University Programs for Preparation of Teachers of Exceptional Children, 1961–1962*, Washington, D.C., Office of Education, U.S. Dept. HEW, 1967.
2   L. Lucito, 'Division of Training Programs—Its Mission,' *Except. Children* (Arlington, Va), Vol. 34, March 1968, p. 531–6.
3   R. Mackie et al., College and University Programs ..., op. cit.
4   H. Saettler, 'Students in Training Programs in the Education of the Handicapped' (doctoral dissertation, Univ. of Illinois, Urbana, Ill., 1969).

increase in student enrolment after federal assistance came into being. In all, there was an increase of almost 67,000 students in all areas of handicap between the 1961/62 school year and the 1968/69 session.

Teacher preparation and research manpower

How many individuals who are trained as special educators devote significant time to research? How many, for example, of the investigators whose work is cited in the present report were trained as educators? These questions cannot be answered at this time. Two studies from general education provide tangential information. A survey of the educational backgrounds of several thousand educational researchers published in 1965 revealed that 46 per cent were trained in psychology, 45 per cent in education and 6 per cent in sociology. These individuals listed their areas of academic affiliation as follows: education, 52 per cent; psychology, 40 per cent; and sociology, 5 per cent.[1] A later study of eighty-seven noted scholars in education inquired into their area of academic specialization. Among these scholars, 61 indicated psychology, 9 identified sociology, and 17 designated an educational speciality.[2] A limited number of special education doctoral programmes are concentrating on the production of graduates who are specially qualified in research. They must overcome several obstacles if they are to be successful. One obstacle is the conflict which is inherent between the demands of a profession and those of science and research. Few individuals can pay allegiance to both a profession and a scientific discipline. This writer believes that the strain of divided loyalties is a greater deterrent to the development of research specialists within a professional field such as special education than is the more widely acknowledged problem of acquiring competence in two or more fields of endeavour. Another serious obstacle to the preparation of research personnel is the chaotic conceptual structure of the field of special education. Much of this chaos begins in the traditional focus on individual handicapping conditions. The student's indoctrination in this view begins in undergraduate training and is emphasized even more in graduate training where he must almost invariably declare his interest in a particular area of handicap. This demand for specialization extends into employment. To teach in public school he must be certified in specific areas of handicap. Should he choose work in a college or a university he must show preparation and promise of achievement in a specific area of handicap so that he can contribute to the sequence of courses which are geared to the demands of teacher certification which graduates must meet.

1   R. Bargar, 'Who is the Educational Researcher?', in: E. Guba and S. Elam (eds), *The Training and Nurture of Educational Researchers,* Bloomington, Ind., Phi Delta Kappa, 1965.
2   G. Buswell *et al., Training for Educational Research,* Berkeley, Calif., Center for Study of Higher Education, Univ. of California (USOE Coop. Res. Project No. 51074).

This focus upon individual categories of handicap poses severe problems to the training of researchers within the framework of special education. Special education does not have unifying paradigms capable of countering the divisive influence of the compartmentalization which results from a preoccupation with individual areas of handicap. When such paradigms are lacking in a field, whether it be a profession or a science, paradigms are imported from more established fields. To date in the United States, the young field of special education has been most dependent upon other professions and disciplines for both paradigms and for methods of inquiry. To prepare research personnel, much of what is to be learned is adopted from other academic disciplines. Importation and adoption of ideas and methods of other fields is not inherently detrimental. In fact it is the pattern of development in most new fields. But the risk in special education is that the new research specialist will be simply a methodologist trained in the techniques of psychology, sociology or some other fields. When a methodology is introduced into a field which lacks intrinsic paradigms the definition of problems and the development of concepts become the province of the methodologist who then introduces the paradigms and the methods of the donor discipline. This occurred in the area of mental retardation when experimental psychologists moved into the field in significant numbers early in the decade.

Teacher training and attitudes toward research

In all professions, the attitudes of the practitioner toward the processes and the findings of research are vital. Progress in the conduct of research and in the adoption of the products of research are quite dependent upon favourable reception by practitioners in the field. There can be no doubt that these attitudes are affected by the experiences of the student in training, although to what extent and in what ways is not clear. The utilization of new knowledge and the significance of the attitude of the practitioner *qua* consumer of research findings were considered in the section 'Research Involving Multiple Handicapping Conditions', above. Little can be added here as there is only very limited hard data regarding teacher training and the formation of these attitudes and dispositions.

The conduct of much of the research which is essential to the progress of special education is dependent upon the full co-operation of teachers and school administrators. Some of the most strategic research will necessitate that the investigator have unimpeded access to interactions among teacher, student and task in classrooms, diagnostic sessions and tutorial exercises. There will be a need for co-operation and collaboration at a very personal and immediate level or else the research might well be viewed as an intrusion into the professional privacy of the teacher and into the sanctity of the classroom or tutorial booth. The tone and quality of these relationships are set by the perceptions which service staff and research personnel have of the relationship of research to service. Furthermore, these perceptions are profoundly influenced by values conveyed from professors to students.

Although the instructional staff of academic programmes in special education almost universally profess their allegiance to the goal of service to exceptional children, in this writer's experience they differ widely in their modes of expressing this allegiance. The three most frequent modes of expression are service through teaching, service through teaching teachers, and service through research. Service through teaching, is the most frequent view and is characteristic of undergraduate teacher preparation from which come the bulk of career teachers. When the second view, service through teaching teachers, prevails, the highest value is assigned to the preparation of teacher trainers. It is as if the primary aim were to create high quality teacher templates as a means of multiplying the number of qualified classroom teachers. This view is generally found among graduate instructional staff and in doctoral training programmes. The third orientation, service through research, is found almost exclusively in doctoral training programmes in major academic centres. Centres and staff which embrace this view are least numerous of all.

The student who is trained in a programme in which any one of these views is paramount is likely to hold this value when he enters the profession. It is obvious that the values given priority in each of these positions is essential to the total educational enterprise. The challenge is to achieve a climate-in-training in which a mutually accepting and reinforcing relationship can develop among those who hold disparate views. This plurality and discrepancy of values is not unique to special education. A comparable circumstance exists in the academic programmes of many fields. It is to be emphasized again, however, that the matter is of special urgency to special education because so much of the basic research of the field will depend upon the most perfect co-operation between school people and research personnel. The foundation for this co-operation must begin early in the student's career. The aim of the programmes which prepare teachers, leadership personnel and researchers must be to inculcate all students with value systems of sufficient scope to embrace the full range of philosophies of service.

E. G. E. de Lorenzo

Uruguay